International Perspectives on Family Support

edited by

W. Hellinckx
M.J. Colton
M.Williams

Published by
Arena
Ashgate Publishing Limited
Gower House
Croft Road
Aldershot
Hants GU11 3HR
England

Ashgate Publishing Company
Old Post Road
Brookfield
Vermont 05036
USA

British Library Cataloguing in Publication Data
International perspectives on family support
    1. Family social work
    I. Hellinckx, W. II. Colton, M.J., 1955- III. Williams, Margaret, 1943-
    362.8'28

Library of Congress Cataloging-in-Publication Data
International perspectives on family support/ edited by Walter Hellinckx, Matthew Colton,
    Margaret Williams.
        p. co.
    Includes bibliographical references
    1. Family services - United States. 2. Family services - Europe. 3. Family social work -
    United States. 4. Family social work - Europe. 5. Child welfare - United States.
    6. Child welfare - Europe. I. Hellinckx, Walter. II. Colton, M.J., 1955- .
    III. Williams, Margaret, 1943- .
    HV699. I54   1997
    362. 82 -- dc21   97-27354
                                                                              CIP

ISBN 1 85742 347 X

Printed and bound in Great Britain by
Biddles Ltd, Guildford and King's Lynn

INTERNATIONAL PERSPECTIVES ON
FAMILY SUPPORT

Contents

Preface

Walter HELLINCKX

Family-centred programmes are one of the fastest growing programme areas in child welfare in the USA as well as in Europe. These programmes are designed to improve family functioning and to realise a number of objectives (Pecora et al., 1992). Placement prevention interventions such as family preservation services reflect the philosophical viewpoint that society should invest as much or more in placement prevention as it would spend for the placement of children.

Within the broad framework of family-centred programmes there is wide variation, and a number of different terms are used according to the type of programme. This book reflects the prevailing variations in terminology. For example, treatment at home is described in such terms as hometraining (Van den Bogaart), home-based services (Baartman), home-based treatment programmes (Vogelvang) or pedagogical help at home. The family-oriented nature of the programmes is reflected in names such as family support (Colton and Williams), family-centred, family support programmes (Van der Meulen and Sipma), and family-based services. The intensity of the treatment offered is emphasised by the use of terms such as intensive family preservation work (Whittaker) or intensive family preservation services.

The Child Welfare League of America (in Pecora et al., 1992) has proposed a trichotomised typology of family-centred programmes:

1. **Family support services.** These are community-based services that assist and support adults in their roles as parents. These services should be equally available to all families with children and should not impose criteria for participation that might differentiate or stigmatise certain parents. These

programmes aim at primary prevention. In many cases they are typically designed for populations at-risk for parenting problems, especially child-abuse and neglect and social isolation. They are preferably applied during pregnancy or in families with young children.

2. **Family-based services.** These services encompass a range of activities for families with problems that threaten their stability. Because in many cases treatment takes place at home, we often refer to them as home-based services. Among other programmes, this type of service includes programmes for families with a developmentally disabled child, where the handicap itself is usually the cause of the child-rearing problem. Here, hometraining tries to acquaint the parents with their child's idiosyncrasies and help them find the best ways of relating to that specific child in that specific situation. Depending on the child's age, the help provided can also be more specifically directed at stimulating certain aspects of the child's development, such as communication and self-help skills, and sometimes at integrating the child into the family's daily routines. The Portage-Project is a well-know example of this kind of family-centred programme.

3. **Intensive family preservation services (IFPS).** These services are meant for families in crisis, when removal of a child is imminent, or when the return of a child from out-of-home care is being considered. They are essentially concerned with normal children who are living in families where the individual, relational, or social problems of other family members cause pedagogical problems and, to a greater or lesser extent, threaten the child's development. The central focus of family preservation is to improve the family's child-rearing abilities so that the family unit may be maintained without endangering the child. Family preservation services have the same philosophical orientation and characteristics as family-based services but differ with respect to two criteria: caseload size and intensity of service. Caseload size is smaller than for family-based services and intensity of service greater: a common criterion for service intensity is at least five contact hours per week.

This book focuses particularly on intensive family preservation services, although some aspects of family-based services are also discussed. The first part of the book provides a general framework, where the five contributing authors discuss theoretical aspects of child-rearing, the causes and characteristics of problems in child-rearing, and the kind of service which may be best suited to particular problematic situations.

In Chapter 1, *Belsky* considers the question of parental influences on child development and the related issue of the determinants of parenting.

In Chapter 2, *Rink* provides a theoretical framework that makes it possible to map all aspects of pedagogical mismanagement in a child-rearing system. He emphasises that the diagnosis and treatment of pedagogical mismanagement requires a standard and accepted orientation and interpretative framework.

In Chapter 3, *Agathonos-Georgopolou, Brown and Sarafidou* present a Greek study on the secondary prevention of child maltreatment. The study aims to identify characteristics which may potentially predispose individuals to child maltreatment, making possible the early identification of families in need of support.

In Chapter 4, *Smit and Knorth* discuss the reasons for involving parents in the residential care and treatment of their children, and ways in which this might be accomplished. An overview is provided of the state of affairs in the Netherlands in this respect.

Finally, in Chapter 5, *Kagan* shares with us an approach to breaking the cycle of perpetual crisis in families where the children have had multiple placements, where abuse and neglect has recurred over generations, and where several previous attempts to avoid placement have been tried with little success.

The second part of the book contains more practice-oriented material. Some family-centred programmes are presented. The authors discuss in some depth the origins of the different programmes, their place in the care process, their essential characteristics and objectives and, finally, their results or effects. Specific directions are provided for the improvement of policy and practice.

In Chapter 6, *Van den Bogaart* presents a historic overview of hometraining practice and evaluation in the Netherlands. He concludes with recommendations for the evaluation of hometraining in the near future.

In Chapter 7, after a general description of the field of home-based services, *Baartman* examines factors which determine the choice between hometraining and traditional ambulant aid, while devoting some attention to the diversity of methodologies in this area. His final focus is on one type of hometraining: 'preventive hometraining'.

In Chapter 8, *Whittaker* reviews the value base, the objectives and the essential components of intensive family preservation services in the United States. He identifies critical challenges for evaluation research, clinical practice and policy.

In Chapter 9, *Colton and Williams* discuss the 1989 Children Act, which gave legislative expression to the idea that children are best brought up by their own families. Their focus is the impact of this Act on the implementation and progress of family support systems in England and Wales.

The basic assumption underlying the 'personal, familial and community help programme', presented by *Palacio-Quintin* in Chapter 10, is the ecological theory of human development and its application to maltreatment. The interventions in this programme allow a simultaneous (re)balancing of individual characteristics, and the organisation of the family and the social network.

Finally, the third part of the book contains three chapters that focus specifically on the evaluation of family preservation work.

In Chapter 11, *Van der Meulen and Sipma* describe the 'Portage Programme' in the Netherlands, with particular attention to the effects of the program, as investigated in six Dutch research projects.

In Chapter 12, *Vogelvang* discusses evaluation research as it applies to home-based treatment programmes. This chapter synthesises theoretical ideas and empirical research findings which contribute to an understanding of the process of change in families. The synthesis is presented in the form of a model of change.

In the concluding chapter, 13, *Jacobs, Williams and Kapuscik* describe three 'waves' of family preservation evaluation research which have been undertaken in the United States. They identify the strengths and limitations of past approaches and summarise the findings from these studies. They conclude with recommendations regarding evaluation activities in the future.

References

Pecora, P.J., Whittaker, J.K. and Maluccio, A.N. (1992), *The Child Welfare Challenge. Policy, practice, and research*, Aldine de Gruyter, New York.

1 Determinants and consequences of parenting: Illustrative findings and basic principles

Jay BELSKY

The ever-growing movement among those in the field of residential and foster care to keep biological families together whenever possible means that, as a developmental psychologist with special interest in parent-child relationships, my 'intellectual distance' from the readers of this volume is probably less than it would have been 10 to 20 years ago. Today, both those with expertise in residential care and those with an interest in so-called 'normal' families share a concern for the dual foci of this chapter - the influence that parents exert on their children and the factors that cause some parents to treat their children one way and some another. Rather than reviewing research on the determinants and consequences of parenting in comprehensive detail, or merely summarising broad conclusions to emerge from these fields of inquiry, it is my intent in this chapter to integrate these two approaches by discussing the results of selected investigations. These nicely illustrate many of the core conclusions which are central to understanding what influence parents exert upon their offspring and why parents parent the way they do.

Parental influences on child development

The first half of this chapter dealing with parental influence on child development is organised on the basis of developmental stages. It begins by considering parental influences during infancy - the first year of life - before moving on to toddlerhood, the preschool and middle childhood years, and finally adolescence.

The focus throughout is primarily on social and emotional development, rather than cognitive or intellectual development.

Infancy

A central developmental task of the infant in the first year of life is the establishment of an affectional bond with his or her primary caregiver. This can be referred to as an attachment relationship and for most infants this affectional bond will be with the mother. It should be noted, however, that there is little if anything to be said on this topic that does not also apply to fathers or other caregivers, including day-care workers and foster carers.

The great English psychiatrist, John Bowlby (1982), argued that, throughout the course of evolutionary history, infants have evolved to develop close, focused, affectional bonds to primary caregivers as a means of promoting their own survival, and that parents, too, have evolved to provide the kind of care and attention that would foster infant attachment and survival. Whereas much of Bowlby's (1944) concern for the infant-mother attachment bond derived from his early work on children whose bonds had been broken, it was his first and foremost American student, Mary Ainsworth (1973), who applied Bowlby's theory to children with more typical childhoods. Perhaps the most significant of Ainsworth's contributions were her conceptualisation of secure and insecure attachments and her creation of a procedure, known as the Strange Situation, for evaluating the security of the one-year-old child's tie to his or her mother (Ainsworth and Wittig, 1969).

Not only did Ainsworth develop a laboratory method for evaluating the security of the infant's affective tie to his or her mother but, just as significantly, she developed a theory concerning, and generated some preliminary evidence about, the influence of maternal care on the development of attachment security. Central to Ainsworth's (1973) theory of attachment is the assertion that it is the sensitivity of maternal care that determines whether an infant develops a secure or insecure attachment. Infants whose mothers are responsive to their needs and provide care that fits the individual attributes of the child in a manner that fosters harmonious and synchronous interactions between mother and child will develop secure attachments. In contrast, those whose mothers are rejecting, intrusive, detached and/or unresponsive in the care they provide will develop insecure attachments.

A decade ago I reported the first of what became a set of three longitudinal studies on this topic (Belsky, Rovine and Taylor, 1984; Isabella, Belsky and von Eye, 1989; Isabella and Belsky, 1990). In these studies, we attempted to link the quality of mothering, observed in the home when infants were 1, 3 and 9 months of age, with security of attachment assessed at 1 year of age. The results of our initial investigation revealed, most interestingly, that at three separate times of measurement mothers of infants who would develop secure attachments provided an intermediate level of reciprocal interaction: a composite construct based principally upon measures of maternal vocalization, stimulation, positive affect and undivided attention (Belsky, Rovine, and Taylor, 1984). We regarded these intermediate levels of stimulating maternal involvement as reflections of sensitive care on the assumption that very high levels of involvement would prove intrusive and would promote, as we found, insecure-avoidant attachment. Conversely, very low levels reflective of detached unresponsiveness would promote, as we also found, insecure-resistant attachment.

This observation, that growth-promoting care might involve neither too much nor too little stimulating maternal involvement - something akin to Aristotle's notion of the 'golden mean' - seemed to be confirmed in a most interesting study of a somewhat related topic: the effect of parental responsiveness to child distress during an entirely different development period. In this work by two Canadian investigators, it was discovered that a significant inverted-U function character-ised the relationship between parental responsiveness to distress and child general competence, comprising friendly, purposive, co-operative and achievement-oriented behaviour (Roberts and Strayer, 1987). As in our infancy work on attachment, more parental care did not seem to be better, as there clearly appeared to be a point of diminishing returns with respect to how responsive parents were to the distress of their four-year-olds.

In this discussion of parental influences on child functioning, it would be misleading not to call attention to the fact that many of the findings reported in this chapter, including the findings I have just described, are open to alternative interpretation. On the one hand, correlational results may reflect effects of children on their parents rather than the effect of parenting on child functioning. On the other hand, genetic influences may simply be masquerading in many studies as effects of parental behaviour. Because parents and children share genes, these common genes may influence both parental behaviour and child functioning and thus result in associations between the two which actually do not reflect parental influence. Needless to say, experimental research is one means of circumventing this interpretative problem: and, fortunately, a recent experimental study clearly chronicles the causal influence of maternal care on the development of attachment security.

In this work carried out in the Netherlands, van den Boom (1994) experi-mented with mothers of 100 carefully selected infants who were highly irritable as newborns. When the infants were 6 months of age, half the mothers were randomly assigned to an experimental treatment that was designed to promote sensitive, responsive care - the very kind that was theorised to promote secure attachment. Not only did the treatment succeed in promoting sensitive maternal

3

responsiveness to positive and negative infant signals, as revealed by pre- and post-intervention comparisons of mothering in the experimental and control group but, just as importantly, this effect on mothering translated into an effect on infants. Those in the experimental group were far more likely to be classified as securely attached (66 per cent) when seen in the Strange Situation at 12 months of age than were those in the control group (22 per cent). Clearly, then, strong causal inferences can be drawn about the effect of sensitive mothering on the development of secure attachment in infancy (Belsky and Cassidy, 1994).

Toddlerhood

Whereas one of the major developmental challenges facing the infant in the first year of life is the development of a close, affectional bond to his or her primary caregiver, during the second and third year of life - the period known as toddlerhood - the child aspires to separate psychologically from his or her parents, a process often referred to as individuation. The developing child learns to walk and talk and expresses his or her own will by saying things like 'mine' to assert a singular claim of ownership or 'no' to reflect unwillingness to co-operate; but, at the same time, the toddler typically retains the infant's desire for connectedness as well. The confusing signals that toddlers often send to parents, and especially their emphatic insistence on having things their own way, challenge parents to exercise their power and influence in a way that does not violate the psychological integrity of the developing child. As we will see when we come to consider parenting during the preschool years and middle childhood, there is theory and evidence to suggest that efforts to overcontrol and dominate the child can backfire, leading to less rather than more co-operation. Interestingly, some of the very same processes seem to be at work during the second and third year of life.

In an ongoing study of the so-called 'terrible twos' - the second and third year of life - my colleagues and I are studying a cohort of boys and their families in attempt to identify why, for some families the 'terrible twos' is an apt description of the toddler years, whereas for others it is not (Belsky, Woodworth and Crnic, 1996a). We are focusing upon families rearing sons because it is well known that, when they grow older, it is boys who are more likely to develop problems managing their impulses (that is, exhibit externalising behaviour). Moreover, we are focusing upon the topic of individual differences in family experiences during toddlerhood because we suspect that, in the main, the 'terrible twos' is a misnomer, since most families do not have major problems managing their young children. In essence, our argument is the same as that of students of adolescence who have come to realise that this developmental period has received a bad reputation despite the fact that most teenagers get along well with their parents, share their parents' values and aspire to be like their parents. To quote an old American saying, it is 'a few bad apples who give the barrel a bad name'.

Given this orientation, our study method consists of observing mothers, fathers and their children on two separate days, for one hour each day, at four different ages - 15, 21, 27 and 33 months. We ask the parents to go about their everyday household routine in the late afternoon/early evening period, when there is much to do. Our observers take detailed notes which they then use, following the home visit, to dictate narrative records of family interaction. These are coded in terms of efforts by parents to control or manage the child and in terms of child responses to such parental control efforts. We pay careful attention not only to how often parents endeavour to control the child, but to how they do it. Do they rely upon simple control statements ('come here', 'stop that')? Do they use 'guidance' (Crockenberg and Littman, 1990) in their efforts to control the child by offering a rationale for their directives ('come here so I can clean your face') or by issuing indirect suggestions which evince respect for the child while simultaneously empowering him ('would you come over here so I can wash your face')? And how does the child react to such control efforts? Does he co-operate by complying immediately with the parent? Does he actively defy the parent by growing angry? Does he just assert his wishes by saying 'no' or the equivalent? Finally, how does the interaction develop following these initial exchanges between parent and child? Is there negative escalation in which both parent and child continue to deliver negative messages at increasing intensity, or is there 'positive closure', a process involving an attempt to re-establish the harmony of the relationship between parent and child?

We subjected our coded narrative records to cluster analysis in an attempt to identify 'patterns' of family interaction and proved successful in identifying a cluster of families at each of our four ages of measurement (15, 21, 27 and 33 months respectively) that seem to be having 'trouble' managing their toddler. One such cluster, in this case at 15 months, nicely illustrates what we have been finding. Consistent with work on problem boys at older ages (Patterson, 1982), we found a subset of families in which parents most frequently tried to control their toddler, relying most frequently upon simple control and least frequently upon control-plus-guidance. Note that negative control which involves the expression of anger or sarcasm by the parent is rarely seen and does not discriminate groups at this age, although it does so later on. In these seemingly 'troubled' families, toddlers complied least frequently and defied most often. Probably in consequence, negative escalation was a more common occurrence than in the other two groups of families identified by means of the cluster analysis.

Two other findings from this study are especially noteworthy. First, measures of child emotionality/temperament obtained when infants were 1 year of age failed to discriminate family groups, though characteristics of parents (for example, personality) did, thereby suggesting that the patterns of family interaction we were discerning did not reflect simple 'child effects'. Second, families repeatedly classified as 'troubled' across the four ages of measurement were more likely to have children who evinced externalising problems involving aggression and disobedience at age three, according to maternal and paternal reports as well as reports by nonparental child-care providers (in the case of children in some kind of day-care arrangement). It is our belief that these results reflect the influence of family processes on child development, though we do have to acknowledge our inability to discount the alternative argument that behaviour is genetically controlled.

I must note, however, that these results may not generalise beyond our sample of boys. That is, we do not know if daughters are similarly affected. This observation raises the important issue of what one American developmentalist, Ted Wachs (Wachs and Chan, 1986), has referred to as the problem of 'organismic specificity'. It refers to the notion that the influence of parenting, or any other experience for that matter, may differ depending upon the characteristics of the child. Thus, boys might be affected in a way that girls may not. Similarly, the effect of some parental practices may vary as a function of the temperament of the child. Recently, Grazyna Kochanska (1995), a Polish emigre now working in the United States, finds that children who are highly fearful benefit far more from gentle maternal discipline which de-emphasises power than do children who are less fearful when it comes to internalising norms of correct and incorrect behaviours. Apparently, this is because the fearfulness of the former children makes even gentle maternal control techniques sufficiently anxiety provoking to motivate compliance and the internalisation of maternal norms.

The preschool and middle-childhood years

With respect to the period just before entry into public school - which, in the United States, means the period from about 3-5 years - virtually all understanding of parental influences on child development derives from Baumrind's (1967; 1971) classic study of a group of middle-class, white children attending nursery schools in California in the 1960s. Detailed observations in the children's homes revealed three main parenting styles. Authoritative parents tended to be high on warmth and on control: that is, while loving and caring, they also had high expectations of their young children and held them accountable for behaving as expected. Permissive parents, in contrast, tended to evince high levels of warmth but low levels of control. Finally, authoritarian parents scored high on control, expecting children to be immediately responsive to them, but provided little of the warmth that might be expected to motivate responsiveness. Detailed observations of the children in the nursery school environment revealed that it was the children of authoritative parents who were most competent with peers, industrious in their work and play at preschool, and co-operative with teachers. Permissively reared preschoolers tended to be impulsive and aggressive, lacking in both self-reliance and self-control, though more cheerful than those whose parents were authoritarian. These latter preschoolers were moody, unhappy, irritable and aggressive.

More recent work dealing with both preschoolers and older children is generally consistent with Baumrind's findings, especially those investigations focused on identifying the etiology of problematic child behaviour, particularly aggressiveness. For example, one set of investigators studying preschoolers found that those whose mothers were hostile and inconsistent in their parenting had children who believed that unfriendly, assertive methods of dealing with interpersonal conflict - such as threatening to hit another child to get one's way - would be most effective in solving conflicts (Hart, Ladd and Burleson, 1990). Perhaps the most well-known findings pertaining to the development of aggressive behaviour derives from the research of Gerald Patterson (for example, Patterson and Banks, 1989). His investigation of 10-year-old boys living in high-crime neighbourhoods indicates that problems with peers involving aggression are associated with coercive parent-child interactions characterised by parental complaining and inconsistent discipline. Not surprisingly, these apparent effects of parenting on child behaviour have consequences for the child's relationships with peers. In fact, it has been shown that mothers' practice and endorsement of physical punishment as a disciplinary strategy predicts 4-year-olds' tendency to propose aggressive solutions for dealing with social problems; and that such social-cognitive orientations themselves predict rejected social status in the peer group (Pettit, Dodge and Brown, 1988). Similarly, other findings indicate that mothers who are more positive and less disagreeable when interacting with their 6- and 7-year-old children and who focus conversation upon emotions (of self and others) have offspring who are more popular in the classroom (Putallaz, 1987).

Adolescence

Findings like these are consistent with common sense and have now been observed many times in relation to the preschool and middle-childhood years. Such findings can easily incline one to conclude that authoritarian or dysfunctional parenting always leads to problematic child outcomes and, conversely, that authoritative parenting always produces competent social and academic functioning. For a long time this was indeed thought to be the case. However, it should be noted that most of the research to date on parental influences on child

7

development has been carried out on a narrow population of families - mostly maritally-intact, middle-class, white families living in the United States. In recent years, investigators have become alert to the possibility that developmental processes, including those pertaining to parental influences, may actually operate differently in different ecological niches. That is, in the same way that we need to think about organismic specificity, or the prospect that developmental processes vary as a function of attributes of the child, there is also a need to recognise that the effects of parenting may well vary as a function of the ecological niche in which the child is growing up.

Intriguingly, the possibility of such developmental and ecological complexity was suggested more than two decades ago in a study by Baumrind on a small sample of African-American children (Baumrind, 1972). In contrast to what she discovered with respect to white, middle-class families summarised earlier, Baumrind discovered in this study that black children whose parents were authoritarian rather than authoritative tended to be the most competent. Recently, studies of parental influence during adolescence have underscored the possibility that processes operative in white, middle-class families may not function the same way in different kinds of households. Such studies alert us to the need to be cautious in generalising from one ecological niche to another, whether a niche be defined in terms of race/ethnicity (e.g., African-American, Asian-American, Hispanic-American, European-American), socioeconomic status (e.g., working class, middle class), family structure (e.g., two parent, one parent) or even, perhaps, geographic region.

Relying on a large data base of over 10,000 high school students, Steinberg and his colleagues (1995) obtained information from the students about the way their parents treated them and, from these reports, were able to classify parenting styles in Baumrindian terms (e.g., authoritarian, authoritative). As anticipated, adolescents raised in authoritative homes proved to be better adjusted and more competent than children raised in families where nonauthoritative parenting practices were the norm. Authoritatively-reared adolescents were confident about their abilities, competent in areas of achievement, and less likely than peers to get into trouble. Most notable, however, was the fact that when the effects of authoritative parenting were examined with regard to school achievement, different results emerged as a function of child race/ethnicity.

Authoritative parenting turned out to have a stronger relation to academic performance among European-American children than among African- or Asian-American children. And this seemed to be the result of the peer group. European-American children with authoritative parents had as friends and associates mostly peers from similar families, so that the values and parenting styles practised in their homes were reinforced in the peer group. In contrast, authoritative parenting exerted a less positive effect on the school achievement of African-

American teenagers because the peer groups that they were most likely to join were least likely to promote academic success. Similarly, coming from a nonauthoritative Asian-American family did not tend to undermine school achievement as might have been expected, because the Asian-American peer group was very encouraging of school achievement. The lesson from this work, then, is not simply one of contextual specificity - namely that developmental processes may operate differently in different ecological niches - but, in the case of school achievement, that peers are critical moderators of parental influence.

Conclusion

Cause and effect remain difficult to disentangle in the large majority of studies linking parenting practices and child development, due principally to rival hypotheses concerning behaviour genetics and child effects in this mostly correlational literature. It is clear that, from infancy onward, affectively negative, demanding, controlling, detached and unresponsive parenting - that is, generally insensitive care - tends to covary with an assortment of negative developmental 'outcomes', ranging from attachment insecurity, to child disobedience, to problems in the peer group and even academic difficulty. In contrast, more positively affective, responsive styles in which control between parent and child is shared if not directly negotiated are associated with a range of competencies: for example, security, co-operation, popularity and achievement (Belsky, 1990). What we must remain alert to, however, is that even these strong trends in the literature may themselves be a function of the rather limited populations of subjects that have been studied. Future work will undoubtedly reveal that many of these findings cannot be generalised across ecological niches. Thus, in addition to the principle of organismic specificity, it will be important to keep in mind contextual specificity.

Determinants of parenting

Having considered in the first half of this chapter the question of parental influences on child development, we now consider the related issue of the determinants of parenting. That is, why do parents parent the way they do? Prior to the 1980s, virtually all research on this issue that did not involve investigations of the etiology of child maltreatment focused upon social class differences in parenting. Repeatedly, such work indicated that parents with more income and education tended to be more involved, less restrictive, punishing and controlling, and more positively affectionate and responsive towards their offspring than parents of lower socioeconomic status; more recent work reveals much the same (Conger et al. 1994; Dodge et al. 1994).

By the 1980s, thanks in large part to arguments advanced by Bronfenbrenner (e.g., Bronfenbrenner and Crouter, 1983), it became apparent that developmentalists needed to move beyond 'social address' models and consider the factors and processes that accounted for these social class effects. Responding to this call for a more refined understanding of the determinants of parental functioning, Belsky (1984) advanced a model of the determinants of parenting that was based upon what was known about the determinants of dysfunctional parenting: that is, the causes of child abuse and neglect (Belsky and Vondra, 1989). This model drew attention to characteristics of the parent, the child and the social context in which the parent-child relationship was embedded. The model presupposed that a parent's own rearing history shaped, even if it did not completely determine, the psychological well being and personality of the parent, and that attributes of the parent influenced the quality of his or her marriage, social relations with others and occupational experiences, which fed back to impact his or her parenting. In addition, attributes of the child, be it his or her temperament, gender or even physical characteristics, to name just a few, also affected parental functioning. Most importantly, the model presumed that because parenting was multiply determined, it was unlikely that any single factor in and of itself would determine how parents cared for their offspring. Central to understanding the determinants of parenting were the notions of stresses and supports or, in the language of contemporary developmental psychopathology, risk and protective factors (Cicchetti, 1984). Parental functioning was seen to be a well-buffered system in which parental dysfunction would most likely occur when risk factors such as a problematic developmental history or an unhappy marriage were many and were not balanced by protective factors like an easy-tempered child or a highly rewarding occupation.

The remainder of this chapter will highlight some findings in the literature which illustrate the potential role played by each of the domains of influence implicated in the model. Evidence will also be presented demonstrating the need to consider multiple factors simultaneously rather than each factor or domain in isolation.

Developmental history

The fact that children who have been abused and neglected are more likely than other children to grow up to become parents who mistreat their own children clearly suggests that one's experiences in the family of origin influence one's parental competence in important ways (Belsky and Vondra, 1989). However, the fact that many parents with such developmental histories do not grow up to

10

be perpetrators of child maltreatment themselves just as clearly indicates that there is no simple one-to-one correspondence between experience in childhood and adult functioning (Belsky, 1993). Most interestingly, evidence from the study of infant-parent attachment security begins to illuminate some of the conditions that might break the intergenerational cycle. By means of a highly sophisticated and probing interview, called the Adult Attachment Interview (Main and Goldwyn, in press), investigators have discovered two important facts about the intergenerational transmission of attachment security. First, adults who describe - in a credible and detailed manner - their childhood experiences in their families of origin as more benign and supportive are more likely to have infants who develop secure attachments to them; and this effect of early child-rearing experience on infant attachment seems to be mediated by the more sensitive and responsive care that parents with positive attachment histories themselves provide to their offspring (for review, see Belsky and Cassidy, 1994)

Second, and perhaps more important, parents with more problematic histories seem to rear insecure infants principally when they have not come to grips with their problematic pasts, either because they deny them in a way that is not fully convincing in the interview or because they remain caught up in the entangle-ments of their early lives. In other words, the past need not mean that those at risk will rear insecure children if, as a result of what might be regarded as emotionally corrective experiences sometime during their lives, they gain perspective on their troubled pasts, acknowledge the pain they have experienced, and resolve the issues that can be so difficult to overcome without the necessary support.

This all-too-brief summary of a rather large literature should make it clear that the developmental impact of factors implicated in my model of the determinants of parenting can themselves only be understood 'in context'. Knowing only about an individual's developmental history, for example, without information about whether the individual has gained perspective on these experiences and/or whether there exist compensating factors, ultimately provides little insight into how an individual will parent.

Personality and personal psychological resources

If developmental history is going to influence the way an individual parents, it is likely that such impact will be mediated by the individual's psychological well being or personality. An abundance of evidence now indicates that, not surprisingly, parents who are more psychologically healthy tend to provide care that is more sensitive, responsive and authoritative rather than detached, intrusive or overcontrolling (see Vondra and Belsky, 1993 for review). Higher levels of self-esteem, ego control and ego strength, as well as an internal locus of control

11

have all been linked in observational studies to more skilled mothering (Biringen, 1990; Mondell and Tyler, 1981; Cox, Owen, Lewis and Henderson, 1989). In our previously mentioned study of toddlers, we find that fathers who are more extroverted - that is, sociable and positively emotional - express more positive affection towards their sons and are more likely to cognitively stimulate them than are less extroverted fathers. Mothers who are more agreeable - that is, friendly, trusting, and caring - also express more positive affection towards their toddlers than do other mothers, and are more involved with their offspring. Finally, the more neurotic mothers and fathers are - that is, prone to the negative emotions of anxiety, hostility, and depression - the lower the quality of care we observe them to provide in their child's second year (Belsky, Woodworth and Crnic, in press).

Clearly, then, the psychological resources that adults bring to their roles as parents influence the way in which they function as parents. This is true whether mothers or fathers are the focus of interest, and whether psychological resources are conceptualised in terms of transient states (e.g., depressed, happy) or enduring traits (e.g., neurotic, extroverted).

Child characteristics

Because the parent-child relationship involves two parties, it is not surprising that attributes of each participating member affect the nature of the interactions that transpire between mother and child or between father and child. Some of the most compelling evidence of the role of temperament in particular in shaping parent-child interaction comes from the aforementioned Dutch study by van den Boom. Prior to implementing her intervention designed to foster maternal sensitivity and thereby attachment security, this investigator compared the mothering provided to her specially selected sample of highly irritable newborns to that provided to less irritable newborns during their first six months of life (van den Boom and Hoeksma, 1994). The results convincingly indicate that infant negative emotionality exerts a strong impact on the nature and quality of maternal care. Mothers of irritable infants, across the first six months, provided less effective stimulation and were less responsive to positive signals from their infants. One of the things that makes these findings so impressive is that, in the main, chronicling consistent effects of infant temperament on parenting has proven quite difficult (Crockenberg, 1986). Earlier in the chapter, I observed that infant positive and negative emotionality measured at one year of age proved unrelated to whether families had trouble managing their toddlers during the second and third year of life (Belsky et al., in press, 1995). As it turns out, child age may be a critical factor, as van den Boom found that effects of infant negativity tended to diminish across her six-month period of study (van den Boom and Hoeksma, 1994).

In any event, we should not lose sight of the fact that the findings of van den Boom just described, like those summarised pertaining to the apparent impact of parental attributes, derive from what are essentially correlational studies. Not surprisingly, this design feature, which impedes our ability to draw strong causal inference, plagues almost all work pertaining to the determinants of parenting. Fortunately, in the area of child effects, investigators have proven creative in generating experimental designs to explore causal influences. In such work, a child actor, known as a 'confederate' is trained to act in a particular manner - for example, aggressive and defiant - and the effect of such behaviour on adults is evaluated (e.g., Brunk and Henggeler, 1984). In another creative design, mothers with and without disordered children are observed interacting with their own child and with another who behaves distinctly different from their own (e.g., Anderson, Lytton and Romney, 1986). In each case, clear evidence emerges that mothers and other adults react to disobedient, negative and/or highly active children with negative, controlling behaviour. Such findings are consistent with the theory that, beyond the infancy period, children with difficult temperaments or behavioral styles are more likely than are other children to evoke from parents 'upperlimit' control, that is, behaviour designed to reduce the child's aversiveness (Bell and Chapman, 1986).

The marital relationship

An abundance of evidence linking marital conflict and child behaviour problems (Emery, 1988) has led many to ponder the developmental and psychological mechanisms that may account for this association. One current prospect is that parenting mediates the relation between marital processes and child functioning (Belsky, 1981; Fauber et al., 1990) and evidence is accumulating that is consistent with such theorising. I have found in my own work, for example, that marital deterioration across the transition to parenthood is more pronounced in the case of mothers whose children develop insecure attachments than in the case of mothers whose infants develop secure attachments (Isabella and Belsky, 1985). In a related study, we further observed that the more the marriage deteriorated, not over just the first nine months of the firstborn's life but over the first three years of parenthood, the more intrusive and negative fathers were observed to be when their children were three years of age. In addition, consistent with the literature linking problem behaviour and marital conflict, the more negative and unco-operative were children with both their mothers and their fathers (Belsky, Youngblade, Rovine and Volling, 1991). Katz and Gottman (1995) recently reported remarkably similar results in a study of families with

13

four- and five-year-olds. The fact of the matter is that numerous studies now reveal relations between marital quality and parenting (see Belsky, 1990, for review). What seems especially interesting is that associations seem stronger for men than for women, which may reflect that fact that, at least in America, the role of father is less scripted by social conventions, resulting in fathers being more susceptible to marital influence than mothers (Belsky, 1990).

Social support

It is not just a parent's relationship with his or her spouse that appears to influence the quality of care provided to offspring, but also the availability and the quality of relationships which parents have with friends, neighbours, relatives and even community organisations and agencies. In the main, the evidence indicates that more support and higher quality of support is beneficial, though there may be a point of diminishing returns (for review, see Belsky, 1990; Belsky and Vondra, 1989). When associates become intrusive and overcontrolling, they may have a deleterious impact rather than a positive one; and then there is also the issue of the nature of support itself. When friends and relatives hold values that are in favour of, for example, physical punishment, their impact may be less positive than might otherwise be desired.

In our own work with toddlers. we have found that in those households in which family interaction is likely to be more rather than less 'troubled', the social support experienced by mothers and by fathers seems to be limited (Belsky et al., in press, 1995). Parents report fewer people to confide in and seek help from, as well as less satisfaction with the support they receive. Such data are consistent with evidence that parents who abuse and neglect their children are more likely to be socially isolated (Belsky, 1993). Before embracing a simple causal connection, however, we should not lose sight of the possibility that a lack of support or low satisfaction with support may be a consequence of an individual's own making (Sarason, Sarason and Shearin, 1986).

In my model of the determinants of parenting, social-contextual influences on parenting are acknowledged to be influenced by attributes of the parents themselves (Belsky, 1984). The sad fact of the matter is that some individuals are simply less skilled than others in recruiting and retaining supportive assistance, be it emotional or instrumental in nature. However, some recent experimental work involving the parents of infants demonstrates that support from professionals can foster the kind of care that promotes attachment security (see Belsky, Rosenberger and Crnic, 1995). This clearly suggests that not all the associations between social support and parental functioning are likely to be a result of third-variable (i.e., noncausal) explanations.

Occupational experiences

Central to Freud's notion of mental health are the concepts of love and work. Having already addressed issues of marriage, we turn now to work. The data summarised earlier pertaining to social class in part reflect the influence of work on parenting, since social class is greatly defined by the occupational prestige of one's job. Extensive studies by Kohn (1995) in both the United States and in Poland further clarify the nature of the process which might explain the aforementioned findings. In general, what Kohn and his collaborators discovered is that adults whose jobs are less substantively complex (in terms of the intellectual demands which work places on the employee) and who are provided little autonomy with respect to decision-making come to demand more subservience on the part of their children. Interestingly, these results obtain even after personal psychological attributes of parents are controlled, so simple third variable explanations do not account for the findings; they appear to be truly causal. Essentially, Kohn concludes that values encountered on the job - for example, not to think and to do as one is told - are carried home to shape the way one parents.

It is not just job values that shape parenting, but stress as well. A fascinating set of studies of air-traffic controllers in the U.S. indicates that elevated levels of stress lead fathers to withdraw from family interaction (Repetti, 1994). What makes this work so interesting is that it involved variation in observed father-child and even husband-wife interaction on different days, when work stress was known to vary as a function of variation in air traffic. This innovative research design discounts the alternative explanation that certain kinds of men, who would parent in certain kinds of ways, simply have different kinds of jobs that are inherently more and less stressful.

Multiple determinants

If nothing else, it should be clear at this juncture that a multiplicity of factors appear to influence how parents care for their offspring. Some of these factors reside within the parent, some within the child, and some are characteristics of the social context which may or may not be directly affected by attributes of the parent. Having examined the sources of influence included in my model of the determinants of parenting one at a time, we now turn to some illustrative research which examines multiple determinants. Two types of investigations can be distinguished: one that focuses upon pathways of influence and a second that examines cumulative influence.

A good example of the former type of work comes from an ongoing investigation of rural families in America who are experiencing stress as a result

15

of economic pressures derived from limited job opportunities (Conger et al., 1993). In this study of adolescent girls, structural equation modelling revealed that greater levels of family economic pressure promoted depression in both mothers and fathers. Moreover, parents who were more depressed experienced greater marital conflict, which in turn undermined the extent to which mothers and fathers alike were involved with and nurturant towards their adolescent daughters. Finally the more nurturant and involved both parents were, the more positively adjusted were their daughters.

I want to contrast this path-analytic approach to examining multiple sources of influence with another, less process-oriented one, that is based on the premise that parenting is a well-buffered system which is most likely to be undermined when risk factors accumulate and are not balanced by protective factors. To illustrate this point, I will rely upon some of my own data, again from our ongoing toddler study but this time focusing upon the security of infant-parent attachments, given evidence that security is influenced by the quality of care that the infant receives from his or her parent (for review, see Belsky and Cassidy, 1994). In this work, we generated composite measures of parent personality (extraversion + agreeableness - neuroticism), marital quality (love + mainte- nance / communication - ambivalence - conflict), social support (number + satisfaction) and infant temperament (positivity - negativity) and then split each of these composites at the median, defining scores below the median as reflecting risk (Belsky, Rosenberger and Crnic, 1995). We then calculated a total risk score reflecting the number of times a particular parent scored in the risk condition; this could range from zero, when no composite scores fell below their respective median, to four, when all four composite scores for a particular individual fell below the median. Next, we plotted rate of secure attachment as a function of the number of risk factors. As anticipated, the probability of the infant developing a secure attachment with his mother and father declined as the number of risks increased. In other words, having just a more difficult temperament, or just a less pleasant personality, or just limited social support - that is, just a single risk factor - did not lead to increased risk of a child developing an insecure attach- ment. Rather, what mattered most were multiple risks. Thus, having a difficult temperament and a parent whose personality was not particularly pleasant plus limited social support was far more problematic than a family experiencing just one or two of these conditions. This is because, as we theorised, protective factors tend to buffer the parental system from risks.

Conclusion

Many of the major conclusions which I have drawn from this illustrative review of the literature bear directly on issues pertaining to residential and foster care. As we have seen, sensitive-responsive care is vitally important to the development of secure attachments in infancy. And from the toddler years onwards, authoritarian approaches to parental control seem likely to backfire. In fact, to the extent that they succeed in the short-term, they are likely to fail in the long-term. After all, few parents or parent substitutes desire to cope with a routinely defiant and unco-operative child.

Under specifiable conditions it appears that the likelihood of problematic parent-child relationships increases. However, central to understanding these conditions is not any single factor, but the patterning of risk and protective factors. Invariably, residential and foster care are judged viable strategies for promoting child well being when multiple conditions lead concerned professionals to the judgement that stressors greatly outweigh supports. The challenge, of course, for such professionals is to make the determination as to whether they can generate a better balance through intervention between these competing forces. To the extent that they can, improved parent-child relations and, ultimately, child well being should result.

References

Ainsworth, M. (1973), "The development of infant-mother attachment" in B. Caldwell and H. Ricciuti (eds), *Review of child development research,* vol. 3, 1-94, Chicago.

Ainsworth, M. and Wittig, B. (1969), "Attachment and exploratory behavior of one-year olds in a strange situation" in B. Foss (ed.), *Determinants of behavior,* vol. 4, 129-173), London, Methuen.

Anderson. K., Lytton, H. and Romney, D. (1986), "Mothers interaction with normal and conduct-disordered boys: Who affects whom?", *Developmental Psychology,* vol. 22, 604-609.

Baumrind, D. (1967), "Child care practices anteceding three patterns of preschool behavior", *Genetic Psychology Monographs,* vol. 75, 43-88.

Baumrind, D. (1971), "Current patterns of parental authority", *Developmental Psychology Monograph,* 4P (l, Pt.2).

Baumrind, D. (1972), "An exploratory study of socialization effects on black children: Some black-white comparisons", *Child Development,* vol. 43, 261-267.

Bell, R. and Chapman, M. (1986), "Child effects in studies using experimental or brief longitudinal approaches to socialization", *Developmental Psychology*, vol. 22, 595-603.

Belsky, J. (1981), "Early human experience: A family perspective", *Developmental Psychology*, vol. 17, 3-23.

Belsky, J. (1984), "The determinants of parenting: A process model", *Child Development*, vol. 55, 83-96.

Belsky, J. (1990), "Parental and nonparental care and children's socioemotional development: A decade in review", *Journal of Marriage and the Family*, vol. 52, 885-903.

Belsky, J. (1993), "The etiology of child maltreatment: A developmental-ecological analysis", *Psychological Bulletin*, vol. 114, 413-434.

Belsky, J. and Cassidy, J. (1994), "Attachment: theory and evidence" in M. Rutter and D. Hay (eds), *Development through life: A handbook for clinicians* (pp. 373-402), Oxford, Blackwell.

Belsky, J., Crnic, K. and Woodworth, S. (In press), "Personality and parenting: Exploring the mediational role of transient mood and daily hassles", *Journal of Personality*.

Belsky, J., Rosenberger, K. and Crnic, K. (1995), "The origins of attachment security: Classical and contextual determinants", in R. Muir, S. Goldberg and J. Kerr (eds) *John Bowlby's attachment theory: Historical clinical and social significance* (pp. 153-183), Hillsdale, NJ, Analytic Press.

Belsky, J., Rovine, M. and Taylor, D. (1984), "The Pennsylvania Infant and Family Development Project, III: The origins of individual differences in infant-mother attachment: Maternal and infant contributions", *Child Development*, vol. 55, 718-728.

Belsky, J. and Vondra, J. (1989), "Lessons from child abuse: the determinants of parenting", in D. Cicchetti and V. Carlson (eds) *Current research and theoretical advances in child maltreatment* (pp. 153-202), Cambridge, MA, Cambridge University Press.

Belsky, J., Woodworth, S. and Crnic, K. (1996a), "Trouble in the second year: Three questions about family interaction", *Child Development*, vol. 67, 556-571.

Belsky, J., Woodworth, S. and Crnic, K. (1996b), "Troubled family interaction during toddlerhood", *Development and Psychopathology*, vol. 8, 845-855.

Belsky, J., Youngblade, L., Rovine, M. and Volling, B. (1991), "Patterns of marital change and parent-child interaction", *Journal of Marriage and the Family*, vol. 53, 487-498.

Biringen, Z. (1990), "Direct observation of maternal sensitivity and dyadic interactions in the home: Relations to maternal thinking", *Developmental Psychology*, vol. 26, 278-284.

Bowlby, J. (1944), "Forty-four juvenile thieves: their characters and home life", *International Journal of Psycho-Analysis*, vol. 25, 19-52.

Bowlby, J. (1982), *Attachment and loss, Vol. 1, Attachment*. 2nd Ed. NY, Basic Books.

Bronfenbrenner, U. and Crouter, A. (1983), "The evolution of environmental models in developmental psychology", in P. Mussen (ed.), *Handbook of Child Psychology* (pp. 358-414), NY, Wiley.

Brunk, M. and Henggeler, S. (1984), "Child influences on adult controls: An experimental investigation", *Developmental Psychology*, vol. 20, 1074-1081.

Cicchetti, D. (1984), "The emergence of developmental psychopathology", *Child Development*, vol. 55, 1-7.

Conger, R., Conger, K., Elder, G., Lorenz, F., Simons, R. and Whitbeck, L. (1993), "Family economic stress and adjustment of early adolescent girls", *Journal of Marriage and the Family*, vol. 29, 206-219.

Conger, R, Ge, X., Elder, G., Lorenz, F. and Simons, R. (1994), "Economic stress, coercive family process, and developmental problems of adolescents", *Child Development*, vol. 65, 541-561.

Cox, M., Owen, M., Lewis, J. and Henderson, V. (1989), "Marriage, adult adjustment and early parenting", *Child Development*, vol. 60, 1015-1024.

Crockenberg, S. (1986), "Are temperamental differences in babies associated with predictable differences in caregiving?", in J. Lerner and R. Lerner (eds) *Temperament and psychosocial interaction in infancy and childhood. New Directions for Child Development* (pp. 53-73). San Francisco, Jossey-Bass.

Crockenberg, S. and Littman, L. (1990), "Autonomy as competence in 2-year olds: Maternal correlates of child defiance, compliance and self-assertion", *Developmental Psychology*, vol. 26, 961-971.

Dodge, K., Pettit, G. and Bates, J. (1994), "Socialization mediators of the relation between socioeconomic status and child conduct problems", *Child Development*, vol. 65, 649-665.

Emery, R. (1988), *Marriage, divorce and children's adjustment*, Beverly Hills, CA, Sage.

Fauber, R., Forehand, R., Thomas, A.M. and Wierson, M. (1990), "A mediational model of the impact of marital conflict on adolescent adjustment in intact and divorced families", *Child Development*, vol. 61, 1112-1123.

Hart, C., Ladd, G. and Burleson, B. (1990), "Children's expectations of the outcomes of social strategies: Relations with sociometric status and maternal disciplinary styles", *Child Development*, vol. 61, 127- 137.

Isabella, R. and Belsky, J. (1985), "Marital change during the transition to parenthood and security of infant-parent attachment", *Journal of Family Issues*, vol. 6, 505-522.

Isabella, R. and Belsky, J. (1990), "Interactional synchrony and the origins of infant-mother attachment: A replication study", *Child Development*, vol. 62, 373-384.

Isabella, R., Belsky, J. and von Eye, A. (1989), "Origins of infant-mother attachment: An examination of interactional synchrony during the infant's first year", *Developmental Psychology*, vol. 25, 12-21.

Katz, L.F. and Gottman, J. (April, 1995), *Marital conflict and child adjustment: Father's parenting as a mediator of children's negative peer play*. Paper presented at the biennial meeting of the Society for Research in Child Development, Indianapolis, Indiana.

Kochanska, G. (1995), "Children's temperament, mothers' discipline, and security of attachment: Multiple pathways to emerging internalization", *Child Development*, vol. 66, 597-615.

Kohn, M. (1995), "Social structure and personality through time and space" in P. Moen, G. Elder and K. Luscher (eds), *Examining lives in context: Perspectives on the ecology of human development*, Washington, DC, APA Books.

Main, M. and Goldwyn, R. (in press), "Interview based adult attachment classifications: Related to infant-mother and infant-father attachment", *Developmental Psychology*.

Mondell, S. and Tyler, F. (1981), "Parental competence and styles of problem-solving/play behavior in children", *Developmental Psychology*, vol. 17, 73-78.

Patterson, G. (1982), *A social learning approach to family intervention: III. Coercive family process*, Eugene, OR, Castilia.

Patterson, G. (1986), "Performance models for antisocial boys", *American Psychologist*, vol. 41, 326-335.

Patterson, G. and Banks, C. (1989), "Some amplifying mechanisms for pathologic processes in families", in M. Gunnar and E. Thelen (eds), *System and development. The Minnesota Symposia on Child Psychology* (pp. 167-210), vol. 22, Hillsdale, NJ, Erlbaum.

Pettit, G., Dodge, K. and Brown, M. (1988), "Early family experience, social problem solving patterns, and children's social competence", *Child Development*, vol 59, 107-120.

Putallaz, M. (1987), "Maternal behavior and children's sociometric status", *Child Development*, vol. 58, 324-340.

Repetti, R. (1994), "Short-term and long-term processes linking perceived job stressors to father-child interaction", *Social Development*, vol. 3, 1-15.

Roberts, W. and Strayer, J. (1987), "Parents' responses to the emotional distress of their children: Relations with children's competence", *Developmental Psychology*, vol. 23, 415-422.

Sarason, I., Sarason, B. and Sheerin, E. (1986). "Social support as an individual difference variable", *Journal of Personality and Social Psychology*, vol. 50, 845-855.

Steinberg, L., Darling, N., Fletcher, A., Brown, B.B. and Dornbusch, S. (1995), "Authoritative parenting and adolescent adjustment: An ecological journey", In P. Moen, G. Elder and K. Luscher (eds), *Examining lives in context*, pp. 423-466, Washington, DC, APA Books.

van den Boom, D. (1994), "The influence of temperament and mothering on attachment and exploration: An experimental manipulation of sensitive responsiveness among lower-class mothers with irritable infants", *Child Development*, vol. 65, 1457-1477.

van den Boom, D. and Hoeksma, J. (1994), "The effect of infant irritability on mother-infant interaction", *Developmental Psychology*, vol. 30, 581-590.

Vondra, J. and Belsky, J. (1993), "Developmental origins of parenting: Personality and relationship factors", in T. Luster and L. Okagaki (eds), *Parenting: An ecological perspective* (pp. 1-34), Hillsdale, NJ, Erlbaum.

Wachs, T. and Chan, A. (1986), "Specificity of environmental action as seen in environmental correlates of infants' communication performance", *Child Development*, vol. 57, 1464-1474.

2 Pedagogical mismanagement in families and other child-rearing systems

Ko RINK

1. Introduction

The Department of Orthopedagogy of the State University of Groningen and the Northern Institute for Orthopedagogical Research (NIVO) have developed treatment programmes for child-rearing systems, such as families and communities, in which pedagogical mismanagement occurs.

Over the past years this has resulted in a theoretical framework that makes it possible to map all aspects of pedagogical mismanagement in a child-rearing system. We will elaborate upon this framework in this chapter.

The following themes will be discussed:
- the child-rearing system and the 4-variable model by which such a system can be shaped;
- the essence of child-rearing and of pedagogical mismanagement as the converse of this rearing process;
- the three most important child-rearing tasks in a rearing situation and an outline of the forms of pedagogical mismanagement during each of these tasks; and
- the necessity for a uniform orientation and interpretative framework in order to diagnose and treat pedagogical mismanagement in an involuntary population.

2. The child-rearing system and the 4-variable model

A system is a coherent whole made up of similar parts. These parts, separately and through their interaction, contribute to a product. When this product happens to be child-rearing, we call this a rearing situation. Such a situation may occur in a family or in a group home or residential institution.

The factors in a child-rearing situation are similar in that they are rearing variables. We talk of a rearing variable when:
- it affects rearing in a relatively autonomous way;
- this effect can vary with respect to its nature (positive/negative) or to its intensity (none/a lot); and
- this effect can be changed by treatment interventions.

The four most important variables which can be identified in a child-rearing situation are as follows: (see, for example, Van Lokven, 1995).

a. The C variable

This variable concerns the child or youth who is being reared. It can affect the rearing process in two ways:
- through the personal characteristics of the child, with respect to cognitive, emotional and behavioural factors; and
- through the way in which the child communicates with the rearing adult and responds to the child-rearing style of the adult; and through the way the child responds to the treatment programme and the situational context in which child-rearing is taking place.

b. The RA variable

This variable concerns the adult who is doing the child-rearing, and it can similarly affect the child-rearing process in two ways:
- through the personal characteristics of the adult, with respect to cognitive, emotional and behavioural factors; and
- through the adult's own child-rearing style and the way in which the adult communicates with the child; and through the way the adult responds to the treatment programme and the situational context in which child-rearing is taking place.

c. The St variable

This variable concerns the situation types (St', St'', St''', etc.) in the child-rearing situation. A situation type is a regularly recurring event in the child-rearing process: for example, getting up in the morning, the child coming home from school, and washing up the dishes after supper in the evening. Such situation types comprise the St variable. Each situation type has three dimensions, the quality of which may have a positive or negative effect on child-rearing. These three dimensions are: the actual activities carried out in the situation; the rules or social expectations accompanying the situation; and the emotional atmosphere belonging to the situation.

d. The Sc variable

The situational context comprises the material circumstances in which child-rearing takes place. It has the following dimensions:
- the functioning of the child-rearing group, whether the group be a family or an institution. Here, we have to consider roles or positions, the formation of sub-groups or factions, group cohesion, and the content and manner of communication.
- the nature of the physical house or home.
- the financial situation.
- the social network of the child-rearing group. This network includes contacts with relatives, the neighbourhood, clubs or religious institutions, and any involved authorities, such as a general practitioner, a family guardian, a magistrate of a juvenile court or an orthopedagogue.
- the child's living environment. This means the environment in which the house is situated: for example, an estate with a play area, or an apartment in a building where there is no room for the child to play.

This child-rearing system with its four variables can be compared to a gestalt in the sense that, as a whole, it has characteristics which cannot be derived separately from its parts. The system as a whole is bounded, as it were, by the Sc variable or situational context, within which the situation types (the St variable) play themselves out. The parents' and the children's functioning in the family is often embedded in these situation types, but may also be demonstrated outside them. The rearing variables (C and RA) determine each other, but not in all respects. From a pedagogical point of view, the partial nature of this interdependence is due, in particular, to the primary responsibility of the parent as manager of the rearing situation, as well as to the increasing responsibility the children may be expected to assume, under normal circumstances, for their own functioning as they grow older. This partial interdependence is illustrated simply in Figure 2.1.

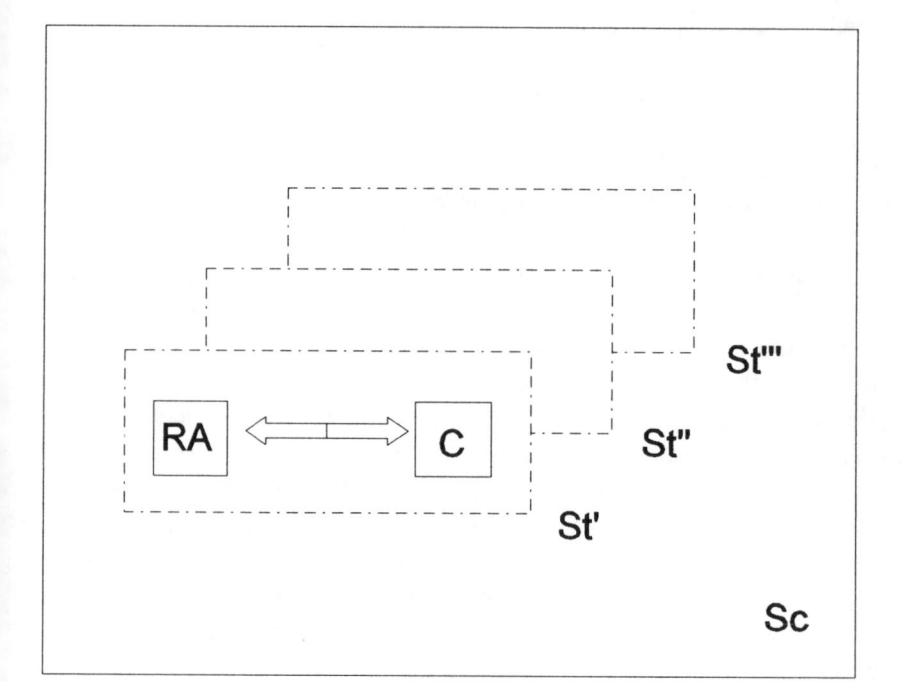

Figure 2.1: Partial interdependence between rearing variables in the rearing situation (Rink, 1995)

The notion of partial interdependence refers to an integrative view of child-rearing (Zandberg, 1992). This view implies that an analysis of child-rearing should not be limited to the way in which parent and child relate to each other during the child-rearing process. Child-rearing is embedded in the whole child-rearing system and the quality of the rearing is co-determined by that whole system.

3. The essence of child-rearing and of pedagogical mismanagement as the antipode of this rearing

In this section we will dwell upon a number of essential aspects of child-rearing and of pedagogical mismanagement.

3.1. Essential aspects of child-rearing as a phenomenon

Within child-rearing, three aspects may be identified: existential, clinical and philosophical. These will be briefly examined.

The existential aspect. This aspect has to do with the level of existential awareness on the part of the parents as rearing adults. First of all, parents have to experience their existence as an existence with a purpose whose realisation is dependent upon themselves. As a result of, for example, a disease or the use of drugs, this existential awareness may have disappeared or been reduced. In order to be capable of child-rearing, a sufficient level of awareness is necessary in this respect. In addition, child-rearing implies that a parent realises that he or she co-exists with a child; the parent is aware of the fact that there is a child in his or her environment. This existential aspect finally implies that the parent realises that this child is in need of her support for its development; she is there to help or guide her child whenever necessary. The existential aspect implies that the parent is there as a child-rearing adult, even before he or she acts as such.

The clinical aspect. This aspect concerns the parent's willingness and ability to act as a child-rearing adult. He or she must be capable of performing two kinds of acts, the one setting up the condition for the other. The parent must be able to enter into or continue a bidirectional communication with the child, as a result of which both parties become or remain mutually accessible in a pedagogical respect. The parent bears primary responsibility for the quality of this communication. In addition, the clinical aspect implies that the parent makes use of this communication to encourage the child's capabilities or to compensate for the child's deficiencies.

The philosophical aspect. The values and norms of the parent as a child-rearing adult fulfil a teleological function in the way that the parent encourages the child's development by means of his or her clinical acts. This function lends a certain substance and direction to the bidirectional communication and to the encouragement and compensation.

   The existential, clinical and philosophical aspects of rearing are summarised in Figure 2.2

26

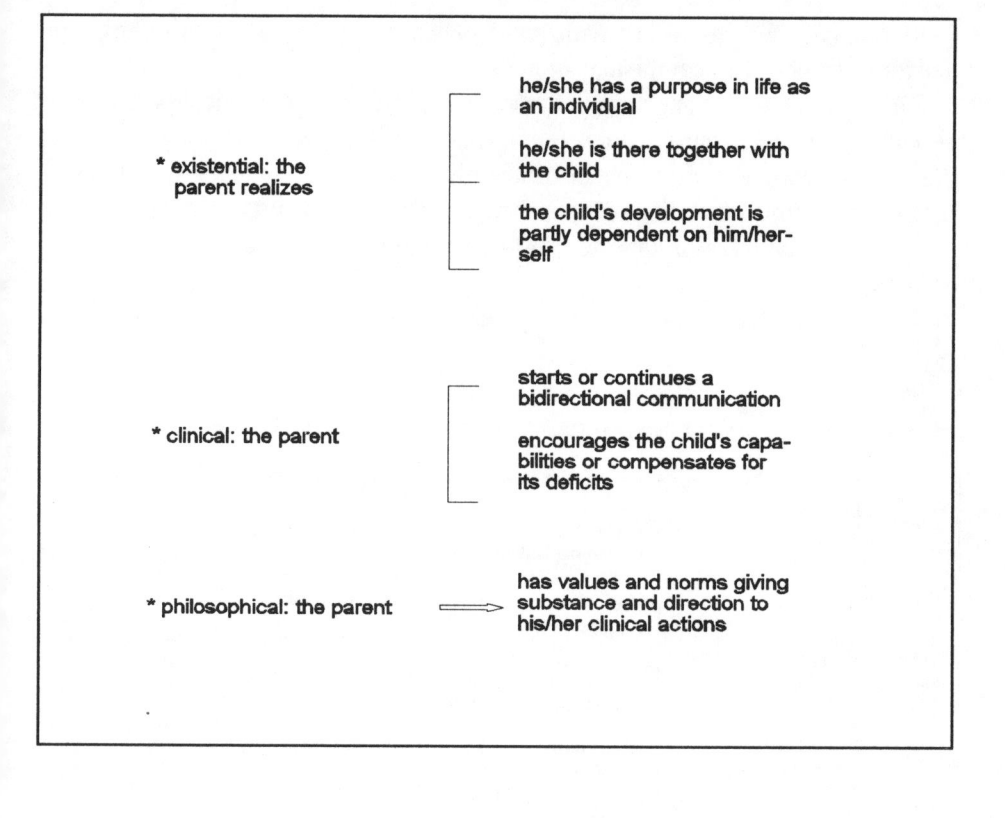

Figure 2.2: Child-rearing as an existential, clinical and philosophical phenomenon (Rink, 1995)

3.2. Essential aspects of pedagogical mismanagement

Pedagogical mismanagement as opposed to child-rearing can similarly be described in existential, clinical and philosophical terms.

Pedagogical mismanagement in an existential sense means that parents have no or too little personal perspective in their lives, have no room in their experience to co-exist with their children, or lack the awareness that their child might need them as rearing adults. The existential cause for pedagogical mismanagement is more basic than any other cause.

Pedagogical mismanagement can also be due to a clinical cause. Parents may lack the willingness or ability to act as child-rearing adults when necessary. When a mother is not willing or able to bring about bidirectional communication with her child or lacks the dedication or capability to recognise and support the child's capabilities or to look for the proper compensation options for the child's shortcomings, then this will provide a clinical cause on her part for the origin or existence of pedagogical mismanagement.

Pedagogical mismanagement can be viewed from a teleological perspective as well. When the parents' values and normative views are inconsistent or when the parents' clinical actions are insufficiently tuned to the child's possibilities in teleological terms, this will undermine the child's existential security or will lead to inadequately encouraging the child's capabilities or compensating for short-comings.

The essential aspects of pedagogical mismanagement are summarised in Figure 2.3.

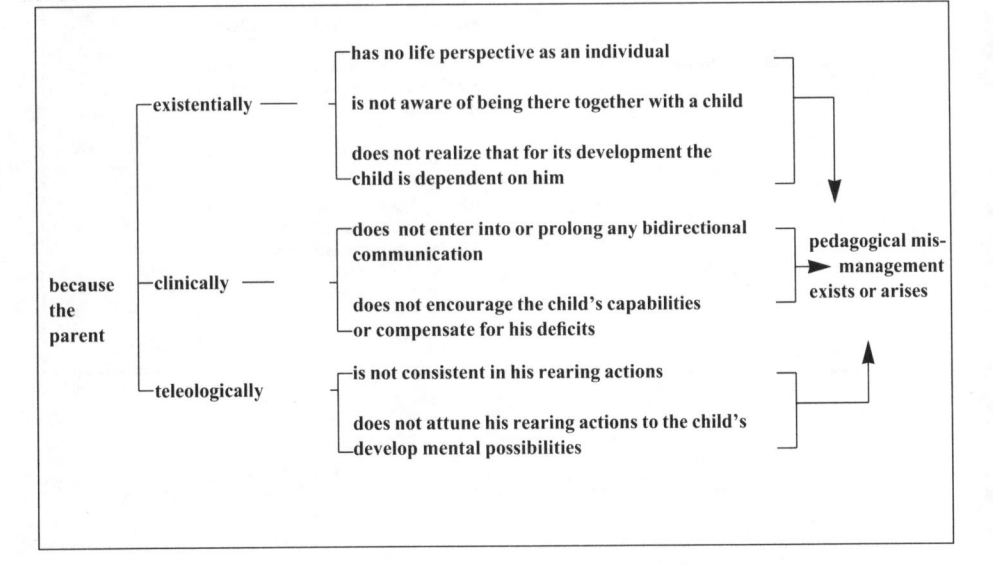

Figure 2.3: The essence of pedagogical mismanagement (Rink, 1995)

4. The three most important child-rearing tasks and the types of pedagogical mismanagement at each of these task levels

In section 4.1, the most important child-rearing tasks will be discussed, and in section 4.2, the types of pedagogical mismanagement will be outlined.

4.1. Three child-rearing tasks

The existential, clinical and teleological aspects of child-rearing are given shape by the rearing adults carrying out three rearing tasks. These tasks are distinguished by the object to which they are directed:
- the first task, the 'essential child-rearing' task, comprises that which is essential to child-rearing and is directed at the child or C variable;
- the second task is concerned with controlling the quality of the infrastructure in the child-rearing situation and is directed at the St and Sc variables; and
- the third task concerns controlling the quality of child-rearing and is directed at the rearing adult or RA variable.

These tasks will be briefly explained.

The 'essential' child-rearing task. The rearing adult performs the first child-rearing task by setting up direct contact between herself and her child. The parent must initiate or continue a bidirectional communication with the child; and must be willing and able to do so. The willingness should be based on the parent's awareness that the child needs her help and guidance in order to develop. The ability aspect demands an effort from the parent in terms of communication. She must try to receive and understand her child's verbal or non-verbal signals. In addition, the child should be able to receive and understand the parent's signals as well. During 'essential' child-rearing the parent should then make use of this communication for encouraging the child's capabilities or compensating for the child's shortcomings. If the parent fails to do this, whatever communication exists is an 'empty dialogue' from the pedagogical perspective and no real child-rearing is taking place. Encouraging and stimulating the child's development is brought about by a combination of accepting the child, being responsive to the child, and being demanding of, and controlling, the child. Maccoby and Martin (1983) call this combination the authoritative child-rearing attitude.

Controlling the quality of the infrastructure in the child-rearing situation. This second child-rearing situation is of an indirect nature. In this regard, Kok (1992, p. 23) speaks about 'creating social situations in which children can blossom optimally'. Controlling the quality of the infrastructure implies two activities. First, the St and Sc variables - that is, the daily child-rearing programme and the social and material context in which this takes place - have to be expressly structured or moulded. As a result, on the one hand, existential security will be provided, particularly to younger children, and, on the other hand, the child's capabilities may be stimulated.

In addition, this structure makes the St and Sc variables accessible to the child. This implies that there should be sufficient variation in the routine for the child to gain the necessary learning experiences, and a sufficient feeling of usefulness and meaning to enable the child to participate willingly in the routine. Children should be enabled to learn at home that later they have to structure their environment in consultation with others and how they can best do this.

The child-rearing principles inherent in the second rearing task are briefly shown in Figure 2.4.

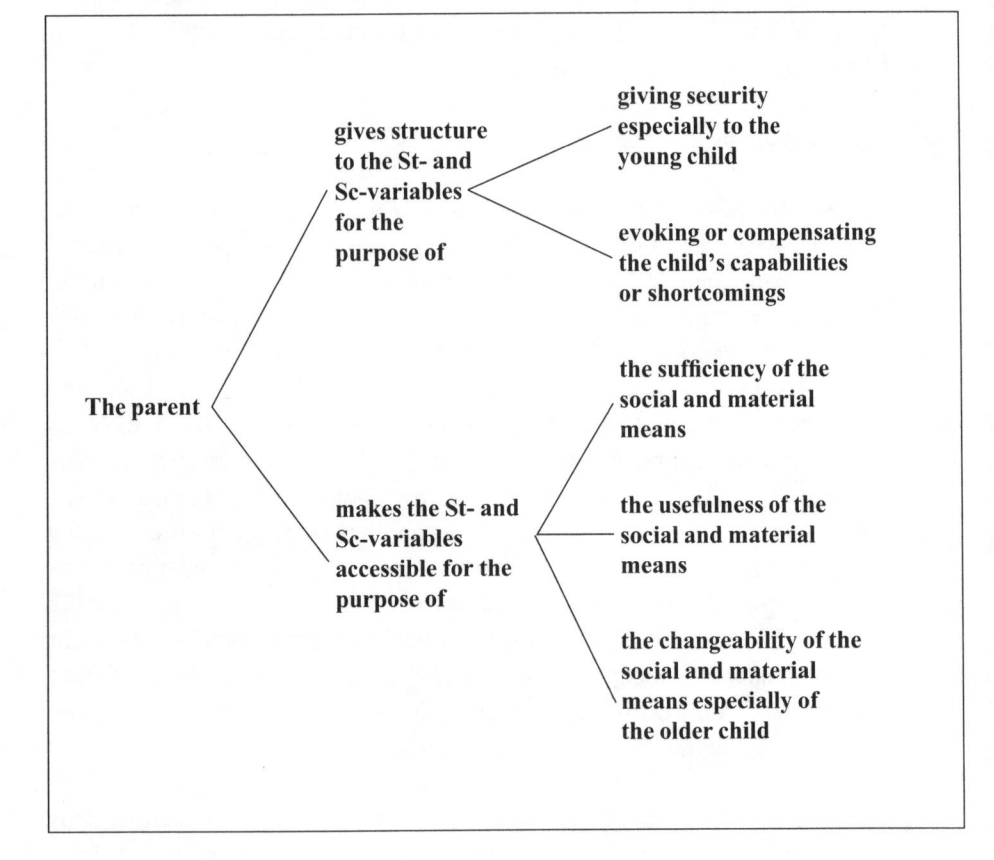

Figure 2.4: Child-rearing principles during the second rearing task (Rink, 1995)

Controlling the quality of child-rearing. This third child-rearing task is directed at the rearing adult or the RA variable. The level at which the first and second child-rearing tasks are carried out is strongly dependent on the parent's capabilities to be really aware of the rearing situation (existential condition) and to be willing and able to enter into it (clinical and teleological conditions). If a parent lacks existential awareness, she cannot be expected to focus attention on the quality of her own child-rearing. However, when this awareness is present, the parent can be held responsible for his or her willingness, capabilities and child-rearing goals. If the parent comes to the conclusion that she cannot properly carry out the first and the second child-rearing tasks, controlling the quality of child-rearing - the third child-rearing task - implies that she should try to access and make use of professional help.

4.2. The types of pedagogical mismanagement at each of the three task levels

The types of pedagogical mismanagement will be briefly explained in the following section. For a more complete description, please refer to Rink (1995: 52-66).

Pedagogical mismanagement at the first task level. The first child-rearing task was concerned with 'essential rearing'. Direct pedagogical mismanagement manifests itself in several ways. First of all, it may be that there is no bidirectional communication at moments when the rearing adult should have been acting in an authoritative way. At these moments, parent and child are pedagogically inaccessible to each other. At this task level, this form of pedagogical misman-agement is basic. In addition, a parent can withhold direct developmental support from the child by adopting an approach that is not authoritative. The best-known pedagogically undesirable approaches are: indulgence, neglect, and physical and sexual abuse. These forms of direct pedagogical mismanagement often occur in families in combination with lack of communication.

Pedagogical mismanagement at the second task level. These indirect forms of pedagogical mismanagement occur when a parent is not able or omits to make use of the St and Sc variables as child-rearing mechanisms. The St and Sc variables are not structured either by organising daily events or by providing material and social structure in a situational context. As a result, existential security is withheld especially from younger children, and these child-rearing methods are not used to reinforce the child's capabilities or to compensate for the child's shortcomings.

At this task level, pedagogical mismanagement also occurs when there is insufficient variation in social and material structures for children to participate in changing the routines, or when the usefulness of the routines is not apparent. Learning in such an environment is difficult, if not impossible.

31

The types of pedagogical mismanagement at the third task level. The third child-rearing task is concerned with the rearing adult or RA variable. Earlier we identified three dimensions of child-rearing: the existential, clinical and teleological dimensions. When existential awareness is lacking, the quality of child-rearing is not controlled at all, at either the first, second or third task levels. The result of this lack of existential awareness is that parents do not realise that pedagogical mismanagement is a problem. Because they are unaware, they are not conscious of their own inability to rear children and they do not they find it necessary to seek professional help. However, when existential awareness *is* present, indirect pedagogical mismanagement will occur when the parents' interest in their own willingness or child-rearing capabilities decreases. This lack of interest may be caused by circumstances inside or outside the family. Pedagogical mismanagement becomes persistent when, as a result of lack of interest, parents are not motivated to call in outside help or are not able to use that help in an effective way.

The types of pedagogical mismanagement at the first, second and third task levels are briefly summarised in Figure 2.5.

Field of the rea-ring task (RT)	Forms of pedagogical mismanagement
First RT	- being pedagogically inaccessible - withholding direct developmental support: . indulgence . neglect . physical abuse . sexual abuse
Second RT	- not organizing/structuring the St- and Sc-variables - not making the St- and Sc-variables accessible to the child; social and material structure is: . not large or varied . not perceived as useful . unchangeable
Third RT	- lack of the existential awareness necessary to a rearing adult - decreased attention to the level of willingness or ability to rear - decreased attention to the controlling function necessary to achieve child-rearing goals - lack of willingness and capacity to make use of outside help

Figure 2.5: Expressive forms of pedagogical mismanagement at the first, second and third task levels

5. The necessity of a uniform orientation and interpretative framework for the diagnosis and treatment of pedagogical mismanagement

From the foregoing, it is clear that pedagogical mismanagement has many forms at different task levels. The causes are also multiple, lying with the child, with the rearing adult, and with the daily programme or situational context.

Possibly as a result of these many forms and causes, several lines of approach have been followed in Holland with respect to the diagnosis of pedagogical mismanagement. The scope of this chapter does not allow for a survey of all the instruments being used in this connection. In child protection, the following, among others, are frequently used: the VSPS (Scholte, 1991), the PSI (Weterings, Pruijs, Bloemberg, Grootes, Pool and Van de Oetelaar, 1991) and the CBCL (Verhulst, Koot, Akkerhuis and Veerman, 1990). Without specifically elaborating on these and other instruments, I would like to comment, more generally, on all these efforts to diagnose pedagogical mismanagement. The following points are particularly relevant:

- Many instruments are not designed to determine the quality of child-rearing and consequently the degree of pedagogical mismanagement. This is especially important in the context of child protection when an indication has to be given of the extent to which a child's mental or physical development is threatened by the quality of the rearing the child is receiving. The orientation and inter-pretative frameworks of many instruments are rarely of a pedagogical nature. No or too little attention is paid to the existential, clinical and teleological dimensions of child-rearing, to the way child-rearing is made concrete by means of the different child-rearing tasks, and to the central dimensions and forms of pedagogical mismanagement as the converse of this model of child-rearing.
- When instruments focus on the family as the rearing system, they mostly limit themselves to only some of the four rearing variables - often the RA and C variables. Thus, no impression of the total rearing system and the other rearing variables in it is obtained. From the System guidance project East Groningen (SEG-project), the relevance of the St variable becomes obvious, both in determining the quality of child-rearing in a family, and in assisting the orthopedagogical home help to reduce pedagogical mismanagement. In many SEG-families with pedagogical mismanagement, it was possible to fight this mismanagement effectively by setting up situation types: that is, by introduc-ing a well-organised daily programme (see Rink, Algra, Van Lokven and Vlieg, 1994, p. 157). Instruments tend to pay too little or no attention to the St variable.
- With respect to child protection, researchers tend to focus on the behaviour problems of the child - the C variable - without determining the quality of

child-rearing in the family in question. As a result, it cannot be ascertained whether the observed behaviour problems are connected with the quality of child-rearing in the family, with the situation at school or, for example, with a club of which the child is a member.

- Finally, there are weighting problems. Workers of Child Welfare Councils are presented with questions concerning the family situation. It frequently remains unclear on what they base their answers and to what extent they differ or agree among themselves as to how they weigh facts or opinions. This can also happen when parents or other child-rearing adults are asked to pass judgement on children's behaviour. Imposing child protection measures on the basis of answers of this sort raises questions since the criteria on which weighting is based have not been made explicit and consequently cannot be verified and politically discussed. These problems are recognised when weighting is left to professionals. Even so, there remain the problems of verification and the impossibility of any political discussion.

This instrumental jungle in terms of pedagogics is hard to disentangle. Moreover, the use of certain instruments is closely linked with financial interests. The Dutch central government, at present in favour of decentralisation in the field of child care, does not respond to appeals for co-operative efforts in exchanging this instrumental jungle for a necessary uniformity in orientations and interpretative frameworks, by means of which the different institutions, especially those in the field of child protection, might diagnose and treat pedagogical mismanagement. It is our opinion that the central government does need to play a guiding role in making these orientations and interpretative frameworks uniform. Diagnosis and treatment of pedagogical mismanagement could take place in preparation for or during a child protection measure. In this context, clients are entitled to a diagnosis that would be essentially the same no matter who was making it.

Our proposal to the central government with regard to making diagnostic and treatment frameworks more uniform contains the following components:

1. The central idea is that making the framework uniform should result in an instrument through which the quality of child-rearing and thus the extent of pedagogical mismanagement can be determined. This instrument should be capable of indicating at what task level this pedagogical mismanagement occurs and in what forms it manifests itself.
2. The instrument should encompass each of the four rearing variables in the rearing system. (This is the orientation framework.)
3. The instrument should make it feasible to determine the way in which each of the rearing variables contributes to the forms of pedagogical mismanagement in question at any particular task level. (This is the interpretative framework.)

34

4. The interpretative framework requires weighting the rearing variables, their characteristics and the different forms of these characteristics. How do they contribute to forms of pedagogical mismanagement at certain task levels?
5. The central government must ask institutions to carry out this weighting as part of their policy at the institutional level and to make explicit the criteria used in that connection. Institutions with the same or similar functions should use the same criteria: for example, the newly institutionalised six jurisdiction areas of the Councils for child protection in Holland. Making these weighting criteria explicit will allow the central government, at the same time, to indicate the margins within which institutions or organisations are allowed to differentiate on the basis of, for example, ideological grounds.

References

Kok, J.F.W. (1992), *Opvoeden als beroep, een inleiding voor groepsopvoeders en leraren*, Nelissen, Baarn.

Maccoby, E.E. and Martin, J.A. (1983), "Socialization in the context of the family, Parents-child interaction" in E.M. Hetherington (ed.), *Socialization, personality and social development*, IV, 1-101, New York, John Wiley.

Rink, J.E., Algra, A.E.T., Van Lokven, H.M. and Vlieg, E. (1994), *Ortho-pedagogische thuishulp in een justitieel kader OTJ. Eindrapport SOG-project*, Groningen, Kinderstudies.

Rink, J.E. (1995), *Pedagogical mismanagement and Orthopedagogy*, Leuven, Garant.

Scholte, E.M. (1991), *De vragenlijst en het hulpverleningsplan Sociale en pedagogische situatie. Handleiding bij gebruik van de VSPS en de HSPS.* Versie 2.0., Delft, Elburon.

Van Lokven, R. (1955), *De noodzaak van een 'herkenbare' pedagogische diagnose voor de AJL*, in AJL Nieuwsbrief, vol. 2, no. 5, 4-7.

Verhulst, F.C., Koot, J.M., Akkerhuis, G.W. & Veerman, J.W. (1990), *Praktische handleiding voor de CBCL*, Assen-Maastricht, Van Gorcum.

Weterings, A.M., Pruijs, H., Bloemberg, W.A., Grootes, C., Pool, W. & Van de Oetelaar, T. (1991), *Signaleren binnen de jeugdhulpverlening. De ontwikkeling van het PSI, Pedagogisch Signalerings-Instrumentarium*, Leiden, Centrum Onderzoek Jeugdhulpverlening (COJ).

Zandberg, Tj. (1992), "Jeugdhulpverlening en integratie", *Pedagogisch tijdschrift*, vol. 17, no. 3, 187-199.

3 Secondary prevention of child maltreatment: The early identification of families in need of support

by Helen AGATHONOS-GEORGOPOULOU
Kevin BROWN
E. SARAFIDOU

Introduction

The prevention of child maltreatment has been addressed primarily at the tertiary level, attempting to cure a problem which has already manifested itself in various pathological ways. This after-effect approach has proved partly effective as it entails multiple intervention strategies whose target population of families have limited inner drive and resources for change. Furthermore, this approach in most countries is based on a complex system of child abuse allegations and reporting which often results in the stigmatisation of families and in pathologising the phenomenon.

At the other end of the spectrum, primary prevention aims at structural societal changes which may prevent the problem before it occurs. These societal changes may include: the elimination of cultural norms and media influences that legitimise and glorify violence; the reduction of violence-provoking stress such as poverty; the enhancement of kin and community ties; and the promotion of education which may change the sexist character of society and violence as a way of dealing with children's 'challenging behaviour' (Gelles and Cornell, 1985). Such fundamental changes require an ideological revolution, an ecological approach to social issues, and the political will of each nation and society.

In the middle of the spectrum, secondary prevention aims at predicting the problem as early as possible. It is based on the early identification of characteristics which have the potential to predispose individuals to child maltreatment. Such predisposing factors may form a basis for intervention with families at 'high risk' for child abuse and neglect (Browne, 1988; Pringle, 1980). Secondary prevention seems to be the most promising and cost-effective solution as the early identification of individuals with child abuse potential, combined with a non-stigmatising supportive approach, may prevent the problem before it occurs.

Incidence

Estimates of the extent of child maltreatment in different countries vary, and each reflects only a portion of the actual prevalence of cases. Three basic factors are responsible for the underestimation (Parke and Lewis, 1981): the failure to detect injuries caused by abuse, the failure to recognise abuse as the cause of a victim's injuries, and the failure to report the case to the appropriate service (Zigler and Hall, 1989).

In the United States, a problem that was thought to affect 447 children in 1960, was found to affect more than 2 million children 30 years later. Current estimates claim that approximately 1-2 per cent of American children are abused or neglected every year (Krugman 1992).

Epidemiological data from the United Kingdom, based on Register Research of the National Society for the Prevention of Cruelty to Children, suggest a rate of 0.85 per 1,000 children 0-14 years old and 1.23 per 1,000 for the 0-4 year-old group (Creighton, 1988). Browne (1989; 1993), claims that 1 per cent of English children under five are abused or neglected.

It is almost impossible to compare estimates for the incidence of child maltreatment among different countries because of national differences in aware-ness and reporting systems, as well as in cross-cultural issues and service systems (Kamerman, 1975).

The incidence of child maltreatment in Greece has not been determined because of the lack of a reporting system. An attempt to estimate it among the in-patient population of Aghia Sophia Children's hospital revealed a rate of 0.64 per 1,000 children, which may easily be projected to at least 1-2 per thousand children, including community samples. Extrapolating from this and from the U.K. findings, and based on the yearly birth rate of 100,000 births, it is expected that 100-200 new cases of child maltreatment will occur annually in Greece: for all children aged 0-18 years, 1,800-3,600 will be experiencing maltreatment at any particular point in time. On the other hand, if we use the incidence rate of 1per cent (Krugman, 1992; Browne, 1993) and apply this to the 100,000 births in Greece per year, we would expect 1,000 to 2,000 new cases annually, or 18,000 to 36,000 cases among children aged 0-18 years.

The effects of maltreatment

A number of studies on the consequences of maltreatment to children, though fraught with definitional and methodological problems, support the widely-held assumption that child abuse and neglect have serious negative effects on the child's physical, neurological, intellectual and emotional development (Toro, 1982).

A disproportionately high number of abused children have been found to perform below the average for their age on I.Q. tests and to show deficits in academic performance (Hoffman-Plotkin and Twentyman, 1984; Martin, Beeley, Conway and Kempe, 1974; Sandgrund, Gaines and Green, 1974).

The areas of emotional development affected have been found to be self-esteem, expectations of self and ambitions for the future.

Language delay has been described as a common developmental problem among abused children. In Lynch and Roberts' (1982) study, one-third of all the preschool children demonstrated marked delays in language, with no differences observed between the abused children and their siblings.

Abused children's behaviour in the home has been characterised by high rates of aggressive and aversive behaviours such as hitting, yelling and destructiveness when interacting with parents and siblings (Lahey, Conger, Atkeson and Treiber, 1984; Reidy, 1977). Similarly, they show aggression towards pre-school peers which later on may be described as bullying.

Little research has been carried out on abused children's resilience, which has been defined as the phenomenon of maintaining adaptive functioning in spite of serious risks (Rutter, 1987). The concept of resilience has been applied in the context of individuals, families and communities (Agathonos 1995). Resilience can change over time and is affected by both environment and genetics (Mrazek and Mrazek, 1987). It is fostered by protective factors or skills which character-ise the individual child, and generic life circumstances such as having good health and access to educational and welfare services. These factors foster resilience in children regardless of the specific nature of the stressor.

All clinical and research findings suggest that maltreatment should be prevented by early identification of the risk factors linked with individual, familial and social characteristics, before violence establishes itself as a family pattern of interaction.

The Greek study

The aim of the study to be presented was to compare the characteristics of abusing and non-abusing families on 118 variables which have been described in the international literature as differentiating between abusing and non-abusing samples. These variables were considered under the following classifications:

1.   Problems in pregnancy and birth.
2.   Problems in the neonatal period.
3.   Problems from the neonatal period to referral.
4.   Child's problems upon referral.
5.   Social and demographic characteristics of families (e.g. parental age).
6.   Problems in living conditions.
7.   Family characteristics (e.g. child not living with both natural parents).
8.   Parental absence.
9.   Other problems.
10.   Serious stressful family relations.
11.   Serious stress with relatives.
12.   Serious stress with others.
13.   Alcohol problems.
14.   Drug problems
15.   Criminal record.
16.   Unemployment.
17.   Physical illness.
18.   Psychiatric illness.

The sample of abusive families used for the research comprises 197 cases of physically abused and neglected children from the Attica region. They were all children aged 0-17 years who were referred to the multidisciplinary team of the Institute of Child Health.

For this research we decided to use the definition by Garbarino and Gilliam (1980), which pertains to a clinical sample by referring to both physical abuse and neglect while also considering the cultural context. The operational definition used is: 'Any acts of commission or omission by a parent or guardian that are judged by a mixture of community values and professional expertise to be inappropriate and damaging'.

Criteria for inclusion in the study

The criteria for inclusion in the study were:

1. Place of origin: Attica region.
2. Age of child: 0-17 years.
3. Children with physical injuries of non-accidental origin upon referral.
4. Children with failure to thrive and physical neglect needing medical intervention.
5. Children with a history of inflicted injuries and/or severe emotional abuse within the last year.

Children in category (5) were those named as 'at risk'.

Control sample

A non-abusing population of 177 children and their families were approached. These families were drawn from primary health clinics in the Attica region belonging to the National Foundation for Social Welfare, a large government organisation. They thus represented a non-clinical community sample. Eight per cent of the control families refused to participate in the study. The remaining 163 children and their families formed the control sample.

Each abused child was matched with a control as to (a) sex, (b) age, and (c) social class as indicated by the parents' number of years of schooling.

In total, 118 variables were statistically compared between abusing and non-abusing families and 86 (73 per cent) were found to have a higher representation in the abusing group.

This shows that the majority of the variables claimed in the literature to be associated with child-abusing families are also associated with child-abusing families residing in the Attica region of Greece.

The findings support the notion that abusing families differ considerably from non-abusing families. The characteristics found to differentiate between the two groups may be used as risk factors to identify high risk families for child maltreatment in Greece. This approach comprises the area of secondary prevention.

Aims of the risk approach

The risk approach to the prevention of child maltreatment has been described as a managerial tool for the distribution of resources and their maximal utilisation, based on the assessment of children and their families as High or Low Risk for child abuse and neglect (Browne and Saqi, 1988). The aim of this approach is to support all those considered as high risk early enough in their role as parents, before child maltreatment occurs. This approach is based on the mobilisation of health and social services at the community level to (1) develop methods for detecting risk factors, (2) train health care and social workers in these methods and (3) provide intervention strategies to prevent or ameliorate undesired outcomes (World Health Organisation, 1978). The risk approach is classical in the field of preventative health, but has never been applied to the early detection and prevention of maltreatment of children in Greece.

The application of a checklist of risk factors may be retrospective or prospective. A retrospective approach to the use of a checklist compares the risk factors in two identified groups, abusing families and control families. This may produce a checklist for screening. The prospective approach refers to the use of the checklist on a specific population followed up over time in order to estimate its sensitivity and specificity. Browne and Saqi (1988), used the results of their retrospective study in a prospective way by having health visitors complete a 13-item checklist.

For reasons of comparison with results of other authors who have chosen discriminant analysis in their prediction work, the data in this study were analysed by discriminant function analysis.

In carrying out the analysis, 'family' variables rather than 'personal' variables were used because of the chosen conceptual approach to child maltreatment. This approach regards the problem of child maltreatment as a function of family interaction rather than of individual pathology. The presence of a serious problem in one parent was assumed to set the climate for the family as a whole. It was possible to apply this concept to all but four of the variables.

Fifteen characteristics were identified in the analysis with a positive standardised canonical coefficient. These were then placed in order of relative importance based on the size of coefficient value, and were categorized into five Heavy-, five Medium- and five Light-weight predictive factors.

Table 3.1 presents this categorisation.

41

Table 3.1
Relative importance of characteristics associated with abuse used for screening, as determined by discriminant function analysis (N=15)

Heavy-weight

Child's bad state of hygiene upon referral.
Parents with mental health problems.
Bad quality of relationship between parents.
Parents with adverse life experiences.
Mother strictly disciplined by own parents.

Medium-weight

Life Events for parents, last year.
Child not with both natural parents.
Mother unable to rely on anybody when in crisis.
Father with unsteady employment or unemployed.
Mother less than 21 years at birth of index child.

Light-weight

Delayed psychomotor development.
Child had 'other illnesses' prior to referral.
Not breast fed as neonate.
Parents expect immediate obedience from child.
Parental absence prior to referral.

Based on the size of their coefficient value, a score of 3 was given to heavy-weight factors, 2 to medium-weight and 1 to light-weight factors. These scores were then applied to the 15 factors, in both groups, abusing and controls (see Figure 3.1). The cut-off point was 9. As shown in the Figure, abusing families scored significantly higher, covering most of the high risk area.

●

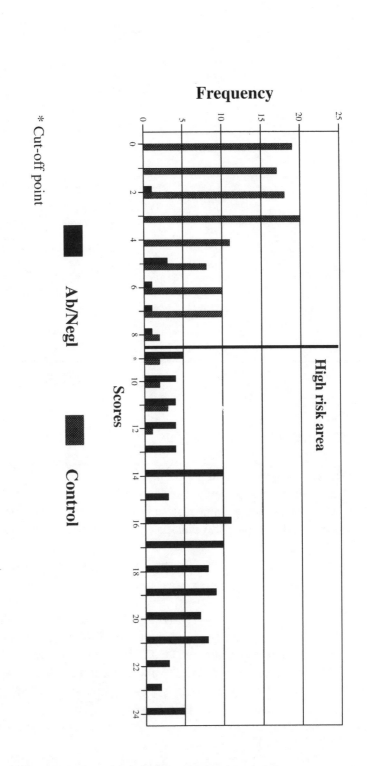

Using the same analysis, the predictive ability of characteristics associated with abuse was estimated. The percentage of families correctly classified as abusing (sensitivity) was found to be 86.8 per cent, while the percentage of families correctly identified as non-abusing (specificity) was 96.3 per cent. Overall, 92.3 per cent of families were correctly classified by this method.

Levels of 85-90 per cent of correct classifications have been the maximum reported for screening procedures so far.

Application of checklist to screening

As an epidemiological exercise, an attempt was made to apply the checklist to the estimated yearly incidence of physical child abuse in Greece, based on the hospital incidence rate of 0.6/1000, which definitely does not represent the true picture in Greece but is the only proximal figure available (see Figure 3.2).

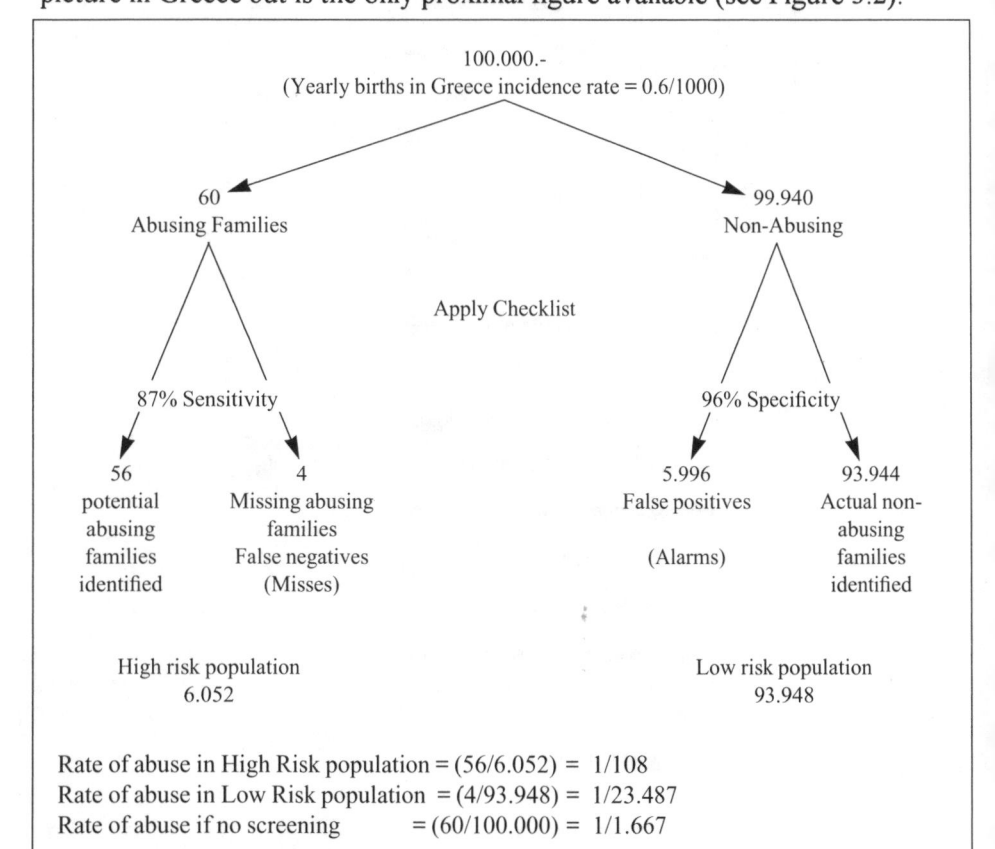

Figure 3.2 Application of the checklist to the annual births in Greece to identify potential abusing families

44

Therefore, with an incidence rate of 0.6 children in 1,000 or 6 children in every 10,000 and a population of 100,000 births annually in Greece, each year 60 abusing families would be expected. An application of the checklist to identify potentially abusing families would mean that 56 potential abusing families would be identified (with 87 per cent sensitivity) and 4 would be missed. However, 5,996 non-abusing families would be incorrectly classified as potential abusers with only a 96 per cent specificity. As Figure 3.2 indicates, the practical problem would be to distinguish the 56 potential abusers from the 6,052 high risk population (i.e. 1/108 high risk families). At the same time, it would be impossible to find the 4 missed potential abusing cases as they would be mixed up with the low-risk population of 93,948.

Therefore 1 in 23,487 low-risk families would go on to abuse their child. This figure adequately demonstrates the limitation of a screening approach if used by itself. Nevertheless, without screening, the health professionals in Greece would be looking for 1 in 1,667 families instead of 1 in 108 high-risk families.

It must be recognised that this investigation into the predictive ability of a checklist as a potential screening tool was based on retrospective data. Therefore, there is no guarantee that the performance would be as accurate when applied prospectively. It is recommended, therefore, that a prospective research programme be carried out before such a checklist is used on a Greek population.

The application of such a screening procedure, regardless of its limitations, may have positive effects on the population of non-abused children identified by the risk index. Even the minimum intervention offered (for example, a home visitor), if it follows a well-planned and ethically sound approach, may be well received and effective with non-abusing families.

The findings of this study raise a number of questions which should be the target of further research in Greece and elsewhere, when appropriate.

A first target would be the prospective use of the checklist of high-risk factors for the prediction of maltreatment, by identifying parents who have a high priority for service provision, with special emphasis on parenting. This should then lead to a pilot project of secondary prevention in a specific geographical area or community. Such a project, following the work of Browne and Saqi (1988), should have three steps. First, all families with a newborn child residing in the area should be screened perinatally using the study's checklist of high-risk characteristics. This will identify a high-risk target group for further screening. Second, all parents of the target groups should be visited at home by health visitors twice during the child's first six months of life. The purpose of these visits is to allow parents to express their thoughts and feelings related to stressful areas of parenting and family life. Finally, at approximately the end of the first year, a home visit should focus on qualitative aspects of mother-infant interaction.

Secondary prevention of child maltreatment may raise serious ethical questions if based on a conceptual approach of abuse as an act of psychopathological perpetrators in need of control. There is now clear evidence that child maltreatment is a result of the interplay of predisposing factors in the parents, the child and the environment, whose mutual interaction with protective factors at the same levels may trigger abuse.

It is, therefore, proposed that in applying secondary prevention approaches, parents and families should be regarded as having high priority for service provision rather than as at high risk for abuse. This conceptual approach may not only promote secondary prevention but may also contribute to changing the philosophical foundation of contemporary child-protection work in many countries.

References

Agathonos, H. (1995), *Promoting resilience in a Greek island community characterized by social exclusion*, Paper delivered at the International Seminar "Children on the Way from Marginality to Citizenship: Childhood Policies: Conceptual and Practical Issues", Montebello, Quebec, Canada, October 16-20.

Browne, K.D. (1993), "Home visitation and child abuse: The British experience", *The Advisor*, vol. 6, no. 4, 11-31.

Browne, K.D. (1989), "The health visitors' role in screening for child abuse", *Health Visitor*, vol. 62, no. 9, 275-277.

Browne, K.D. (1988), "The nature of child abuse and neglect: An overview", in K. Browne, C. Davies and P. Stratton (eds.), *Early Prediction and Prevention of Child Abuse*, Wiley and Sons, Chichester.

Browne, K.D. & Saqi S. (1988), "Approaches to screening for child abuse and neglect", in K. Browne, C. Davies and P. Stratton (eds), *Early Prediction and Prevention of Child Abuse*, Wiley and Sons, Chichester.

Creighton, S.J. (1988), "Child abuse in 1987: Initial findings from the NSPCC's Register Research", *Child Abuse Review*, vol. 2, no. 9, 15-16.

Gelles, R.J. and Cornell, C.P. (1985), *Intimate Violence in Families*, Sage, Beverly Hills, California.

Hoffman-Plotkin, D. and Twentyman, C.T. (1984), "A multimodal assessment of behavioural and cognitive deficits in abused and neglected preschoolers", *Child Development*, vol. 55, 794-802.

Kamerman, S. (1975), "Eight countries: cross national perspectives on child abuse and neglect", *Children today*, vol. 4, 34-37.

Krugman, R.D. (1992). "The battered child at thirty: What can be learned from Paul Krugman at eighty?" *Pediatrics*, vol. 90, no. 1, Part 2, Saul Krugman Festschrift, 154-156.

Lahey, B.B., Conger, R.D., Atkeson, B.M. and Treiber, F.A. (1984), "Parenting behavior and emotional status of physically abusive mothers", *Journal of Consulting and Clinical Psychology*, vol. 52, 1062-1071.

Lynch, M.A. & Roberts, J. (1982), *Consequences of Child Abuse*, Academic Press, London.

Martin, H.P., Beezley, P., Conway, E.S. and Kempe, C.H. (1974), "The development of abused children", *Advances in Pediatrics*, vol. 21, 25-73.

Mrazek, P.J. and Mrazek, D.A. (1987), "Resilience in child maltreatment victims: A conceptual exploration", *Child Abuse and Neglect*, vol. 11, 357-366.

Parke, R.D. and Lewis, N.G. (1981), "The family in context: A multilevel interactional analysis of child abuse", in R.W. Henderson (ed.), *Parent-Child Interaction - Theory, Research Prospects*, Academic Press, New York.

Reidy, T.J. (1977), "The aggressive characteristics of abused and neglected children", *Journal of Clinical Psychology*, vol. 33, 1140-1145.

Rutter, N. (1987), "Psychosocial resilience and protective mechanisms", *American Journal of Orthopsychiatry*, vol. 57, 316-331.

Sandgrund, A., Gaines, R. and Green, A. (1974), "Child abuse and mental retardation: A problem of cause and effect", *American Journal of Mental Deficiency*, vol. 79, 327-330.

Toro, P.A. (1982), "Developmental effects of child abuse: A review", *Child Abuse and Neglect*, vol. 8, 423-431.

Zigler, E. and Hall, N.W. (1989), "Physical child abuse in America: past, present, and future", in D. Cicchetti and V. Carison (eds.), *Child Maltreatment* (38-75), University Press, Cambridge.

4 Parental involvement in residential care: Fact or fiction?

Monika SMIT
Erik J. KNORTH

1. Introduction

Traditionally, an important purpose of residential placement was to limit the damaging influence by the family of a 'problem child'. This was accomplished by breaking off or minimising the contacts with the family, in the child's interest. Residential homes served as replacements for the parents (Jenson and Whittaker, 1987; Günder, 1989).

Nowadays, in the Netherlands as elsewhere, we try to prevent out-of-home placement of children as much as possible, and to provide children with care that is as light, as short-term, and as close to home as possible. That means that we first try to help children in their own family situation. For this purpose several kinds of home treatment methods have been developed (Vogelvang, 1995). In addition, the capacity of various kinds of day treatment has increased considerably over the last few years (Hermanns, 1993). However, if a residential placement is called for, that rarely means that contacts with the natural parents will be completely broken off. We have begun to realise that, no matter how difficult the parent-child relationship is, the parents are still very important for children in care (Ainsworth, 1991). From the early 1970s on, family-oriented residential care has been advocated and family-focused care has become a generally accepted principle in the Netherlands (De Ruyter and Van Weelden, 1986).

This development is closely connected with the idea - especially advocated in the USA - that residential care, just like other less far-reaching interventions, is a *temporary support system* whose purpose is to support the family and especially the parents: '.... therefore, (residential) child treatment programmes should not be regarded as substitutes for family living but rather as instruments for helping natural or foster parents or other guardians develop successful methods of caring for children with special life adjustment problems' (Whittaker, 1979, p.7; see also Whittaker, 1992). Programmes for intensive home care, day treatment or residential care do not challenge this view: they simply represent different ways to organise professional support.

Adherence to a principle does not mean that the principle reflects reality. Therefore, in the following sections, we will examine the actual participation in residential care of parents in the Netherlands.

2.   Reasons to involve parents

There are several reasons why the original family, and especially the parents, should be involved in the care and treatment process. These reasons include pragmatic and theoretical considerations as well as empirical results and legal obligations.

2.1.   Pragmatic and theoretical considerations

One *pragmatic* consideration is that parents, as experts through experience, are an important source of information. Especially at the beginning of the treatment process, they are the ones who know most about a particular child.

In addition, a child in a residential home should not be viewed as an isolated individual. Children remain strongly linked to their families (De la Marche, 1989) and maintain feelings of loyalty towards their parents after admission. Therefore, the family is 'present' in the residential home, even when this is physically not the case. Involving parents in the treatment process can reduce the probability that children will experience conflicts of loyalty. As well, involvement may serve to overcome the parents' possible resistance to the placement.

It is also important to involve the parents in the care process on the basis that the family may eventually be reintegrated. From the child's point of view, parental involvement can prevent estrangement from his or her natural environment, isolation, and the loss of important socialisation models (Van Acker, Mertens and Verwaaijen, 1986). While the child is in residential care, efforts will be underway to make conditions in the family as favourable as possible for a return home (see also Dresen, 1987; Smit, 1993). But, even if children do not return to the parental home, it is important to work on the relationship with the parents

49

because the parents, if not totally absent, will still be an important resource for the child (Martone, Kemp and Pearson, 1989).

Considerations of a more *theoretical* nature include increased insight into the importance of attachment and into the influence of traumatic separation experiences: for example, due to a residential placement. We should also mention the shift in orthopedagogical/psychological approaches from a primary focus on the problems of the individual child to a focus on the problematic family situation (Hellinckx, 1983). Closely connected with that is the preference for an approach aimed at the family system.

2.2. Empirical results

Two kinds of empirical results provide relevant arguments to involve parents in residential care. First, research data show that problems reside not only in the children admitted to residential care but in their parents and original families as well. Second, there are data to indicate that involving parents has positive effects.

With respect to parents and natural families, the results of Van der Ploeg and Scholte (1988) provide us with valuable information. In their study *Tehuizen in Beeld (Residential Homes in Focus),* these authors analysed, among other things, the situations and characteristics of the original families of 337 children in 58 residential homes. The data show that 58 per cent of the parents were divorced, and in 55 per cent of the families the relationship between the parents was considered 'bad'. Problems among parents included emotional disturbances (54 per cent of the fathers; 69 per cent of the mothers) and addiction (19 per cent of the fathers; 13 per cent of the mothers). In 54 per cent of families, there were also considerable problems with other children (see also Knorth and Van der Ploeg, 1994). Thus, in this study at least, the families of the admitted children also had problems.

Further, evidence from research data shows that contacts between the child and the family and involvement of parents in the treatment of their child are important predictors for final family reunion or successful reintegration into society (Taylor and Alpert, 1973; Fanshel, 1975; Millham, Bullock, Hosie and Haak, 1989; Ainsworth, 1991). In a somewhat different way, the importance of co-operation with parents of admitted children is demonstrated in a recent study by Walton, Fraser, Lewis, Pecora and Walton (1993). They tried to find out whether a family preservation programme, aimed at preventing children from being placed out-of-home, could also be used to establish a family reunion after a placement. One hundred and ten families with a child placed out-of-home (ages between one and 17 years; average age 10.7 years) participated in the study. In all of these cases, return to the parental home was a treatment goal, but in no case had this transition already occurred. The families were randomly assigned to the experimental condition (n=57) or the control condition (n=53). The experimental group received intensive in-home care for three months (a home visit at least three times a week), aimed at tangible support (e.g., transportation, financial aid, clothing, food, repairs) and at learning new skills (communication, child-rearing, handling conflicts, and so forth.). At the same time, efforts were made to place the child back home short- term. In the control condition, the usual care was offered. The results showed that 93 per cent of the children in the experimental condition were home again after three months of special care, compared with 28 per cent of the children in the control group. A year after the programme ended, 75 per cent of the experimental group of children were living at home, as opposed to 49 per cent of children in the control group.[1]

2.3. Legal obligations

Ever since the Dutch Law on Child Care (Wet op de Jeugdhulpverlening) came into force, child-care institutions have been obliged to involve parents in the treatment of their children. For example, it is required that the parents or guardian of the child have to be consulted when a (semi)residential institution is chosen (Art. 29, 2nd part, and Art. 22, 1st part). Further, there has to be a treatment plan for every admitted child, containing '.... a statement about the way in which eligible members of the child's family will be involved in the treatment or a mention of the reasons why not' (*Besluit Kwaliteitsregels*, Art. 5, 2nd part, c). The document continues: 'A treatment plan shall not be established or altered until at least (....) the parents and the legal representative of the child have been consulted, unless there happens to be an acute emergency and it is expected that consultation will harm the child ....'(*Besluit Kwaliteitsregels*, Art. 5, 3rd part). The 'executor' - 'the person who maintains a provision' (*Leeswijzer bij de Wet op de Jeugdhulpverlening*, p. A2) - prepares a report at the end of his involvement with the child, where he describes the way in which he has done his duty. The report is added to the treatment plan. The executor sends a copy of the report with the treatment plan to (at least) the parents and the legal representatives of the child (*Besluit Kwaliteitsregels*, Art. 5, part 6).

In sum, the Dutch Law on Child Care determines that parents have to be involved in several aspects of the (residential) care to their child, but the way in which this is done is left to the executor.

51

3. Ways to involve parents

At its least intensive, parental involvement may mean nothing more than keeping parents informed on a regular basis about, for instance, the progress of their child. At its most intensive, parental involvement can mean placing not only the child but also the parents in residential care and aiming the treatment at the entire family. In between these two extremes lie other forms of involvement, such as contacts between the parents and the treatment team in the home, parent groups and parent training, counselling of parents and family therapy.

In this regard, Jenson and Whittaker (1987) wrote an interesting review article about the ways in which parents can play an active role in the process of residential child care. These authors distinguish three phases of care: a) preplacement and admission; b) treatment; and c) departure, reintegration and aftercare. In a publication of the (German) Verband katholischer Einrichtungen der Heim- und Heilpädagogik (1989), an overview is given of various ways in which one can work with families. The following Tables present, in three parts, the methods mentioned in these two publications. Jenson and Whittaker's classification is largely used as a point of reference.

Table 4.1 shows how parents can be actively involved in the care process of their child in the *preplacement and intake-phase*. Key concepts here are 'exchange of information' and 'clarification of expectations' (concerning, among other things, the role that parents are expected to play while the child is in the residential home). Through putting appointments with parents in writing (see point 2.c), they are shown that they are viewed as important players whose co-operation is sought.

Table 4.1:
Parental involvement in preplacement and intake

1. Visits:
   a) Preadmission orientation is conducted with all family members through visits to the institution
   b) Residential treatment personnel arrange visits to each child's family and community
2. Individual treatment plans are formulated at intake with co-operation from parents:
   a) parents' rights, roles and responsibilities are identified and discussed;
   b) parents are asked to specify the child's behaviour, peer relations, and family interactions in the weeks preceding placement;
   c) (preliminary) treatment plans are formalised through written agreements or contracts between child, parent, and residential staff
3. Parents with children already in treatment welcome new parents to existing family support groups and therapy sessions

Source: Jenson and Whittaker (1987)

Table 4.2 shows the methods used to involve the parents and other members of the family in the *treatment phase*. Here we distinguish five modalities (see the columns in the table): a) contacts between residential home and parents; b) parental involvement in the daily routine of the treatment programme for the child; c) training of parents to enhance their child-rearing skills; d) support groups through which parents of admitted children can give each other support, especially by exchange of experiences and by networking; and e) various forms of family treatment. The Table also shows that involving parents does not always imply that something is undertaken with the parent; parental involvement may occur through an assignment or an activity with the child.

Table 4.2: Parental involvement in during-treatment strategies

Contact between residential home and treatment parents	Parental involvement in everyday care and treatment activities	Parent training and education	Parent support groups	Conjoint family treatment
1 Brief informal talks between parents and residential care workers 2 Informal telephone conversations between parents and residential care workers 3 Sending a newsletter from the residential home to the parents 4 Sending fliers on specific topics to the parents	1 Visits by or with parents: a) Parents attend weekly events in the group (e.g. having tea on Friday afternoon) b) Parents visit on weekends (sometimes with an overnight stay) c) Children go for weekend to parents d) Parents visit the group at special events (e.g. birthday) e) Parents invite the group (e.g. as a checkpoint for a bicycle tour) 2 Parents are given certain responsibilities for their child's care during treatment: a) Purchase of clothing and daily needs b) Daily scheduling of child's activities (e.g. homework times, music lessons, arrangements concerning meals) 3 Parents are requested to help solve a specific behaviour problem encountered in treatment 4 Parents are contacted weekly by staff and receive written reports on their child's progress 5 Children are given the responsibility of planning and carrying out activities with their parents (e.g. going together to a soccer game on the weekend)	Several possibilities such as: 1 Group training in applying behavioural principles (e.g. contingency management and contract negotiation) 2 Instruction of parents in communication, management in coping skills 3 Modelling problem-solving skills for parents through the use of role playing, video-tapes and reading assignments	1 Organising informal activities for the parents (open house, fancy fair, video nights, etc.): a) informal activities to reduce family anxiety and isolation b) informal activities with self-reflection on the functioning of parents and residential workers (with the option to use social workers and other parents as role models) 2 Short-term support groups present a series of guest speakers to answer questions and discuss issues related to placement and treatment (e.g. drugs, sexuality, children's assessment) 3 Long-term support groups allow parents to share feelings and experiences with family members of other children in placement	1 Application of family therapy (e.g. children are encouraged to understand the behaviour of their parents, to cope with their frustration and anger at their parents, and to develop appropriate ways of interacting with them) 2 Parents attend family treatment sessions hosted by professionals at the residential facility 3 In group sessions with the children the influence of family processes on their functioning in the residential milieu (and vice versa) are examined and used in a therapeutic sense 4 Through extensive family therapy, parents and children develop and implement behavioural contracts that outline specific treatment and reentry plans 5 For several weeks key family members live with the admitted child in the residential milieu; family co-patients attend all therapy activities together

Sources: Jenson and Whittaker (1987); Verband katholischer Einrichtungen der Heim- und Heilpädagogik (1989).

In Table 4.3, we find some variants of methods that residential institutions can use with regard to the parents in the *community reintegration and aftercare phase*.

Table 4.3:
Parental involvement in community reintegration and aftercare

1. Parent support groups are formed during treatment to discuss community reentry and 'what to expect after placement'
2. Aftercare family support groups are established according to the following discharge plans: a) Child returns to biological family; b) Child is placed in adoptive home or other alternatives
3. Aftercare teams composed of social workers, child-care workers, educators, and community service workers assist parents with their child's reentry plans and reintegration:
   a) Prerelease meetings are held to set goals for the child and the parents
   b) Contracts for weekly family counselling are made
   c) Limitations in parenting and family management skills are outlined and specific interventions are planned
   d) Parents help their child develop an educational plan following treatment
   e) Residential treatment staff members act as resource persons by accompanying parents to meetings with school personnel, therapists, and other helping professionals for a specified period following treatment
4. Liaison specialists work with children and parents to facilitate linkages between placements and home. E.g. specialists help youths find employment and solve practical problems during reintegration

Source: Jenson and Whittaker (1987)

The importance of family- and parent-oriented activities, especially at the end of the residential stay, cannot be emphasised enough. In many publications, we find that a successful treatment result can easily break down when reintegration of the child into the next living environment (such as the family) is not supported by specific guidance of the client system (for a review see Smit, 1993).

4. Getting parents involved is no small matter

The fact that care givers are required by law to involve parents in the treatment of their child and that the importance of this is widely recognised, does not mean that it is easy. In the literature, we find all kinds of bottlenecks. The following will systematise the obstacles and objections on the part of parents as well as on the part of the residential organisation and its staff.

4.1. Bottlenecks on the part of parents

According to Günder (1989), the geographic distance to the home where their child has been placed is a problem for some parents. Furthermore, not all parents are able to, or willing to, co-operate in the treatment process. This lack of co-operation is suggested to be the biggest bottleneck both by Conen (1990; 1994), based upon research in more than 300 German institutions, and by Smit (1993), based on research in 53 Dutch residential homes.

An important reason for the documented lack of co-operation is that some parents are so extremely overburdened with other problems (their own or other family members') and by their work, that they do not see how they can contribute (Jenson and Whittaker, 1987). Furthermore, some parents regard the residential placement of their child as a punishment and as unjust and have a negative image of a residential home. Parents can have feelings of guilt about their child's admittance and about their own failures which led to that admission (Heun, 1981). They can be hurt and jealous, especially if their child is doing a little better because of the treatment. Often, the distrust of parents towards the group workers, who are viewed as competitors, also plays a part. Parents sometimes find it difficult to consider the often-young care givers, who have not yet raised children of their own, as serious partners.

Among parents who do not necessarily reject involvement per se, there are those who alternate between commitment and indifference. Such parents do not always keep appointments and tend to turn up unexpectedly at times which are often not convenient for residential home staff (Günder, 1989).

4.2. Bottlenecks on the part of the residential home

Residential care workers sometimes lack the desire to co-operate as well. This may be because they regard the biological parents as an irritating interruption to the residential home's routine (Heun, 1981), or they view them as inadequate and blame them for the problems of the child (Ainsworth, 1991). Residential care givers may want to protect these children against their parents (Günder, 1989) and may not want to 'share' the child with the parents whom they see as competitors.

Even if the desire to co-operate is there, the circumstances of work may thwart it. Working with parents means extra tasks and this costs extra money (Börsch, 1987). In addition, care givers are not always sufficiently qualified to work with parents (Heun, 1981). There may also be a lack of clarity concerning the formal responsibilities of parents and care givers. Based on the research study previously mentioned, Conen (1994) has identified four institutional factors which have equally been found to be obstacles to parental involvement: shift rotations of care givers; shortage of staff; tight budgets; and insufficient staff expertise. With regard to lack of staff expertise, Ainsworth (1991) points out that little is known about the way in which a residential setting can work effectively with parents. Practical guidelines for group workers are especially scarce.

5. The state of affairs in the Netherlands

So far, in this chapter, various reasons have been given for involving parents in the residential care of their child. It has also been made clear that co-operating with parents may be desirable but is not always easy. A number of recent Dutch studies have examined the state of affairs in the Netherlands regarding these matters. We will examine the results from two of these studies.

5.1. The study by Jansen and Oud

All 12 residential institutions in the province of Noord-Brabant participated in a study by Jansen and Oud (1992; 1993). These institutions accept children with psycho-social problems, aged nine to 15 years. The care process of 141 children was monitored over two years, and the parents of 90 children (64 per cent) were also involved in the study as informants. An important focus of attention was the degree of *family focus* of the offered care. This is defined as the degree to which the parents and other members of the family stay in touch with the admitted child, and are involved in caregiving during the residential stay (Jansen and Oud, 1993). Following is a selection of results. The data are based on the first six months of the children's residential stay.
-   In nine out of 10 cases family circumstances are put forward as a partial cause of the child's problems. Yet, in only 32 per cent of cases do residential care givers mention improving the family situation or family relationships as a treatment goal.
-   Almost one third of the children spend a weekend at home with their family every two weeks; the frequency varies between never (13 per cent) to once a week (10 per cent). In 60 per cent of cases, the parents have a (shared) say when it comes to setting up a weekend schedule.
-   Two thirds of the parents continue to take care of clothes and shoes for their child. A minority (30 per cent) have contacts with their child's school during the residential stay. Most parents (68 per cent) feel at ease during visits in the group. However, participation in daily events, such as sharing dinner, playing a game, cleaning the room or doing crafts, seldom occurs. A small group of parents (14 per cent) participate in conferences about the progress of their child.

- With regard to the guidance of parents through the residential institution, on average, parents have personal contact with a group worker once every four weeks, while telephone conversations take place once every two to three weeks. However, parents vary a great deal in the amount of contact they have.[2] The frequency of personal and telephone contacts between parents and representatives of other disciplines - social work and other staff such as the child psychologist, psychiatrist, and general manager - is a lot less. With respect to methods of contact, more intensive ways of family and parent guidance occur infrequently: only 10 out of 90 families received family therapy or family discussions in the first six months, and with six of these 10 families only a few sessions were held. Other kinds of parental guidance, such as discussion groups, parent classes or psychological/educational skills training in the group home, did not occur in the research group.

It is interesting to see which *subjects* are broached in contacts between parents and residential staff. Table 4.4 shows this for parents who had a sufficient number of contacts to make the question meaningful.

Table 4.4:
Topics of discussion during contacts with residential care staff (in %)

topic	residential child care workers (n=84)	other residential home staff (n=71)
Behaviour of child at home	86	86
Behaviour of child in living group	85	83
Weekend and vacation schedule	71	68
Behaviour and performance of child at school	70	56
Advice about managing the child	50	42
Feelings of parents towards out-of-home placement	49	55
Practical matters (clothes, school things, etc.)	35	28
Personal problems of parents	20	34
Material problems of parents	20	21
Partner relationship problems	12	21
Development in therapy	0	9
Other issues	25	28

Source: Jansen and Oud (1992).

It is clear that, in the contacts that parents have with group workers and other residential staff, the *behaviour of the child* at home and in the group is the main subject of conversation. Often, arrangements for weekends and vacations as well as the child's behaviour at school come up in the discussion. One out of two parents indicate receiving advice and suggestions about how to handle their son or daughter. In contacts with other staff, this issue is voiced as well. Much less attention, proportionally, is paid to the parents' personal problems, except for the feelings provoked by the out-of-home placement.

Furthermore, it was established that parents, on average, have discussions with a worker of a community-based service once a month. However, there is a wide range here also: one quarter of the parents never speak with a social worker from this kind of service, whereas almost a quarter do so once every two weeks or more frequently. There are more house calls (an average of 3.8 over six months) than conferences at the office (an average of 2.6 over six months). The main topics of conversation are the same: the behaviour of the child at home and in the group and the child's functioning at school. Compared with residential care workers, the topics discussed with community workers focus a little less often on weekend and vacation schedules, and more often on parents' feelings about the placement (49 per cent) and parents' personal and material problems (42 per cent). Partner relationship problems are not often discussed in contacts with community workers (16 per cent).

To some extent, it can be affirmed that there are more contacts with representatives of community-based services in those cases where parent guidance from the residential home is minimal: there is a significant negative correlation with the general dimension 'parent counselling by the residential home'. Further, guidance by a community-based service also seems to relate significantly to the number of contacts between parents and child: when there is more guidance, there are fewer parent-child contacts and less parental involvement in the residential admission procedure. Not surprisingly, therefore, Oud and Jansen (1993) question whether it would not be better in the end for residential homes to provide parental guidance themselves whenever possible (p.153).

The main finding of Jansen and Oud's research is that, in reality, residential settings are less family-oriented than one would expect from reading the clinical literature. Jansen and Oud link this finding, among other things, to:

a) the complexity of the problems and the low expectations that caregivers sometimes have about the possibilities of change in a family (girls with complicated problems experience less family-oriented care);
b) the age of the child (the older the child, the less family-oriented care);
c) the kind of institution to which the child is admitted (child psychiatric centres tend to be more family-oriented than other centres).

5.2. The study by Smit

In a study about discharge from residential care (Smit, 1993), attention was also paid to parent involvement. Care givers from a total of 53 institutions for children (aged 12 to 21, with psycho-social problems), were asked to what degree the parents of 149 of these children were involved in important decisions. The focus was on decision-making about admission, treatment planning and the discharge of children who returned to the parents' home after the residential stay or who started independent living. Residential staff filled out information about the part the parents played on a five-point scale: 1 'determinant'; 2 'co-determinant'; 3 'advisory'; 4 'informed afterwards'; 5 'not-involved'. Table 4.5 shows the results. The first two scale points have been collapsed to prevent the cell frequency from being too small.

Table 4.5:

The part parents play in decision-making about admission, treatment planning and discharge; residential home information (in %)

part parents play in decision-making	back home (n=82)			indep-endent (n=67)			totals (n=149)		
	I	II	III	I	II	III	I	II	III
(partly) determinant	69	23	85	35	20	11	55	22	55
advisory	8	3	3	4	2	17	6	3	9
informed afterwards	20	60	10	46	60	60	31	60	31
not-involved	3	14	2	15	18	13	8	16	6

I = decision about admission; II = decision about treatment planning; III = decision about discharge.

The following stand out in this table:
- the involvement of parents in decision-making about important aspects of their child's care depends to a great extent on the future whereabouts of the child; participation is greater when the child returns home after the residential stay. Parents of children who go on to independent living are often informed afterwards about various decisions, or are not involved at all;
- parents of children who return to the parental home have more input into decision-making about discharge. In making decisions about admission, many parents of this group of children are (partly) determinant;

- the involvement of parents in treatment planning is limited, regardless of where the child lives after discharge: in most cases information is given afterwards. Comparatively often, parents are not involved at all in treatment planning.

The study also paid attention to the degree of 'family orientation' of the care process. In 78 per cent of the cases, parents seemed to receive some kind of care or guidance during their child's residential stay. This was provided by the residential home (in 16 per cent of the cases), by a non-residential organisation such as the placement agency (35 per cent), or by both the home and the non-residential organisation (27 per cent). Mostly, the care was individually focused on the parents (in 56 per cent of the cases in which there was care/guidance). The study also showed that more in-depth kinds of care to families were rarely offered: family therapy was offered in 17 per cent of the cases in which there was care/guidance; and training in parenting skills (educational, social and communication) was offered in 18 per cent of the cases.

6. Conclusions

In this chapter, we have stated that family-oriented care is a widely-accepted principle and well worth the effort. Dutch residential institutions are required by law to involve parents in the care of their child. However, because the literature suggests a number of reasons why this is difficult in practice, we asked what the situation was regarding parental involvement in residential child care in the Netherlands. The overall picture shown by the empirical studies discussed is that the role of parents in residential care is quite often limited.[3] More specific findings are as follows.

The results of the Jansen and Oud study show that parents have by far the most contacts with the group worker. The most frequent topic of conversation in these contacts is the *behaviour of the child* in the institution and at home on weekends. In about half the cases, these conversations include offering advice on child rearing. Much less frequent are contacts with parents in which *their own functioning*, whether related to their child or not, is the issue. Here, we must add that in the contacts parents have with community-based services there is more often room for discussing personal problems. Moreover, this study showed that there is a large variation in the frequency of parent-institution contacts. This may mean that 'care-to-order' is offered; in one case a comparatively high frequency of contacts is desired or seems possible, whereas, in another case, such a high frequency seems less desirable or not feasible. Parents are sometimes not very accessible to caregivers. However, we do not know whether the intensity of parent contacts is always the result of a conscious choice or treatment strategy. More research could clarify this matter.

The role parents are offered in decision-making about the care process is limited. Smit's study showed that in about three quarters of the cases parents are either informed afterwards or not involved at all in decisions about treatment planning. Decisions about the admission and discharge of children show a more favourable picture, especially when the child is expected to return to the parental home. In general, this expectation occurs more often when the child is younger.

We may conclude that parental involvement is generally higher for young children than for adolescents, especially when returning home is not seen as a possible goal for the adolescent. It is doubtful that any theoretical support can be found for this. In order to improve the parent-adolescent relationship - a process which can lead to tensions even in 'normal' families (Meeus, 1994) - parent contacts are essential, especially for adolescents with severe psycho-social problems (see Klomp, 1992; Scholte, 1994).

The attention that nowadays is paid to intensive treatment at home and especially to intervention projects designed to prevent a residential placement (Baartman, Bakker, Jagers and Slot, 1993; Spanjaard and Berger, 1994; Jagers, 1995) can and, so far as we are concerned, must give a new impulse to family-oriented care *in* the residential homes. We aim at a broader goal for so-called family preservation programmes: not only should they focus on preventing out-of-home placements, but they should also be intended to increase the chance of family reunion after the placement (see also Whittaker, 1992; Pecora, 1994). The USA has interesting results in this area. We refer to the results of the research by Walton et al. (1993), discussed in paragraph 2.2. We feel that there are reasons enough to experiment, in the Netherlands as well, with family reunion programmes in which close co-operation between community-based services and residential care is deemed to be essential.

A matter which deserves particular attention is the central position of the group worker in relation to parent contacts. Opinions differ as to whether or not this is desirable. For example, Gunning and Verhey (1986) feel that guidance and treatment of parents is a task for specialised staff (such as social workers with a training in family therapy). Others (De Vriendt, De la Marche and Pyck, 1985) hold the opinion that group workers specifically should be closely involved in parent/family counselling. The discussion does not have to be abstract, however; as we saw, in everyday practice group workers are precisely the persons who have by far the most contacts with parents. Family-focused residential care must take advantage of this. However, it is still necessary to question whether every group worker has sufficient skills for parent or family-oriented interventions. Examples in the field where group workers play an important role in this respect (Smeets and Welzen, 1984; De Vriendt et al., 1985; Verzaal, 1991) show that, in these organisations, good conditions have been created for training and supervision.

Group workers not only exchange information with the parents about the well-being of their child, but they also give advice. Now that the importance of parent contacts has been highlighted, we think it would be interesting to examine the impact of the group worker's actions compared with the impact of workers in other disciplines. Very little is known about this. There are no solidly-based answers to questions such as 'what is the advice that is offered?', and 'do parents follow the advice?' (see Gerards, 1993). Research into these questions would have theoretical as well as practical value.

Notes

1. The authors find the results promising, but warn against too-hasty generalisations. For one thing, care givers in the experimental programme were found to have more experience in child care. Also some preselection of families took place: no families where the child was considered to be in direct danger from an imminent reunion were included in the sample.

2. For example, 28 per cent of the parents have no contact at all whereas, in 9 per cent of cases, weekly discussions take place. Even in telephone contacts with group workers, we find a large variation.

3. This view corresponds with the findings of the Inspectorate of Child Care (Inspectie Jeugdhulpverlening, 1993). The Inspectorate compared institutional policies in two Dutch regions with the stipulations in the Child Care Law concerning the involvement of parents in residential child care.

References

Ainsworth, F. (1991), "A 'No Blame' approach to work with families of children and adolescents in residential care", *Child and Youth Care Forum*, vol. 20, 301-311.

Baartman, H., Bakker, K., Jagers, H. and Slot, W. (1993), *Ambulante hulp aan huis. Van Projecten naar Programma*, Utrecht, NIZW.

Besluit Kwaliteitsregels Jeugdhulpverlening (1991). In *Wetgeving Jeugdhulpverlening* (D.1-D.20). Den Haag: Ministerie van Welzijn, Volksgezondheid and Cultuur/Ministerie van Justitie.

Börsch, B. (1987), "Einführung der Arbeit mit Familien; eine Erleichterung der Heimalltags?" in B. Börsch and M.L. Conen (eds.), *Arbeit mit Familien von Heimkindern* (9-23), Dortmund, Modernes Lernen.

Conen, M.L. (1990), *Elternarbeit in der Heimerziehung*, Frankfurt, Internationale Gesellschaft für Heimerziehung.

Conen, M.L. (1994), *Family involvement in residential homes for children in Germany.* Paper presented at the 1994 International Child and Youth Care Conference, Milwaukee (Wisconsin), USA, June 20th-24th.

De la Marche, J. (1989), "De relatie instelling - ouders, belicht vanuit een aantal theoretische referentiekaders", in A. De Vriendt et al. (eds.), *Groepsopvoeders en ouders; tegenstanders of medestanders?* (45-74), Leuven, Acco. (2nd ed.)

De Ruyter, P.A. and Van Weelden, J. (1986), "Taak en functie van de residentiële hulpverlening", in R. De Groot and J. Van Weelden (eds.), *Van gisteren over morgen. Een orthopedagogische overzichtsstudie* (176-198), Groningen,Wolters-Noordhoff.

De Vriendt, A., De la Marche, J. and Pyck, K. (eds.) (1985), *Groepsopvoeders en ouders: medestanders of tegenstanders?* Leuven/Amersfoort, Acco.

Dresen, M.C.J. (1987), "Ouderbegeleiding in de residentiële hulpverlening", *Tijdschrift voor Jeugdhulpverlening*, vol. 15, no. 10/11, 380-384.

Fanshel, D. (1975), "Parental visiting of children in foster care", *Social Service Review*, vol. 49, 493-514.

Gerards, F.M. (1993), "Pedagogische advisering en gedragsbehoud. Een stappenplan", *Tijdschrift voor Orthopedagogiek*, vol. 32, 463-473.

Günder, R. (1989), *Aufgabefelder der Heimerziehung,* Frankfurt am Main, Deutscher Verein für öffentliche und private Fürsorge.

Gunning, C. and Verhey, F. (1986), "De driehoek ouder-kind-instituut in de residentiële behandeling", *Kind en Adolescent*, vol. 7, 12-25.

Hellinckx, W. (1983), "Gezinsgerichte orthopedagogische hulpverlening aan een emotioneel- en/of gedragsgestoord kind", in J. Van Weelden et al. (eds.), *Onvoltooid of onbegonnen? Hulpvragende kinderen 1* (185-205), Groningen, Wolters-Noordhoff.

Hermanns, J. (1993), "Daghulp als werkveld van de orthopedagoog", in J.D. Van der Ploeg (ed.), *Orthopedagogische werkvelden in kaart - Nederland* (67-78), Leuven/Apeldoorn, Garant.

Heun, D.H. (1981), "Elternarbeit in Kinder- und Jugendheimen", *Unsere Jugend*, vol. 33, 100-107.

Inspectie Jeugdhulpverlening (1993), *Het betrekken van ouders bij de hulpverlening. Thema Rapport Inspectie Jeugdhulpverlening regio's Oost en Zuid-West*, Rijswijk, Inspectie Jeugdhulpverlening/Ministerie van WVC.

Jagers, J.D. (1995), "Programma-evaluatie als een instrument bij innovatie in de jeugdhulpverlening: een illustratie aan de hand van Families First", in M.G. Boekholdt (ed.), *Programma-evaluatie; sleutel tot kwaliteit* (57-65), Utrecht, SWP.

Jansen, M.G. and Oud, J.H.L. (1992), "Gezinsgerichtheid in de residentiële hulpverlening: begeleiding van ouders en gezin", in J.R.M. Gerris (ed.),

Opvoedings- en gezinsondersteuning. Gezinsonderzoek deel 6 (101-122), Amsterdam/Lisse, Swets and Zeitlinger.

Jansen, M.G. and Oud, J.H.L. (1993), *Residentiële hulpverlening geëvalueerd. Een onderzoek naar de ontwikkeling en het behandelingsverloop van residentieel opgenomen jeugdigen in Noord-Brabant. Eindrapport.*, Nijmegen, KU Nijmegen, Instituut voor Orthopedagogiek.

Jenson, J.M. and Whittaker, J.K. (1987), "Parental involvement in children's residential treatment: from preplacement to aftercare", *Children and Youth Services Review*, vol. 9, 81-100.

Klomp, M. (1992), *Hulpverlening aan adolescenten*. PhD dissertation, Rijksuniversiteit Groningen.

Knorth, E.J. and Van der Ploeg, J.D. (1994), "Residential Care in the Netherlands and Flanders: Characteristics of Admitted Children and their Family", *International Journal of Comparative Family and Marriage*, vol. 1, 17-27.

Leeswijzer bij de Wet op Jeugdhulpverlening (Guide to the Law on Child Care) (1991), in *Wetgeving Jeugdhulpverlening* (A.1-A.30). Den Haag: Ministerie van Welzijn, Volksgezondheid and Cultuur/ Ministerie van Justitie.

Martone, W.P., Kemp, G.F. and Pearson, S.J. (1989), "The continuum of parental involvement in residential treatment: engagement - participation - empowerment - discharge", *Residential treatment for children and youth*, vol. 6, no. 3, 11-37.

Meeus, W. (ed.) (1994), *Adolescentie. Een psychosociale benadering*, Groningen, Wolters-Noordhoff.

Millham, S., Bullock, R., Hosie, K. and Haak, M. (1989), *Lost in care. The problems of maintaining links between children in care and their families*, Aldershot, Gower.

Oud, J.H.L. and Jansen, M.G. (1993), "Hoe gezinsgericht is de residentiële hulpverlening?" *Gezin, Tijdschrift voor Primaire Leefvormen*, vol. 5, 128-156.

Pecora, P.J. (1994), "Are intensive family preservation services effective? Yes", in E. Gambrill and T.J. Stein (eds.), *Controversial Issues in Child Welfare* (290-301), Boston, Allyn and Bacon.

Scholte, E.M. (1994), "Adolescent probleemgedrag", in W. Meeus (ed.), *Adolescentie. Een psychosociale benadering* (254-299), Groningen, Wolters-Noordhoff.

Smeets, P. and Welzen, K. (1984), "Groepsleider tussen ouder en kind", *Kind en Adolescent*, vol. 5, 213-221.

Smit, M. (1993), *Aan alles komt een eind. Een onderzoek naar beëindiging van tehuishulpverlening*. PhD dissertation, Rijksuniversiteit Leiden.

Spanjaard, H. and Berger, M.A. (1994), "Families First. Hulp aan gezinnen ter voorkoming van uithuisplaatsing van kinderen", *Jeugd en Samenleving*, vol. 12, 720-729.

Taylor, D.A. and Alpert, S.W. (1973), *Continuity and support following residential treatment*, New York, Child Welfare League of America.

Van Acker, J., Mertens, H. and Verwaaijen, S. (1986), "Hulpverlening aan gezinnen met adolescenten", *Tijdschrift voor Orthopedagogiek, Kinderpsychiatrie and Klinische Kinderpsychologie*, vol. 11, 31-43.

Van der Ploeg, J.D. and Scholte, E.M. (1988), *Tehuizen in beeld*, Leiden, Rijksuniversiteit Leiden, Vakgroep Orthopedagogiek/Centrum Onderzoek Jeugdhulpverlening.

Verband katholischer Einrichtungen der Heim- und Heilpädagogik (1989), *Familienarbeit in der Heimerziehung*, Freiburg im Breisgau, Lambertus Verlag.

Verzaal, H. (1991), *Niet uit huis zonder thuis. Ervaringsgerichte gezinsbehandeling als basis voor residentiële hulpverlening aan jongeren*, Amsterdam, Op Dreef.

Vogelvang, B.O. (1995), "Hometraining", in G. Gluckers et al. (eds.), *Handboek kinderen en adolescenten*, number 25 (ther-Hom 1-15), Houten, Bohn Stafleu Van Loghum.

Walton, E., Fraser, M.W., Lewis, R.E., Pecora, P.J. and Walton, W.K. (1993), "In-home family-focused reunification: an experimental study", *Child Welfare*, vol. 72, 473-487.

Whittaker, J.K. (1979), *Caring for troubled children; residential treatment in a community context*, San Francisco, Jossey-Bass.

Whittaker, J.K. (1992), "Enhancing social support for high risk youth and their families following residential care", in J.D. Van der Ploeg et al. (eds.), *Vulnerable Youth in Residential Care. Part I: Social Competence, Social Support and Social Climate* (81-100), Leuven, Garant Publishers.

5 Breaking the cycle of perpetual crisis[1]

Richard KAGAN

My colleagues and I work with families where children have had multiple placements, where abuse and neglect has recurred over generations, and where several previous attempts to avoid placement have been tried with little change. The children we see may be in a crisis group care facility, an emergency foster home, or at imminent risk of placement. They may have slashed at their parents with butcher knives, put electrical cords around their necks, set their beds on fire, or hung by their fingertips from third floor balconies. Parents may look hopelessly depressed or like the stalker from the latest horror movie.

Crises are exciting. A family member in trouble can have teachers or police chasing them. It is a little like going on a roller coaster. Once it has started, there is no way that you can get off. You hold on, experience the thrill, and feel alive.

Crises can become a way of life which seems to go on forever with no clear origin or conclusion. The family seems to be always on the move, running from what is too painful to be fixed. Families spin from one crisis to another in what may appear to be a never-ending cycle which brings in authorities and helping professionals.

Our job is to quickly engage families in a non-shaming manner and find a way to turn a dangerous situation into a turning point which can end the cycle of crises. In this chapter, we will look at an approach which helps me focus my work and engage families in the midst of crisis.

The split

Children growing up with abuse and neglect learn that crying over a scraped knee may mean getting a hard whack with a hand, belt or board and hearing their parent scream, 'Don't bother me right now! Can't you see I'm busy with your brother? You kids are driving me nuts. One more problem and I'm out of here. ... Now get back outside ... If I don't get some peace, I'm putting you in a home [2]...'

The child's head goes down. Her eyes narrow and the tears stop. She has learned a vital lesson for survival in her family: don't upset your parent at all costs. The child learns to ignore the pain in her leg and to keep her mouth shut. It's best not even to look at it. She learns to carry on pretending nothing happened.

Later in the day, she may hear a very different message. 'Come here baby' coos the same mother who shunned her hours before. 'Rub Mommy's back ... You're my sweetie ... You're Mama's special one ... None of the others are worth a damn ... I could never make it without you.' The girl is drawn into a special role with her mother - a companion who watches over and cares for her parent.

The memories of the scraped knee and her mother's rejection are blocked. I love my Mommy! she'd tell anyone who asked about her mother. It's 'the two of us against the world'.

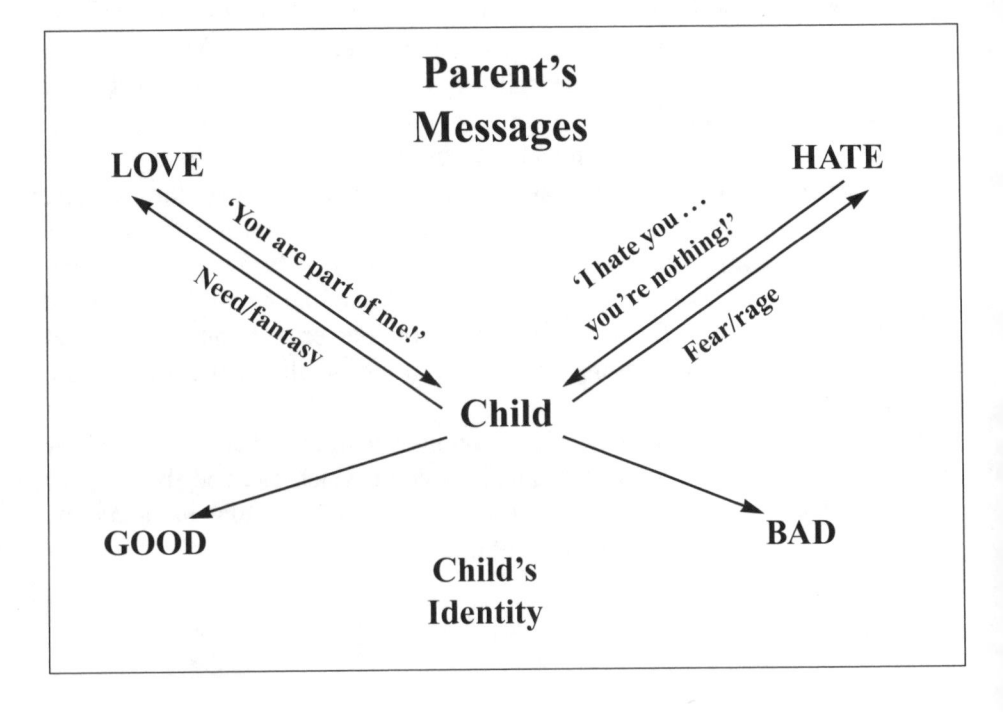

The child grows up (according to Masterson, 1976) hearing two conflicting and powerful messages from her primary parent: 'I love you. You're a part of me.' and 'Get out! I hate you.' Living day to day with both messages leads the child to split her own identity into two parts (See Figure 5.1).

The 'good' daughter is always there for her parent, ready night and day to hold, serve, and care for. The 'bad' daughter acts out the fear and rage, often repeating what she has heard but dare not say at home. She calls her teacher 'a fucking bitch', smacks the girl in front of her in the lunch line, and takes what she wants from another child's locker.

Living with the threat of abandonment

Families revolving in crises are continually on the edge of falling apart and dissolving. The critical element in these families is symbolised by the child threatened with placement. Abandonment and eviction from the family system are real threats established over generations with siblings, cousins, parents, grandparents, aunts and uncles ending up outside the family in residential treatment, foster homes, drug/alcohol rehabilitation, prisons, or simply scattered, living on the streets.

Temporary living arrangements may be the norm in the family for everyone by age 14. Very often, one parent has abandoned the child at an early age. Children may spend their first years with grandma before moving in with their birth mother at age five when grandma gets too tired, becomes sick or needs to care for a younger grandchild. By 13 or 14, they may be looking for any means possible to get away.

Peers provide excitement, escape and brief moments of intimacy. Gangs provide substitute families. Pregnancy is often seen as a second chance to create the intimacy and attachment that a teenage girl lost (or never had) with her own parents.

Born under a bad sign

A child can become the focal point of a family's struggle by picking up on festering emotional wounds and her parents' traumas. The child learns to act out what cannot be said, and, from this perspective, is acting in a competent way in her family system (Ausloos, 1981; Waters and Lawrence, 1993). Her bad or crazy behaviour helps to balance a system in crisis.

A child who becomes tied in with traumas in a family may learn over time to carry on the tension, the stress, and the fighting of the past. The child and other family members remain unbalanced with conflicting pressures reflecting the split messages: love/hate; loyalty/defiance. As the pressure moves too far in one direction, the crisis cycle is engaged. According to Berenson (1976) and Fossum and Mason (1986) the family oscillates from shame to rigid perfectionism.

Secrets lead to splitting and fractures of each family member. A child cannot deal with what has happened when she sees her father on the verge of exploding in rage or abandoning the family and her mother hiding in fear or threatening to hit someone or kill herself. The things that cannot be said often represent the terrors and fears of abandonment (Ausloos, 1986). These are the focal points (Pittman, 1987) which lock a family into revolving patterns of crises and block change. The broken pieces of the child's life cannot be put together because this would mean facing the threat of abandonment and the break up of the family.

Working with time

Families embroiled in one crisis after another appear to be dealing only with the present (Ausloos, 1986). Stress is dealt with by creating and responding to events of the moment. Family crises escalate directly in response to pressures from inside or outside the family. Outsiders usually see these families as chaotic.

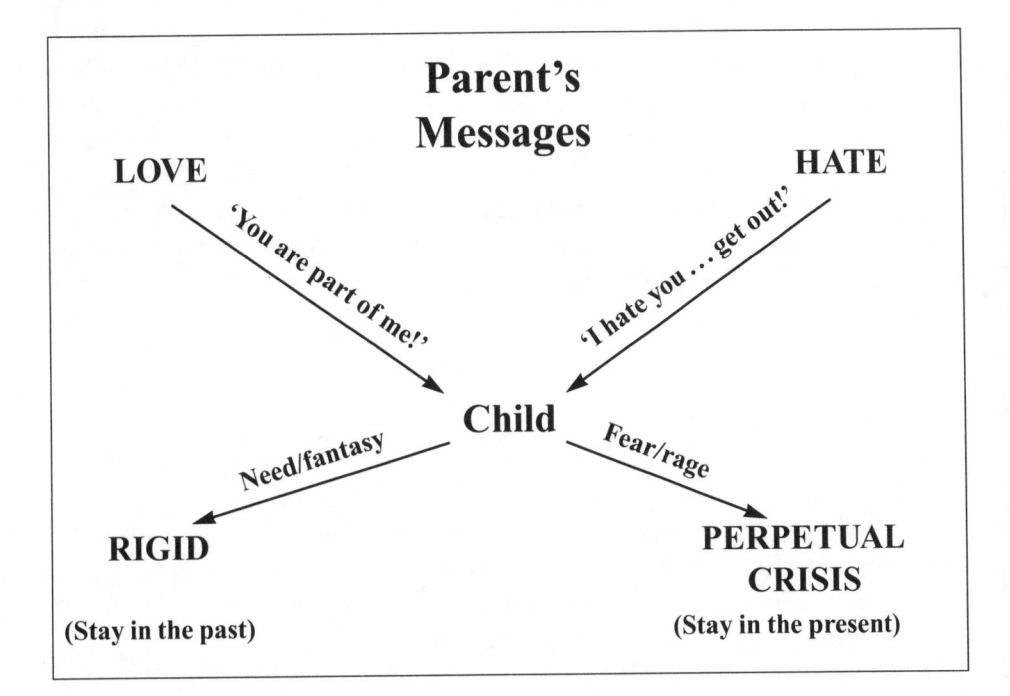

Practitioners quickly become immersed in crises and feel pressured to act immediately to rescue or protect.

Crisis-prone families often revolve between a rigid, 'walking on eggshells' orientation and an intense, crisis stage (See Figure 5.2).

This shift corresponds to the split messages given and received by generations of family members (again, see Figure 5.2)

'You are part of me!' and other all-encompassing messages of love renew a child's desperate wish and need to cling to the parent she has become so terrified of losing. Because the parent-child attachment is so weak and often threatened, the child acts in a very constricted and immature manner, trying to recapture the bond she may have had as a toddler. This is the rigid side of the split.

A few hours or moments later, the child may once again hear a hate/rejection message from her parent. This generates an almost immediate and often over-powering sense of fear. The child may react with rage and begin to get into trouble outside the family. Children often act out the abusive messages and violence experienced within the family.

Painful dilemmas are avoided when family members become restricted within a predominant time zone of awareness and action. This, in turn, constrains how they see the world and how they act. The challenge for families is to regain the lost dimensions of time and thus open up previously blocked perspectives and possibilities for resolving traumas. For families in seemingly perpetual crises, we engage family and network members to face the past and make choices for the future.

Healing involves family members slowing down time (Ausloos, 1986). Time-lines of key family events, photo albums, genograms, family stories, and visits with relatives to find out about the past are useful assignments to help family members regain and share with each other a sense of the past. The power of these assignments lies in family members becoming safe enough and feeling strong enough to share what happened before.

Countering split messages

Haley (1977) described 'perverse triangles' between two parents and a child in which parents detour conflicts through an acting-out adolescent. Systems messages have been used in family therapy (Watzlawick, Beavin and Jackson, 1967; Nichols, 1984) to counter the paradoxes experienced by family members. For instance, therapists may give a message stressing both how a family maintains its balance with a cycle of interactive behaviours and the necessity for a child to continue enacting a problematic behaviour in order to protect the family (Papp, 1983).

Ferreira (1960) described delinquent behaviour evolving from the 'split double bind' in which a youth hears conflicting messages from two parents. Ausloos (1981) found that giving chaotic families paradoxical injunctions led to more crises. A group care facility could counter this split double bind by having a family worker stress how the youth's behaviour (running away, stealing, for example) played a critical and competent role in maintaining his parents' and family's homeostasis. The youth's primary child-care worker would then stress that this was true but, at the same time, the worker saw the positive potential shown by the youth and would work with the youth to make small changes to avoid going back to court.

Dual centring messages

I have found dual messages very effective in dealing with splits experienced by a child who is facing the very real threat of abandonment by his or her *primary* parent (See Figure 5.3).

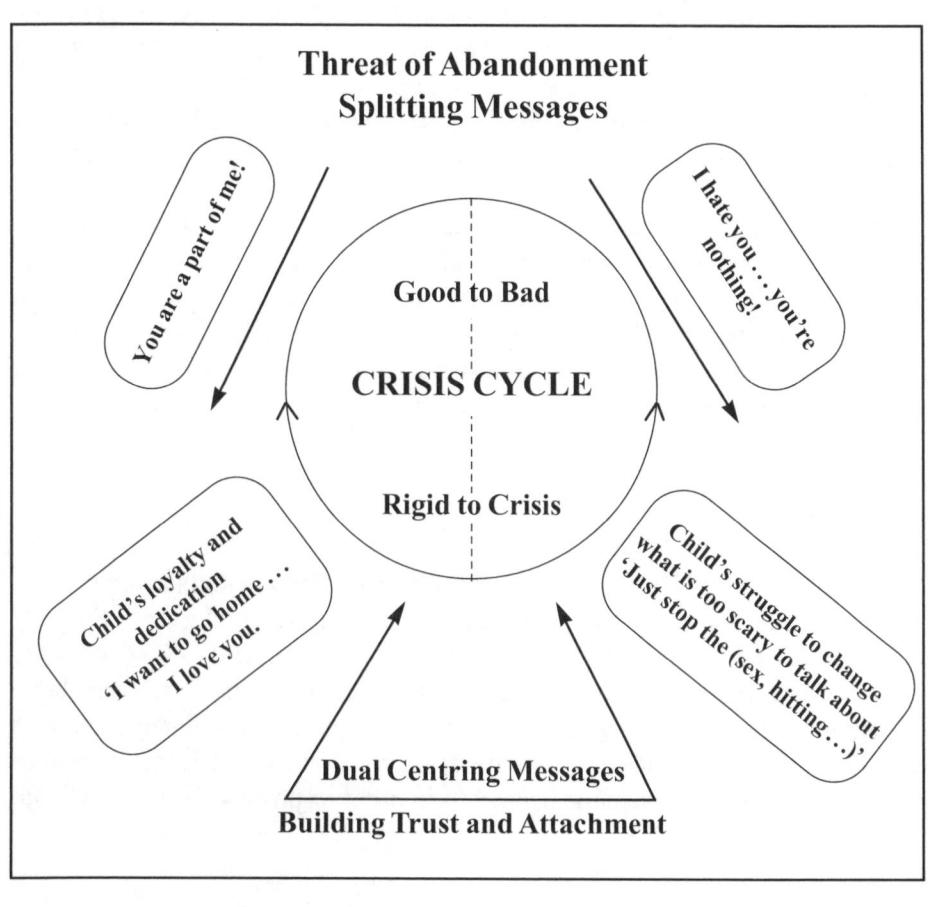

Children in crisis-addicted families have often experienced the loss of one parent and are desperate to keep the fragile threads which connect them to their remaining Mum or Dad. Therapeutic messages can stress *both* the child's loyalty and dedication to her parent and the child's struggle to change what is terrifying and too painful to talk about in the family.

A boy in a crisis residence told his father he wanted to go home. '... Just stop the sex'. Another boy demanded to go back to his Grandpa but showed everyone that he was scared to be alone with him. In each case, we needed to focus on both messages.

This is contrary to what is generally expected of therapists in child and family services. Parents often expect that we will advocate for the child and cast blame on the parent for a child's problem. Such parents are prepared to fight for their self-esteem and see practitioners as the enemy. Or conversely, we may be expected by many parents and most children to fix a 'bad' or 'sick' child. We become locked into a 'no-win' struggle if we advocate for one position or the other and soon find ourselves immersed in a family's serial crises.

We often feel pressured or compelled to push one side of a dilemma or another. This would be like pushing on one side of a canoe in the middle of a storm. The canoe would tip and someone in the family system (perhaps the grandparents or other professionals) would feel compelled to quickly apply an equally powerful (or more powerful) counter-force on the other side of the canoe.

The resulting battle would in effect keep the canoe afloat, though tipping from side to side in a cycle of crises, with the family always in jeopardy of sinking. Working with 'both/and' messages allows us to centre our work on the family's need for balance with powerful forces impinging from different sides.

'Bad' boys and 'bad' parents

Bill, another boy I saw at my agency's crisis residence, had a reputation for stealing and defiance to teachers. I asked his mother what she liked about him, what good things he did, and what they did for fun together. We talked about his defiance and stealing as his way to show what he could not say and that he could be a very caring and likeable boy. Bill's mother warmed up in our session, dropped her animosity towards therapists and agreed to participate in counselling with her son. At the end of our session, she said that after years of work with school officials and several previous therapists, 'You're the first person who told me that he's not a bad boy'.

In mainstream American culture, 'bad' boys or girls are often assumed to come from 'bad' parents. Labels of 'bad' and 'sick' can perpetuate perceptions that change is impossible and foster continued hunts for someone to blame. Our task is to get beyond a blaming orientation without neglecting real problems.

I assume that each parent and child has their own 'both/and' dilemma. If a child feels torn in two directions - for example, a boy pulled between his mother and grandmother - I would ask if others felt the same way. I encourage each family member to express their own dilemma and look for common themes. In this way, I can validate the dilemmas experienced by each family member and avoid adding to feelings of shame.

In another family, Joan placed her nine-year-old son in a crisis residence after he set a fire in her kitchen. The affection Joan and her son once shared had evolved over the previous five years into an escalating pattern of taunting by her son and rebukes and slaps by his mother. After two weeks of placement, Joan confided that she often felt like killing her son. In a family session involving Joan, her mother, and her son, Joan's mother shared how she had felt like killing Joan when Joan was a child.

If a child feels torn between love and hate towards a parent, it is very likely that the parent grew up feeling the same way towards their parent. This split becomes the focus of our interventions. Our challenge is to help family members to reweave the torn fragments of their lives.

Mending the split

The child threatened with placement is torn between the need to love and care for their parent and at the same time, the child's fears and anger. The child struggles to maintain the image of a loving parent while suppressing memories of being hurt, rejected or abandoned. The fragility of the parent (depression, threats of suicide or violence, and the likelihood that the parent might run away, or be hospitalised or incarcerated) makes it impossible to voice the fear and hate side of the split.

A child needs a secure attachment in order to heal from trauma (Bettelheim, 1960; Bowlby, 1969; 1973; Erikson, 1963). The child growing up with mixed messages ('I need you.', 'You're everything to me!', 'You're a bitch!', 'I hate you!') learns to numb her own pain, to withdraw, and to dissociate in order to manage her distress. She cannot let go of her parent and yet feels a drive to escape which escalates as the child enters adolescence.

The child absorbs the split by incorporating both sides - the good child who is loving and loyal to her parent and the bad child who rebels, defies and becomes the 'bitch' provoking more of her parent's wrath. When it is too dangerous to rebel against one's own parent, the child learns to defy and resist other adults who act as authority figures, provoking the child's fears and anger.

Dual, centring messages can be used to link a child's split responses to the conflicting messages she has received from her primary parent. In this way, we can frame a 'both/and' message which directly counters and relinks the split message received by the child over time. Such a message focuses the family's struggle for change on the primary dilemmas which have threatened the family's collapse while at the same time validating the family's experience in a balanced way. The canoe does not have to tip.

Writing to Mum

Kristen, a nine-year-old girl, was placed in a crisis residence for biting and hitting peers, siblings, and teachers. She had been expelled from school and Janet, her mother, said she was unable to handle her any more despite a year of family counselling.

The first night in residence, Kristen begged her mother to get rid of Janet's boyfriend and was overjoyed when Janet told her she would ask him to leave. Kristen then shared with staff that Janet's boyfriend had hit her mother, Kristen, and her siblings.

The next day, however, Janet came to visit Kristen in the crisis residence and let Kristen know that Bill, her boyfriend, would be cooking dinner that night. Kristen flew into a rage, called her mother a 'fuckin' bitch', and began from that day to kick and hit other children in the crisis residence. She would not respond to staff and had to be held. She then repeatedly bit staff who in turn felt that she would have to be hospitalised.

Kristen needed the hitting to stop at home but learned that her mother needed Bill and would keep him. When child protection services staff interviewed Kristen, she yelled 'Nothing happened!' and ran out of the room.

We could have tried to push Janet to move her boyfriend out in order to stop the violence at home. On the other hand, a one-sided message would have invalidated Janet's position that she was unable to manage without her boyfriend and that he helped her and her other children. If we pushed for Bill's removal, Kristen would have likely seen us as enemies of her family and accelerated her biting and hitting in the crisis residence. Or, her mother may have chosen to extend Kristen's placement by saying she could not take Kristen back at that time.

In our family session, Kristen climbed onto her mother's lap. I told Janet that this did not surprise me since, when I met Kristen, the first thing Kristen showed me was that she was writing a letter to her Mum. 'She loves you very much, more than anything. She's also got things that she cannot say, that's she's too scared to say and that she even warned me not to say.'

I wanted to accentuate both Kristen's devotion to her mother and her terror of her mother getting hit and to reframe Kristen's rages and cuddling as a desperate effort to save her mother. 'She both loves you and is terrified of you and others in the family getting hurt. She's afraid of Bill hitting you and the kids but told me when I saw her that she loved everyone in the family and saw Bill as part of the family.'

There was a real basis for Kristen's rage at her mother and the fragility of her attachment. Kristen had grown up feeling loved then hated and rejected. She modelled her own behaviour after the hitting, kicking and biting she witnessed in her biological father's terrifying but powerful rages. Kristen raged whenever she saw her mother pulling away and had learned, like many children, that it was much safer to act out your rage with teachers and child care workers than with your mother, father, or mother's boyfriend.

With permission from Janet, we were able to talk about the violence the children experienced when she lived with their biological father. Janet's older brother shared how their father had ordered Kristen and him to stab her mother with a butcher knife and beat her repeatedly. Kristen would try to protect her mother. She desperately wanted to gain her mother's love and raged against her mother's repeated rejections and allegiance to her boyfriend over Kristen. Talking about the past took the pressure off Bill and Janet's need to keep him.

I could then go back to Janet later in our session to tie Kristen's current behaviour with the past. 'She's always afraid of losing you, of you being killed. I need to ask if anything was happening that made it worse in the last year or in the last month when Kristen has been getting into so much trouble at school.'

To my surprise, Janet affirmed this. 'She saw Bill and me get into a fight about a month ago. I sent the kids over to a friend's house but she brought them back.' I asked Bill and Janet if there had been any hitting since Kristen was doing a lot of hitting in school and at the crisis centre. Janet shared that Bill had struck her on the face. 'It happened when he was knocking the door open.'

This was, of course, only one of many secrets in the family. Still, after this session, Kristen calmed down, did not provoke other children into fights, focused her attention on school work, and bit no one. She listened to staff in the crisis centre and they were able to relax and enjoy her feisty spirit.

Kristen was brought home by her mother a few days later and returned to her classroom behaving like a fourth grader. I was very pleased that Kristen and her family had trusted us enough to talk about how frightened the children were of their mother being killed and to make a commitment to continue this work in counselling. The family's mental health worker and school officials were not able to make this session but were involved in later work to help Janet and Bill stop the violence and for Janet to care for and manage the children without threats of abandonment.

We had helped Kristen send her letter in a way that Janet could accept. Kristen was desperately struggling to keep her mother and at the same time was trying to stop the violence. Kristen's message, in turn, spurred Janet to share what everyone had been too afraid to say out loud.

Validating the positive

The split responses of the child can be used as a metaphor for the splits experienced by all family members. I tell parents and siblings that when I see one family member feeling such a desperate struggle between the need to love and protect their family and their fears or rage at what has happened, I have to expect that other people in the family feel the same way.

It helps me to find out how children understand what happened to family members at critical times in a family's history. I ask parents for permission to ask their children what they learned about important events. Why did Mum and Dad separate? What helped Mum get by in the terrible year when her parents died, the children's father left, and she was hurt in a car accident? What was it like for Mum or Dad at the same age as the child in placement?

Such questions open the door for parents to talk about what was good and bad in their own experience and how children may experience traumatic events. This approach also allows me to validate the healthy striving and yearning for love and attachment of all family members, not just the child at risk of placement.

Dual, centring messages allow me to validate the positive striving of a child or parent: for example, a child's yearning for her Mum or Dad, or a father's efforts to give his child more than he received growing up. This validation of the positive and accentuation of real signs of competence allows family members to avoid feeling that they are being shamed and symbolically pushed up against a brick wall with no escape. I can then add, 'At the same time, your son is struggling to manage his terror that the beatings will happen again and that no one is safe.'

The dual message leaves a way out. We demonstrate that we are not afraid to hear or talk about the frightening or harmful things that have happened, and at the same time we respect the loyalty of family members (Boszormenyi-Nagy, 1972) and their need to maintain the family's balance. This is an implicitly empowering message. We are telling family members that we are not afraid to validate what is real but will do so in a non-shaming manner. This understanding allows us to engage family members to begin working on what is not being said directly.

Stating the duality of a child's perspective opens up previously hidden forces which drive a child's acting out behaviour. Parents are implicitly challenged to take responsibility for their homes. Each family member, including children, is challenged to recognise what leads up to crises and to make choices about continuing typical responses in escalating crises or slowing down the crisis and experimenting with a different stance or response.

Yelling, screaming, hitting, running away, or evicting become choices which tell everyone whether or not the same old crisis cycle will go on. The dual, centring message provides a way for family members to reintegrate conflicting pressures and asks them to decide whether they will replace cycles of crises day-by-day with choices to provide consistency, safety, nurture, and trust.

The metaphor of the child's crisis

Children like Kristen who are threatened with placement symbolise the family's struggle and serve as a focal point for family pressures to both remain the same and change. The child shows the splitting in the family and how family members have learned that they can only be half-good or half-bad, half-right or half-wrong. Pushing to any one side triggers the crisis cycle.

If the child is an 'angel' today, her sisters and brothers may be 'devils' getting into trouble. And, today's angel knows that tomorrow she, too, may be castigated as 'the bad one'. Today's good feeling of being wanted is precarious. According to Minuchen (1974), family members balance themselves with a multi-step dance around the pit of abandonment.

Crises become addicting in the family as they provide both thrills, intimacy, and relief from greater threats. It is safer and easier to battle a teacher, fight off the police or defy the warnings of child protection workers than to directly face unspoken traumas in the family or the prospect of Dad or Mum leaving for good. Crises provide a break from feeling, thinking about, or doing something about the greater threats.

Masterson (1976) described how a child cannot individuate if she fears her mother's withdrawal of affection and availability. The child, over time, learns that she cannot tolerate intimacy because intimacy is tied in with rejection. At the same time, the child cannot develop autonomy because she has learned over and over that to do this means threats and experiences of abandonment, and often an overwhelming sense of responsibility for her parent's rage and depression.

The child learns that to grow and achieve means to lose her parents' love and to feel alone in a barren world. The only way to get attention is to regress, to cling, to have tantrums. The child, in effect, learns she must remain emotionally like a toddler.

The child learns to be hypervigilant and hyperactive, to act before the wound can be touched. She must remain on guard, paying attention to the signs of a dreaded event and then move quickly, becoming a major part of the crisis cycle of the family.

Revolving through the cycle of crisis generates thrills, intimate encounters and provides a sense of balance like a teeter-totter moving back and forth. The family's dance mirrors their struggle with unresolved conflicts: enmeshment versus isolation; avoidance versus traumatisation; shame versus rigidity.

Metaphor, the link

I want to find a metaphor which can link both sides of a split message and frame the struggle embodied by the family members at most risk. By focusing on where the child in placement became stuck in her own development, I usually learn about a traumatic event which symbolises the primary splits and dilemmas represented by the child in placement or at risk of placement.

When I met Kristen, she was writing to her mother. Kristen needed to find out if her mother would care for Kristen and protect Kristen and herself from the death threats dating back to when Kristen was a toddler.

Metaphors help parents to move away from shame-based thinking - good versus bad. Parents and children can use a metaphor to validate the split messages coming down over generations. By owning a metaphor, the parent can take charge. Kristen's mother needed to decide what she was 'writing back' to her daughter.

Taking charge means moving away from the good/bad splits and slowing down the spin of events. It means learning to recognise triggers and developing a safety system - who will do what - when anyone in the family once again perceives the early warning signs of a return to the old patterns of crisis. Who can a child or parent go to for help? How can family members signal each other? What is the agreed-upon plan for dealing with the threat of Mom's relapse into alcoholism, Dad's losing his temper, or Billy running off with his old gang?

Family members can be challenged to move from dissociation to reality, from incompetence to skills and achievements, from depression (anger directed inwards) to self-care, from violence (anger directed outwards) to a series of safety steps, and from depersonalisation to respect for self and others.

Centring on the metaphor and need for a secure attachment also provides a way for different practitioners and family members to join together and provide a consistent message. Consistency is necessary in order to help clients to slow down time and move out of battles and crises. Without a united approach and common goal, different service providers will be quickly drawn in to re-enact the different messages and battles which have kept family members in crisis.

79

I want to find a metaphor which family members can own and use to frame choices. Use of the metaphor helps clients regain a sense of control and move past obstacles that have appeared insurmountable in the past.

Rebuilding attachments

Choice by choice, hour by hour, parents and children have the opportunity to mend the splits which have torn them apart. Each choice provides a new, albeit tentative link pulling together the traumatic splits from the past. Like a seamstress reknitting a torn garment, parents are helped and challenged to sew together the split parts of themselves and their children. The first stitches are tentative but mark the beginning of a new chance for the family to heal and grow.

The child threatened with placement is like a two-year-old with a scraped knee, hurting and bleeding. The child needs a parent who can validate the physical pain and the emotional hurt. Attachment means being attuned to a child, recognising her thoughts, what she sees, how she responds, and working with a sense of time which includes both the past and the future.

When a mother or father hugs their hurt two-year-old, they are saying 'I will not abandon you. I will help you survive the pain. You are not alone.' When a parent becomes strong enough to say 'I know you were scared I'd kill myself (or be killed)', the child can begin to see and hear a little more. When a little girl sees day by day that her parent is working to end the violence, stop an addiction, and care for his/her children, the girl can start to feel safe enough to trust again.

When a child is in a crisis placement or at imminent risk of placement, the first step is to validate the conflicting message - of love and hate, loyalty and fear, affection and rejection - which drive the crisis cycle. Focusing on the child in placement's struggle with these conflicts presents parents and children with both the challenge and the opportunity to face what could not be talked about, with support for their efforts to make things better. Family members can begin to relink the torn fragments that make up each person's identity and open up possibilities to see, hear, feel, think and talk about the past, the present and the future.

The safety and trust established in a non-shaming relationship with a therapist provides the context within which parents can show their children that it is safe enough to share their experiences of trauma, the terror of abandonment, and their hopes for a better future. The child can then move beyond split messages and develop positive relationships with peers, teachers, and other adults without having to be disloyal and risk the break up of a family.

Real world therapy

No magic words exist to heal the traumas of children facing abandonment. Not all parents can raise a child. But I believe that children and parents can face the realities of their lives. Facing the reality of who cares enough and is strong enough to parent a child is painful work but also sends a message of hope. The answer to threats of abandonment is the struggle of family members and practitioners to help each child gain a safe, secure home and a bonded relationship to someone the child can count on now and into the future.

The rewards for practitioners such as myself come in small but real changes in a child's trust and in a parent's commitment - in a child who entered a crisis placement at great risk of hurting herself or someone else, but who now feels believed and can learn and grow again within a family she can call her own. Over time, these changes make the difference between perpetuating histories of trauma and giving the next generation a better life.

Notes

1. This chapter was adapted from Kagan, R. (in press) *Turmoil to Turning Points; Building Hope for Children in Crisis Placements*, New York: W. W. Norton 8 Company. The foundation for this approach was based on Kagan, R. and Schlosberg, S. (1989). For this chapter ,'she' is used to refer to both girls and boys. Families described represent composites from different families and are not intended to represent any real people. Quotes are not exact.

2. Referring to an institution for children.

References

Ausloos, G. (1981), 'Systemes, Homeostase, equlibration', *Therapie Familiale*, vol. 2, 187-203.

Ausloos, G. (1986), "The March of Time: Rigid or Chaotic Transactions, Two Different Ways of Living Time", *Family Process*, Vol. 25, 549-557.

Berenson, D. (1976), *Family therapy theory and practice*, New York, Gardner Press.

Bettelheim, B. (1960), *Surviving and other essays*, New York, Vintage Books.

Boszormenyi-Nagy, I. (1972), *Invisible loyalties*, New York, Harper and Row.

Bowlby, J. (1969), *Attachment and loss: Vol. 1. Attachment*, New York, Basic Books.

Bowlby, J. (1973). *Attachment and loss: Vol. 2. Separation*, New York, Basic Books.

Erikson, E. (1963), *Childhood and society*, New York, W.W. Norton and Company.

Ferreira, A. (1960), "The double bind and delinquency", *Archives of General Psychiatry*, vol. 3, October, 359-367.

Fossum, M.A. and Mason, M.J. (1986), *Facing shame: Families in recovery*, New York, W.W. Norton and Company.

Haley, J. (1977), "Toward a theory of pathological systems", in P. Watzlawick and J. Weakland (eds), *The interactional view*, New York, Norton .

Kagan, R. and Schlosberg, S. (1989), *Families in Perpetual Crisis*, New York, W.W. Norton and Company.

Masterson, J. F. (1976), *Psychotherapy of the Borderline Adult; A Developmental Approach*, New York, Bruner/Mazel.

Minuchin, S. (1974), *Families and family therapy*, Cambridge, Mass., Harvard University Press.

Nichols, M. (1984), *Family therapy concepts and methods*, New York, Gardner Press.

Papp, P. (1983), *The Process of change*, New York, Guildford Press.

Pittman, F.S. (1987), *Turning points: Treating families in transition and crisis*, New York, W.W. Norton and Company.

Waters, D. and Lawrence, E. (1993), *Competence*, New York, W.W. Norton and Company.

Watzlawick, P., Beavin, J. and Jackson, D. (1967), *Pragmatics of human communication*, New York, W.W. Norton and Company.

6   The application of intensive family support programs: Hometraining in the Netherlands. Evaluation and its impact on practice

Peter VAN DEN BOGAART

Introduction

In the Netherlands, a rather unique kind of intensive family support programme is practised on a broad scale by youth welfare agencies. This kind of programme is commonly called 'hometraining', although other terms such as 'treatment at home', 'practical pedagogical assistance at home', 'intensive family treatment' or simply 'help at home' are occasionally used.

Hometraining is not a specific treatment programme or method but a general way of delivering assistance. It has the following characteristics (Van den Bogaart and Wintels, 1988).

1. Hometraining is delivered at home.
2. Hometraining is intensive: the practitioner visits the family one or more times a week for one hour or more.
3. Hometraining is practised with multi-problem families who have one or more children at risk. The families are more or less resistive to professional assistance and therefore difficult to treat.
4. Hometraining takes everyday family-life events as a starting point of treatment and is based on the wishes and needs of the family members. Therapeutic schools or scientific theories play no or only a secondary role.
5. Hometraining is directed at the family as a whole and not at individual members.

6. The goal of hometraining is to support the family in such a way that it stays together and will be able to function autonomously or with minimal support when hometraining is finished.
7. Hometraining in most cases is delivered by trained social workers or family workers.
8. Hometraining in most cases is a co-operative effort between two or more agencies in a geographical region.

In this chapter, a historical overview of hometraining practice and evaluation in the Netherlands will be presented. I begin with a short description of the dawn of hometraining in the post-war period. Next, the roots of modern hometraining methods are presented. Then, experimental hometraining policy and the results of its evaluation will be discussed. Recent trends in hometraining practice and evaluation in the post-experimental hometraining period will conclude the history of Dutch hometraining practice and evaluation. The historical presentation is followed by some recommendations for the evaluation of hometraining in the near future.

Early examples of family-centred projects: 1945-1963

An early example of the kind of support programmes that are to be discussed here is the 'Family-Centred Project of St. Paul' in the United States. This project started in 1947 and was based on the research finding that a small percentage (6 per cent) of the families registered by welfare agencies in St. Paul, Minnesota took a disproportionately large share (50 per cent) of social welfare services. In these relatively few families there was a high concentration of serious problems such as dependency, ill health and maladjustment. The family-centred project aimed to develop and administer methods for effective treatment of these multi-problem families. It had many features in common with hometraining as defined above: support was delivered at home; it was directed at multi-problem families; it was directed at the family as a whole; and it was implemented through a co-operative effort by various welfare organisations in the region. Furthermore, it contained elements which have recently been rediscovered in the Netherlands, such as the involvement of lay people from the community as support figures for the families, and the use of social support facilities in the families' neighbourhood. Evaluation research showed positive results for many of the supported families (Birt, 1956).

The experiences of St. Paul were brought to the Netherlands by Kamphuis, a prominent and well-known Dutch social work teacher (Kamphuis, 1963a; 1963b). The work of Kamphuis and others led, in the post-war reconstruction period, to many family-centred projects with elements of hometraining (Kamphuis, 1951; Hoytink, 1948; Van Rooy, 1948; Thierry, 1985). These projects were strongly encouraged by the Minister of Social Work.

Most of the family-centred projects were rather abruptly terminated in about 1963, owing to a general change in cultural values. Particularly relevant here is the shift from valuing 'adjustment' to valuing 'emancipation'. All family-centred projects were directed at the adjustment of families to society. This was now viewed as paternalistic and therefore the projects were discredited on ideological and political grounds (Milikowski, 1961; Van Wel, 1986; De Regt, 1986). Somewhat later, the emancipation of adolescents and young adults, accompanied by the decline of traditional family values, accelerated this termination of family-centred projects.

Until recently St. Paul and the many Dutch family-centred projects of the reconstruction era had been forgotten by most social scientists and practitioners. Somewhat surprisingly, these projects do not seem to have influenced the development of modern hometraining practice in a direct way. They can therefore be considered as 'prehistory'.

The origins of modern hometraining methods: 1974-1985

Most hometraining methods that are practised in the Netherlands nowadays were developed in the second half of the 1970s and the first half of the 1980s. The six most prominent methods will now be chronologically introduced.

The first method was originally called Intensifying Treatment and later on *Very Intensive Family Treatment (VIFT)*. It was initiated in 1974 by the municipal agency for social psychiatry of the city of Nijmegen, and, in 1984, it was adopted by the Institute for Family Guardianship and Advice of Friesland (Coenegracht, Maas and Roosma, 1991). The motives for the initiation of VIFT were very much the same as the motives for the Family-Centred Project of St. Paul: the inability to help a particular group of multi-problem families who were resistant to treatment. The most outstanding characteristic of VIFT is that the hometrainer develops a very close relationship with the treated family. The hometrainer spends a lot of time with the family and becomes in many ways part of the family. In the early 1980s, the role of hometrainer was filled by apprentices of the Leeuwarden School for Social Work. Nowadays, professional workers of the Institute for Family Guardianship and Advice visit the families. With this change to professional workers, the time spent with the family has been reduced from almost daily to about 12 hours a week, and the treatment period has been reduced from one year to about 8 months.

The second method was originally called Orion and later on *Video Home-training (VHT)*. This method was developed from 1977 onwards by Biemans (1980) and others (Aarts, 1991) in a residential centre for youth welfare, called 'De Widdonck'. The original objective of what was later called VHT was to enhance the involvement of parents in the treatment of their children. Results of research on the first relationship between mother and child by Trevarthen (1979) formed the basis of a method practised by group workers in the day-care centre of De Widdonck. Later on, this method was practised more and more at home. A special centre for the utilisation and further development of this home-based method, called Orion, was founded. Now VHT was no longer used to enhance the involvement of the parents in the treatment of their residentially-placed child but to assist the parents in their parental task at home and in this way to prevent placement of the child. The most outstanding characteristic of VHT is that parents are made responsive to contact initiatives by their children. Responsive-ness consists of positive contact initiatives towards the child and positive reactions to contact initiatives by the child. Especially in problem families, parents often do not recognise the weak, hidden or ambiguous contact initiatives tried by their children. To support parents' recognition, interactions between parent and child are systematically video-taped and selected fragments of successful contacts are played back for the parents and discussed with them. Parents learn to show responsiveness to their child through verbal and body language such as babbling, smiling, repeating utterances, making eye contact, saying yes, and so on. If successful, this is claimed to result in so-called positive interaction spirals (Dekker, 1994).

The third method is called *Practical Pedagogical Home Treatment (PPHT)*. This method has its roots in the care of mentally-disabled people. At a conference in 1977, parents of disabled children expressed the wish to take care of their disabled children at home. To enable them to do this, PPHT was developed at the Free University in Amsterdam (Oosterhof Beugelink, 1984) and later on also practised with parents of autistic children (Davies, 1989). In 1979, the day-care centre 'De TweeGelanden' decided to study the feasibility of PPHT for their clients: that is, children with psychosocial problems. In co-operation with other welfare agencies, they started a project. Later on, PPHT became a standard treatment method at 'De TweeGelan- den'. The most outstanding characteristic of PPHT is learning by modelling. In a structured way, parents are trained to act competently in child-rearing situations that cause them problems. The home-trainer or one of the parents plays the part of a role model whose actions are imitated by the other parent in real life situations (Goede, 1991).

The fourth method is called *Family Project (FP)*. FP was developed by Van Acker (1991a; 1991b; 1992) at the University of Nijmegen from 1982 onwards. The development of the method was motivated by the absence of effective treatment methods for behavioural problems in adolescents. Furthermore, FP was presented as an alternative for placement of these adolescents in residential homes. FP is directed at the stimulation of the adolescent's autonomy without creating conflict with the parents. The most outstanding characteristic of FP is the systematic way in which problems are analysed and concrete engagements between family members are formulated, planned, acted out and evaluated. The techniques used are eclectic, mainly borrowed from systems theory and family therapy.

The fifth method is called *Project at Home (PaH)*. From 1983 onward, PaH was developed in a co-operative effort between a Regional Institute for Community Mental Health Care (RIAGG) and the intramural sociotherapeutic institute 'De Triangel', both located in Amsterdam (Garnier and Van Vugt, 1991). The development of PaH was motivated by the inability to effectively treat families with very severe problems and the wish to effectively help intramural clients of 'De Triangel' in a less intensive way: that is to say, extramurally. The most outstanding characteristic of PaH is that assistance is given in all kinds of family situations that cause problems, including assistance in practical day-to-day activities. Attention is, however, focused on relationship problems. The hometrainer is supposed to develop a strong empathic relationship with the parents and other family members.

The sixth method is *Home training using Directive Family Therapy (HDFT)*. HDFT is an application of Directive Family Therapy as developed by the Dutch psychologist Lange (1985). This therapy is based on social learning theory and systems theory. HDFT has been practised by an Institute for Family Guardianship and Advice in Gouda since 1985. The most outstanding characteristic of HDFT is that the hometrainer together with the family members systematically analyses family structures, family patterns and problematic communications. The hometrainer gives concrete directives and instructions which are evaluated afterwards, thereby explicitly using communication techniques.

In recent years, attempts have been made to support the presented methods with a theoretical base (e.g., Wels and Oortwijn, 1992) or to compare methods on theoretical and methodological dimensions (e.g., De Ruyter, 1992; Vogelvang, 1992). Although these studies have led to interesting results, up to now it has been impossible to classify hometraining methods in accordance with theoretical schemes: for example, therapeutic schools. Perhaps, eventually, this will prove entirely impossible because of the eclectic nature of hometraining. Hometraining is principally practice-based. The needs and wishes of clients and day-to-day events in family life are chosen as starting points for interventions. Therapeutic and theoretical notions are explicitly and expressly given second place. All hometraining methods are the same in this respect, and it makes evaluation, comparison or even description of hometraining methods very difficult. The methods used prove to be somewhat elusive. Furthermore, because hometraining techniques and practices change very rapidly, every evaluation or description of a hometraining method may be out of date a year after its publication. Even the names of the methods change over time. VHT for example is nowadays called VHT+, Trajectory Hometraining or Region Hometraining. These ultra-modern versions of VHT render traditional VHT obsolete according to one of the founders of VHT (Biemans, oral communication).

The development of hometraining methods between 1974 and 1985 coincided with specific developments in youth welfare practice in general and in governmental youth welfare policy. This is not the place to discuss these developments in detail. It will suffice to say that family-oriented approaches and traditional family values came to be re-evaluated more and more. This even culminated, for example, in an appeal for an Ethical Revival by the leader of the most prominent Christian Political Party (A. van Agt) during his election campaign in 1976 (Napel, 1992). In this same period, residential treatment of children was vehemently criticised for various reasons (IWAPV, 1984; IWRV, 1984; Hekken, De Ruyter and Sanders-Woudstra, 1988). Hometraining therefore proved to fit very well with the ideological and political *Zeitgeist* of the era in which it originated.

Experimental Hometraining Policy and its evaluation: 1985-1987

Experimental Hometraining Policy

Especially because hometraining promised substantial cuts in governmental youth welfare expenditures, the preventive function of hometraining was music to the ears of national policy-makers in the middle of the 1980s, a period of strong economic recession (Brinkman, 1987; 1988). It was at least five times less expensive to implement and complete hometraining in a family than to treat a child residentially. For these reasons, in 1985, the department of Welfare, Public Health and Culture and the department of Justice set up a Hometraining Support Committee. This Committee was commissioned to support, monitor and evaluate experimental hometraining projects. This was called Experimental Hometraining Policy and was made part of Additional Policy, later called Substitution Policy. Additional Policy aimed to increase ambulant youth welfare and Substitution Policy aimed to substitute residential treatments for ambulant treatments.

Ambulant youth welfare agencies were invited to participate in Experimental Hometraining Policy through initiating new hometraining projects. These projects were financially supported by the national government over a period of two years. Participating projects were to subscribe to three objectives: to prevent placement of children at risk; to promote co-operation between local youth welfare agencies; and to organise the implementation and practice of home-training.

Eleven projects were admitted to Experimental Hometraining Policy. Five of them started to implement hometraining in 1985, the other six started implementation in 1986. The projects were supported, monitored and evaluated by the Hometraining Support Committee, which reported its findings to government in 1988.

Five projects implemented VHT, three implemented FP, one PPHT, one HDFT, and one a mixture of methods. The projects using FP and HDFT were supposed to treat families with adolescents at risk, and were called Adolescents Projects. The projects using VHT and PPHT were supposed to treat families with babies, toddlers and primary-school children at risk, and were called Infants Projects.

Empirical evaluation of Experimental Hometraining Policy

During the last year of Experimental Hometraining Policy, August 1987, the department of Welfare, Public Health and Culture asked the Leiden Institute for Social Policy Research (LISPOR) of the University of Leiden to conduct an independent empirical research study to evaluate the effects of hometraining. This research was at first conducted by LISPOR, and later on it became a co-operative effort between LISPOR and RCYW.

Ten projects participated in the evaluation research. For practical reasons, the project using mixed methods was excluded. The research aimed to measure the successes and failures of the implemented hometraining treatments, together with facilitating and constraining factors. A conceptual framework was used to classify possible facilitating and constraining factors (Mesman Schultz and Van den Bogaart, 1992). This framework differentiates five classes of variables that are supposed to be causally related to the effects of treatments: features of the project plans; organisation of the projects; so-called bridging variables; features of the actual treatments; and features of the treated families. A rather extensive selection of these variables was measured by: analysis of documents; interviews with hometrainers, project managers, change agents and developers of the hometraining methods used; and questionnaires filled in by hometrainers, project managers and parents. The interview schedules and some of the questionnaires were specially designed for the research. Other questionnaires were validated research instruments, already used in other evaluation research.

It must be noted that, according to the research design, the successes and failures of specific treatments were not only studied in relation to the variables associated with the implementation of these treatments and features of the treated families; but, on a higher level, the organisational and administrative context in which the treatments were implemented were also taken into account. For this reason, an interactional multi-level research design was needed. However, these kinds of designs had, at that time, hardly emerged from their primary stage of development (see for example: Mooij, 1987). Using a multi-level design could therefore be very risky. Furthermore, the use of such a design would certainly lead to a sharp reduction in variables (with possibly detrimental effects on the domain validity and practical utility of the results) and to very high costs. Neither of these consequences was desirable, so a complex design was developed using a combination of qualitative analyses and quantitative, statistical analyses. For a full description of this design the reader is referred to the research report (Van den Bogaart and Wintels, 1988; for a short presentation see: Wintels, Van den Bogaart and Mesman Schultz, 1989). For an independent and comparative evaluation of the validity of the research project, the reader is referred to a state-of-the-art study by Van Gageldonk and Bartels (1990).

The most important result of the evaluation research was a distinctive affirmative answer to the main research question: Is Home training effective?. According to the various measures of success and failure, it was shown that most of the hometraining treatments had positive or very positive results. According to the hometrainers, treatment objectives had been attained to a high degree in most families and significant decreases in individual and family problems had occurred. Most hometraining treatments were evaluated very positively by the hometrainers. Only six children out of the 55 treated families had left home during treatment for negative reasons. Almost all parents were satisfied or even highly satisfied by the support they had received. Most of them experienced fewer problems in the handling of their children and reported a significant decrease in their children's adjustment problems. All in all, these results indicated hometraining to be a very effective way of delivering treatment. Furthermore, the correlations between the various measures were moderate to high. Therefore, the multi-method validity of these results is good. To be somewhat more specific, evaluations by parents were on the whole more positive than evaluations by the hometrainers. Client satisfaction levels were extremely high.

Second, the children in most of the treated families were indeed at risk. Psychosocial and behavioural problems of the children at the beginning of treatment were established by means of the Start Questionnaire of the COM-procedure (Brinkman and Kars, 1974; Mesman Schultz, 1977; Mesman Schultz, Depla and Nelen, 1987; Van den Bogaart, Mesman Schultz, Naayer and Zandberg, 1989; Van den Bogaart and Joosten, 1993). This questionnaire is validated and equilibrated. Scores can be obtained on 15 variables, each of which refers to a specific psychosocial or behavioural aspect of the child and his or her environment, such as completeness of the family, relationships with other family members, occupational aspirations, behaviour problems, and so on. By way of a COM-formula, a selection of these scores can be combined into a so-called COMHPG score. This score is a validated predictor for the success of ambulant versus residential treatment. The mean COMHPG-score of the 71 children in the research sample was -.19, indicating problems of such a severity that placement of the child is advisable.

Third, the implementation of the hometraining methods proved to be very successful in most projects. The training of hometrainers was undertaken systematically and according to plan, most hometrainers and project managers were enthusiastic about the training method, their new jobs and the way they were informed, prepared, trained, coached and supervised. Furthermore, the hometrainers were able to implement hometraining treatments according to the method they had learned and to do this consistently in most families. Inconsistencies in implementation were mainly attributed by the hometrainer to specificities of the problems in the treated families and their own lack of experience.

All in all, the main results of the evaluation of Experimental Hometraining Policy were very positive indeed. More specific results, however, gave rise to some tempering of the euphoria. They suggested that positive effects of hometraining were not achieved in all families and that not all projects were implemented successfully.

Closer examination of the results proved the success of the hometraining treatments to be significantly related to three important factors.

The first factor is the age category of the child at risk in the treated family: that is to say, according to almost all effect measures, the Adolescents Projects had clearly less positive results than the Infants Projects. This can be simply illustrated by the fact that five of the six children who left Home for negative reasons were treated by the Adolescents Projects. Between methods, within age-based project categories, no significant differences could be established due to an insufficient number of treated families in the research population.

Whether age-based differences should be attributed to age or to the method used could not be established either because the two factors are nested. However, the data suggested that, within age-based categories, hometraining methods do not differ strongly in effectiveness.

The second factor is the severity of the psychosocial problems of the child. The effects of hometraining were significantly and moderately related to the COMHPG-score. The correlations between COMHPG-scores and different effect measures ranged from .20 to .50.

The third factor is the willingness of families to co-operate in treatment. In the Adolescents Projects, the willingness of adolescents was significantly and moderately related to hometraining success (correlations were about .40). The willingness of the parents had no significant influence. In the Infants Projects, on the contrary, the willingness of the parents was significantly and moderately influential (correlations varying from .17 to .53) whereas the willingness of the children had no or even negative relationships with success.

Like treatment success, the success of hometraining implementation and the adequacy of hometraining practice seemed to differ between the Adolescents and Infants Projects. Because only ten projects were involved, statistical significance of differences could not be established. But it is remarkable that all the Infants Projects were implemented successfully or very successfully, while the implementation of FP in two Adolescents Projects were troublesome, even leading to conflicts between project management and change agents.

All in all, the results of the evaluation research showed that hometraining is a feasible and effective method for youth welfare, that it can be effective in multiproblem families with children at risk for placement, and that the success of hometraining seems to be systematically influenced by factors that can be established and measured beforehand.

One more specific result of the evaluation research deserves to be mentioned separately because it is important for the evaluation of hometraining in its post-experimental period. In almost all projects, but especially in the Infants Projects, practitioners desired to apply hometraining also in families not belonging to the target group: that is to say, in families without children at risk. The argument for this broadening of the target group was the wish to intervene in families where problems have not yet accumulated. Some projects have actually already included these families in their hometraining pool. These hometraining cases were, however, not involved in the official evaluation.

Use of evaluation results

The results of Experimental Hometraining Policy and its evaluations by the Hometraining Support Committee and by LISPOR/RCYW were made public in various ways on a large scale in 1988 and 1989. This campaign was very intensely directed at youth welfare agencies, but to a lesser degree also at the public in general through interviews and articles in magazines and newspapers. Furthermore, anticipating the positive results, government had already, in 1987, set up and financed a Foundation for the Promotion and Dispersion of Hometraining (in Dutch abbreviated to SPIN, which acronym has the very symbolic meaning of spider). SPIN was financed by government and was commissioned to promote, disseminate and implement various hometraining methods. It was also made responsible for systematic quality control in the local hometraining projects it supported.

Upon completion of the evaluation research, the national government invited RCYW to set up a proposal for a scientific sequel. In line with the results of Experimental Hometraining Policy, two possibilities for future research were proposed: (1) research to further develop a good hometraining method for adolescents at risk and (2) a comparative evaluation of different hometraining methods for infants at risk, possibly leading to a merging of the best elements of these methods (Van den Bogaart and Mesman Schultz, 1989). Neither of these proposals were considered adequate to be financed by government. Arguments adduced in support of this rejection were that hometraining methods should have the chance to prove themselves in practice without the interference of researchers and that the proposed research activities were already commissioned to SPIN.

Recent trends in hometraining: 1988-1995

The last eight years of hometraining practice can be characterised as a period in which hometraining has conquered a large area of Dutch youth welfare. Recently, hometraining has even spread to other countries such as England, Sweden, Israel and Belgium. This is called the International Initiative. This war of conquest is clearly led by SPIN. SPIN tries to obtain and keep control of all hometraining activities in the Netherlands. A strong hierarchical structure, called the hometraining supervision ladder, is used to maintain a centralised control of local activities and local hometraining practice. SPIN also grants certificates to hometrainers trained and supervised by SPIN. Despite all these measures, independent initiatives to 'rebuild' local youth welfare by means of hometraining flourish. Heretic groups even seem to be active in some places: these groups practise hometraining methods promoted by SPIN and are supervised by SPIN, but they do not implement hometraining exactly according to the rules set by SPIN.

   These rather turbulent recent developments have confused many practitioners and even some scientists. In order to shed some light on this troubled situation, five trends in recent hometraining practice and evaluation will be highlighted.

1 Domination by Video Hometraining and Directive Hometraining

When SPIN was founded, one of the developers of VHT was appointed general manager. As might be expected, VHT was originally the only method promoted and disseminated by SPIN. Because VHT is directed at young children, SPIN actually promoted no method for adolescents. This was not caused by malice on the part of the general manager of SPIN. He sincerely tried to involve developers of FP - which is intended for adolescents at risk - while promoting the activities of SPIN, but met with little success. For this reason, SPIN decided to develop its own hometraining method for adolescents: a method called Directive Hometraining (DHT). It was based on those elements of FD and HDFT that were thought to be the most effective and feasible (Smits, 1992; Muller, 1993). Use of a video recorder, as in VHT, was a feature added to these two methods.

Since the beginning of its development in about 1990, DHT has been effectively promoted by SPIN. Consequently VHT, and to a lesser degree DHT, are by far the most practised methods in the Netherlands. In 1993, VHT was practised in all 42 geographical regions of the Netherlands and DHT in 13 regions. In that same year, 148 youth welfare agencies implemented hometraining according to VHT and 39 according to DHT (SPIN, 1995). Other methods are practised in three regions at most and by only a few agencies.

The domination of hometraining by VHT has caused much confusion about the essentials of hometraining. Many people believe that hometraining is the same thing as VHT and that the principles of VHT are the principles of Home training. For example, they believe that the essential feature of hometraining is the use of a video recorder; or they believe that it is essential for hometraining to use so-called video interaction principles.

The domination of hometraining practice by VHT and DHT would of course be all right if those two methods were proven to be the most feasible, effective or efficient methods. The only two systematic empirical comparisons of hometraining methods so far are the evaluation of Experimental Hometraining Policy and, to a lesser degree, the dissertation of Vogelvang (1993). Neither of these evaluations suggest VHT or DHT to be the best methods. On the contrary, Vogelvang's results suggest that VHT in the post-experimental period is inferior to PaH in various respects: it is less feasible, it is practised with less problematic families and it is less effective. One of these results - the finding that problems in families treated with VHT are relatively mild - is in line with a recent small scale comparative study of VHT and DHT (Bijl, Van den Bogaart & Mesman Schultz, 1994). The children and families treated by VHT proved in various respects to be less problematic than the children and families treated by DHT. The research sample used in this study was not representative and the results could therefore be accidental. However, in combination with Vogelvang's results and the fourth trend - to be discussed shortly - they are sufficient to warrant a systematic empirical comparison of the various hometraining methods which is less biased in favour of VHT over other hometraining methods.

2   Decline and rise of evaluation research

At least one shelf of a library bookcase could be filled with Dutch publications on hometraining, starting in 1988. Publications on valid empirical research evaluating the results of hometraining would probably fit into a medium-sized handbag. Most of these empirical studies are small-scale studies of particular hometraining projects or applications of hometraining in specific cases (e.g. Wels,

Jansen and Pelders, 1994; Jongbloed and Tavecchio, 1995; Muris, Vernaus, Van Hooren, Merckelbach, Heldens, Hochstenbach, and Postema, 1994; Bijl et al., 1994).

At present, research activities directed at the evaluation of hometraining seem to be increasing. The university of Nijmegen, the university of Utrecht, and a co-operative effort by practitioners in three provinces of the Netherlands, are evaluating different hometraining methods by way of more extensive research projects. Results are not yet available.

Hometraining effects, treatment process and characteristics of the treated families are generally not systematically monitored either by hometrainers or by SPIN. Exceptions exist. Two locations, for example, have a computer data file containing data on almost one thousand families treated with Video Home training. So far, however, these data have only been scantily and incompletely analysed (Bouman and Van der Heide, 1993; Keulen and Bruijn, 1995) and admission to these data is not granted to outsiders.

Lack of valid empirical evidence makes it is impossible to systematically judge the effectiveness of home training as it is presently practised, let alone to compare the effects of different methods or the effects in different kinds of families. Consequently, the rapid changes in hometraining practices, previously mentioned, are uncontrolled changes. No-one can tell whether they are for the better or for the worse.

Although systematic empirical evidence is lacking, there are two sources from which some data on the effectiveness and target groups of hometraining can be obtained.

The first source is research conducted by RCYW which, while not specifically directed to evaluation of hometraining, did gather data on hometraining cases. An advantage of these RCYW research studies is that they all used the same instrument to measure the effects of treatment and the characteristics of the treated children. This instrument is the COM-procedure, mentioned previously. The Start Questionnaire of the COM-procedure is used to measure psychosocial problems at onset of treatment, and the Exit Questionnaire and Follow-up Questionnaire are used to measure the effectiveness of treatment at the end of treatment and six months later.

The second source partly overlaps the first. It consists of a computer data file, called the COM-file, which has been compiled using COM-procedure data gathered from RCYW research projects and other research centres. These data are periodically supplemented with data supplied by agencies which routinely use the computerised version of the COM-procedure for evaluating their treatment. At present, the COM file contains data on almost 10,000 children receiving child welfare services, including 594 children whose families receive hometraining.

These two sources will be used to demonstrate the next two trends in post-experimental hometraining practice.

3 Continuation of positive hometraining results

Data based on the Exit Questionnaire of the COM-procedure will be used to evaluate trends in the effectiveness of hometraining. Data based on the Follow-up Questionnaire are less extensive, but are in line with the data provided by the Exit Questionnaire.

Table 6.1 shows results pertaining to children in the COM-file. These results are based on data gathered by one large-scale national research project (Van den Bogaart, Bijl, Huisman and Mesman Schultz, 1992) and data supplied by four agencies. As might be expected, by far the most cases have been treated with Video Hometraining (see, the first trend). The other cases have all been treated with DHT.

Table 6.1

Trends in the effects of hometraining based on data in the COM-file

	Mean scores on effect measures*		
Period	AC2	AC3	N
1988-1990	-.76	-.93	94
1991-1992	-1.02	-1.18	142
1993-1995	-1.06	-1.23	19

* High scores indicate problematic adjustment of the child at the end of treatment. AC2(Adjustment Criterion 2) is the overall adjustment of the child, and AC3 is the relational adjustment of the child. AC1 is not presented because its equilibration is not yet reliable. The scores presented are standardised scores (z-scores) equilibrated on a representative group of children admitted to Children's Homes.

COM-procedure data from one recently concluded research project (Bijl et al., 1994) have not yet been added to the COM-file. These data concern Video Hometraining and Directive Hometraining cases from 1994. In this study, scores on AC2 and AC3 were -.73 and -.53 respectively (N=29). Although these scores suggest a somewhat less positive hometraining result than the scores presented in Table 1, they do not differ significantly.

The Exit Questionnaire results suggest hometraining to be consistently very effective in the post-experimental hometraining period. Naturally, this conclusion should be treated with caution because the sample included only VHT and DHT cases and was therefore not representative.

4 Shifts in the target group

Table 6.2 presents Start Questionnaire results with respect to children in the COM-file. Scores on COMHPG are used to indicate the severity of psychosocial and behavioural problems. The Start Questionnaire data in the COM-file are based on the same sources as the Exit Questionnaire data presented above. To this has been added data from cases treated in Experimental Hometraining Policy.

Table 6.2
Trends in the target group of hometraining based on data in the COM-file

Period	Mean scores on COMHPG*	N
1985-1987	-.19	54
1988-1990	-.33	151
1991-1992	-.74	292
1993-1995	-.20	106

* High scores indicate severe psychosocial problems of the child at the onset of treatment. The scores presented are standardised scores (z-scores) equilibrated on a representative group of children admitted to Children's Homes.

The Start Questionnaire data from two recent research studies (Van den Bogaart and Mesman Schultz, 1994; Bijl et al., 1994) have not yet been added to the COM-file. Both these studies concern families treated between 1993 and 1995. The first study only includes VHT cases, while the second includes VHT and DHT cases. The mean COMHPG-scores in these studies were -.77 (N=43) and -.60 (N=42).

The results in Table 2 suggest a curvilinear trend in the severity of psychosocial problems of children whose families have been treated with hometraining: first there is a steady decline and then suddenly problems increase again in the last two years. This trend is statistically significant (p<.001). However, supplementing the results with the two research projects not included makes the trend less curvilinear. After a steady decline, COMHPG-scores stabilise at the level of -.40 to -.80 after 1991. Closer inspection of data suggests that the increase of severe problems during the last two years according to data in the COM-file can be attributed to the fact that the 1993-1995 data in the COM-file were mainly supplied by one specific agency. Therefore this curvilinear trend may be due to heavily biased data.

It may be concluded that a gradual decline in the severity of problems occurred after the termination of Experimental Hometraining Policy. This concurs with information received from practitioners. The tendency to practice hometraining in families with children not yet at risk - a tendency already present during Experimental Hometraining Policy - seems to have continued and grown in the post-experimental period. However, this does not apply to all hometraining. The data from hometraining cases in the COM-file suggest that there are still agencies which do not take the preventive function of Home training seriously!

5 Conquests of new areas by Video Hometraining and other Hometraining methods

Video Hometraining not only dominates the field of hometraining in child welfare: during the post-experimental years, many attempts were made to apply the principles of VHT in environments other than the family. Principles of Video Hometraining are nowadays used in day care (Rosmalen, 1991; Van de Zande and Rosmalen, 1994), in residential care (Dekker, Scholte and Mullens, 1992; Houwing, 1994; Van den Bogaart, Van der Weijden and Van der Veldt, 1995)[1], in schools, and even in industrial organisations. The application of Video Hometraining principles in day care and residential care is actually an unconscious movement back to the original Orion method as used in the day-care centre De Widdonck 20 years ago.

At present, many different projects have already been set up with the aim of developing residential and day-care applications of Video Hometraining principles. In 1995, the managers of these projects organised themselves into a national working committee. This committee has agreed that the methods being developed are variants of Video Interaction Treatment (VIT). The committee is presently comparing variants of VIT that have already been implemented during the last five years.

During its development one of the variants of VIT has been systematically accompanied by empirical research (Van der Veldt, Van den Bogaart and Mesman Schultz, 1992; 1994; Van der Veldt, Van der Weijden and Van den Bogaart, 1993). This variant has already been disseminated to a few agencies other than the one it was developed in (Van der Weijden and Van der Veldt, 1995; Van der Veldt and Van den Bogaart, 1995; Stokman, 1995). At the moment, a research project is being prepared in which this variant of VIT will be developed into a 'solid' residential treatment method (Van den Bogaart, 1995). This project will be a co-operative effort between RCYW and four or five child welfare agencies.

Besides VIT, one other hometraining method has been developed systematically for day care and is being implemented in one day-care centre. It is called Learning to Parent with Video and is based on transactional analysis (Heijkoop, 1992; Vogelvang, 1995).

In areas other than child welfare, many hometraining methods and Hometraining-like methods are coming into being very rapidly. These methods are, for example, directed to children with psychotic parents, to psychotic children, to children with terminal diseases in hospital, to mothers in maternity hospitals and to patients with dementia.

Conclusions and recommendations

The history of hometraining and its evaluation lead to the conclusion that a very fruitful way of treating multi-problem families with children at risk has been developed during the past 20 years. Hometraining developed gradually up to the termination of Experimental Hometraining Policy. Since then, its development has accelerated enormously. SPIN, the national foundation designed to promote and disseminate Home training, is probably most responsible for the rapid development of hometraining over the last eight years.

In some respects, the tumultuous post-experimental developments can be looked upon as advances: in other respects, they can be seen as pauses or even backward steps. The large-scale dissemination of hometraining has no doubt been enormously beneficial to child welfare and can therefore be viewed as an advance. It is no exaggeration to say that modern Dutch child-welfare policy is hardly conceivable without hometraining. Hometraining has certainly weakened the boundaries between residential and ambulant child care and has rightfully claimed its own place in the structure of Dutch child welfare. It has, furthermore, played an important role in the development of thoughts on coherent, connected, individualised treatment paths for children and their families. It has empirically proven to be most successful in many cases.

The advances of hometraining are substantial, probably more substantial than the backward steps.

The most important backward step is the absence of empirical data on Home training practice. This makes all the progress mentioned above very uncertain. At the moment, empirical knowledge on everyday hometraining practice is scantier than in 1988. SPIN was commissioned to promote and disseminate hometraining and to monitor its quality. The first two tasks were carried out remarkably well but the last one was largely neglected. Probably it was not such a good idea, after all, to entrust quality control to the promoter of a product.

The second major backward step in hometraining practice is the domination of the field by one or two methods. Of course, a situation in which a thousand different budding and blossoming flowers cover the field of hometraining methods is not a situation to be pursued. But natural selection of methods by means of a centralised foundation is not desirable either. Methods should be selected based on evidence that they are the best in terms of feasibility, efficiency and effectiveness, not because they are promoted by a national foundation. In 1988, some healthy rivalry existed between adherents of different methods, tempered by the wish to try out new ways of treatment. At present, one sometimes gets the impression that even the adherents of the two methods promoted by SPIN are hostile to each other in some respects. Healthy rivalry has certainly regressed to a unhealthy animosity. When a representative of the national government stated in 1988 that hometraining methods should be given the chance to prove themselves in practice without interference by researchers, he probably did not expect the consequences which actually followed - consequences caused by the very absence of researchers.

In order to stop the backwards movement, a large-scale independent national empirical evaluation of hometraining practice and methods is recommended. This research should not be directed at the intricacies of hometraining practice and treatment process, but should focus on simple questions, such as: 'Which method works best in which kind of families?' and 'What are the differences between families treated with different methods?' Perhaps even a national prohibition against further development of hometraining methods should be recommended, at least until contemporary practice has been thoroughly evaluated. These further developments are uncontrolled and can be detrimental to the utility of home-training: for example when the target group is purposely or unwittingly changed. The third recommended measure is an obligation to monitor hometraining cases routinely with a uniform, validated and equilibrated instrument.

Aside from the advances and backward steps in hometraining development, the conquest of new areas by hometraining deserves special notice. Particularly, the development and implementation of residential and day care variants of hometraining provide a great opportunity to bring more continuity to the treatment of children and their families. It is recommended that the systematic development, evaluation and dissemination of these methods should be undertaken.

Notes

1. To our knowledge there is only one example of another Home training method that has been practised in residential care. It is PPHT in a residential centre in Amsterdam (Gelens, 1991).

References

Aarts, M. (1991), *Orion Hometraining*, Weert, Orion.

Acker, J. van (1991a), "Het gezinsproject (The Family Project)" in H. Baartman (ed.), *Praktisch pedagogische thuishulp in bewerkelijke gezinnen (Practical Pedagogical Home Support in families difficult to support)*, Houten/Antwerpen, Bohn Stafleu Van Loghum.

Acker, J. van (1991b), *Ouders en kinderen in conflict: Theorie en praktijk van de hulpverlening aan gezinnen*, Houten/Antwerpen, Bohn Stafleu Van Loghum.

Acker, J. van (1992), "Basisstrategieën bij thuishulp (Fundamental strategies in Home Treatment)" in L. Muller (ed.), *Thuisbehandeling en Hometraining. (Hometreatment and Hometraining)*, Utrecht, SWP.

Biemans, H. (1980), *De therapeutische werkplaats. (The therapeutic workshop)*, Roermond, De Widdonck.

Bijl, B., Bogaart, P.H.M. van den & Mesman Schultz, K. (1994), *Videohometraining en directieve thuisbehandeling. Eerste fase van een onderzoek naar de mogelijkheid en wenselijkheid om twee methoden van intensieve thuisbehandeling te combineren (Video Hometraining and Directive Hometraining; First part of a research on the feasability and desirability of combining two methods of intensive home treatment)*, Leiden, COJ.

Birt, C.J. (1956), "Family-centered Project of St. Paul", *Social Work*, vol. 1, no. 4, 41-47.

Bogaart, P.H.M. van den (1995), *Video-interactiebegeleiding, van prototype naar solide methode (Video Interaction Treatment, from prototype to solid method)*, Leiden, COJ.

Bogaart, P.H.M. van den, Bijl, B., Huisman, P. & Mesman Schultz, K. (1992), *Vernieuwingen in de jeugdhulpverlenin. (Innovations in youth welfare)*, Leiden, COJ.

Bogaart, P.H.M. van den & Joosten, W.G.M. (1993), *The COM-procedure; the use of a program evaluation instrument by organizations for youth welfare.* Paper presented at the third EUSARF-congress "Love is not enough", Lüneburg, Germany.

Bogaart, P.H.M. van den & Mesman Schultz, K. (1989), *Voorstellen voor vervolgonderzoek naar Hometraining (Proposals for continuation research on hometraining)*, Leiden, COJ.

Bogaart, P.H.M. van den & Mesman Schultz, K. (1994), *Psychosociale problemen en meervoudige gezinsproblemen bij de cliënten van RIAGG-Flevoland, afdeling jeugd (Psychosocial problems and multiple family problems of clients of RIAGG-Flevoland, youth division)*, Leiden, COJ.

Bogaart, P.H.M. van den, Mesman Schultz, K., Naayer, P.H.M. & Zandberg, Tj. (1989), *Instrumentarium voor programma-evaluatie in de residentiële jeugdhulpverlening; betrouwbaarheid en validiteit. (Instrument for programme evaluation in residential youth welfare; reliability and validity)*, Leiden/Groningen, LISBON/COJ/RUG.

Bogaart, P.H.M. van den, Weijden, J.A.M. van der & Veldt, M.C.A.E. van der (1995), *Video in de leefgroep. Handleiding voor een prototype van Video-interactiebegeleiding (VIB)*. (Video in residential care. Manual for a prototype of Video Interaction Treatment (VIT)), Leiden, COJ/De Mare.

Bogaart, P.H.M. van den & Wintels, P.M.A.E. (1988), *Evaluatie van intensieve thuisbegeleiding (Hometraining). Resultaten van een onderzoek onder tien experimentele projecten. (Evaluation of Intensive Home Support (Hometraining). Results of a research on ten experimental projects)*, Leiden, LISBON/COJ.

Bouman, M. & Heide, E. van der (1993), *Het beeld stilgezet, een onderzoek naar vijf jaar video- hometraining. (The picture stopped, a research of five years Video Hometraining)*, Utrecht, Vakgroep Kinderstudies, RW.

Brinkman, L.C. (1987), *Toespraak door de Minister van Welzijn, Volksgezondheid en Cultuur t.g.v. het congres over ambulante jeugdhulpverlening. (Speech by the minister of Welfare, Public Health and Culture on the occasion of the congress on ambulant youth welfare)*, Rijswijk, Ministerie van WVC.

Brinkman, L.C. (1988), *Brief van de Minister van Welzijn, Volksgezondheid en Cultuur aan de Voorzitter van de Tweede Kamer der Staten Generaal, nr. 172. (Letter from the Minister of Welfare, Public Health and Culture to the President of the House of Commons, nr. 172)*, Rijswijk, Ministerie van WVC.

Brinkman, W. & Kars, H. (1974), *AEPRA, Aanpassing en predictie van aanpassing. (AAPRA, Adjustment and prediction of Adjustment)*, Den Haag, Staatsuitgeverij.

Coenegracht, A., Maas, V. & Roosma, D. (1991), Intensivering Hulpverlening: helpen waar al het andere ophoudt ofwel helpen voor er geholpen kan worden. (Intensifying Treatment: supporting where everything else stops or supporting before support is possible), in H. Baartman, (ed.)

Praktisch-pedagogische thuishulp in bewerkelijke gezinnen. (Practical Pedagogical Home Support in families difficult to support), Houten/Antwerpen: Bohn Stafleu Van Loghum.

Davies, M. (1989), Hometraining bij kinderen met autistisch gedrag. (Hometraining for children with autistic behavior), in A. Stavast & R.N.Schaap-Paauw, R.N. (eds), *Hometraining, Beleid en Methodiek. (Hometraining, Policy and Method)*, Utrecht, SWP.

Dekker, T. (ed.) (1994), *Video-hometraining in gezinnen. (Video Hometraining in families)*, Houten/Zaventem, Bohn Stafleu Van Loghum.

Dekker, T., Scholte, W. & Mullens, H. (1992), *Het gebruik van de basiscommunicatie in de leefgroep. (The use of fundamental communication in the residential group)*, Amsterdam, SaC.

Gageldonk, A. van & Bartels, A. (1990), *Evaluatieonderzoek in de jeugdhulpverlening; deel 1: Resultaten van een overzichtstudie. (Evaluation research in youth welfare. Part 1: Results of a state-of-the-art review)*, Leiden, DSWO-Press.

Garnier, M. & Vugt, M. van (1991), "Hometraining in het Project aan Huis. (Hometraining in the Project at Home)", in H. Baartman (ed.) *Praktisch-pedagogische thuishulp in bewerkelijke gezinnen. (Practical Pedagogical Home Support in families difficult to support)*, Houten/Antwerpen, Bohn Stafleu Van Loghum.

Gelens, L.J.G.M. (1991), *"Thuiszorg in een tehuis"; een onderzoeksverslag naar een experiment 'hometraining' binnen een residentiële voorziening. ("Home care in a Home"; a research into a experiment 'hometraining' in a residential setting)*, Amsterdam, Tehuis Annette.

Goede, A. de (1991), "Praktisch Pedagogische Thuishulp. (Practical Pedagogical Home Treatment)", in H. Baartman (ed.), *Praktisch-pedagogische thuishulp in bewerkelijke gezinnen. (Practical Pedagogical Home Support in families difficult to support)*, Houten/Antwerpen, Bohn Stafleu Van Loghum.

Heijkoop, J. (1992), "Leren Opvoeden met Video. (Learning to Parent with Video)", in L. Muller (ed.), *Thuisbehandeling en hometraining. (Hometreatment and Hometraining)*, Utrecht, SWP.

Hekken, S.M.J. van, Ruyter, P.A. de & Sanders-Woudstra, J.A.R. (1987), *Residentiële hulpverlening, voorwerp van aanhoudende zorg. (Residential treatment, Cause of continuing worry)*, Rijswijk/Den Haag, Ministerie van WVC/Ministerie van Justitie.

Houwing, C. (1994), *Notitie implementatie Video-interactiebegeleiding in het residentiële werk; een procesbeschrijving. (Note on the implementation of Video Interaction Treatment in residential care; a process description)*, Santpoort, OCK.

Hoytink, M.J. (1948), "De zorg voor het onmaatschappelijke gezin in nieuwe banen. (The care of the dissocial family in new approaches)", *Tijdschrift voor Maatschappelijk Werk*, vol.2, no. 24, 374.

IWAPV (1984), *Tussen droom en daad. (Between dream and deed)*, Rijswijk, Ministerie van WVC/Ministerie van Justitie/ Ministerie van O&W.

IWRV (1984), *Eindrapport. (Final Report)*, Den Haag, Staatsuitgeverij.

Jongbloed, M.H.B. & Tavecchio, L.W.C. (1995), *Eindproject Gezinsinteractie Training: Ontwikkeling, evaluatie en methodiek. (Final project Family Interaction Training: development, evaluation and method)*, Rotterdam/Leiden, Paedologisch Instituut/Vakgroep Algemene Pedagogiek, RUL.

Kamphuis, M. (1951), *Wat is social case work? (What is Social Case Work?)*, Alphen a/d Rijn, Samson.

Kamphuis, M. (1963a), *Nieuwe wegen in het werk met probleemgezinnen. (New directions in the treatment of problem families)*, Alphen a/d Rijn, Samson.

Kamphuis, M. (1963b), *Het avontuur in St. Paul. (The adventure in St. Paul)*, Alphen a/d Rijn, Samson.

Keulen, T.P. & Bruijn, A.M. (1995), *"Wel thuis". Evaluatieverslag video-hometraining Regio Den Haag/Zoetermeer e.o. ("Have a good trip Home". Evaluation report Video Hometraining in the Region The Hague/Zoetermeer and surroundings)*, Den Haag.

Lange, A. (1985), *Gedragsverandering in gezinnen. (Behavior modification in families)*, Groningen, Wolters Noordhoff.

Mesman Schultz, K. (1977), *AEPRA-2, aanpassing en predictie van aanpassing. (AAPRA-2, Adjustment and prediction of adjustment)*, Den Haag, Staatsuitgeverij.

Mesman Schultz, K. & Bogaart, P.H.M. van den (1992), *Interventie-Onderzoek en Ontwikkeling in de jeugdhulpverlening. (Intervention Research and Development in Youth Welfare)*, Leiden, COJ.

Mesman Schultz, K., Depla, M. & Nelen, M. (1987), *Evaluatie van gedifferentieerde residentiële hulpverlening aan jeugdigen. (Evaluation of differentiated residential treatment of juveniles)*, Leiden, LISBON.

Milikowsky, H.Ph. (1961), *Sociale aanpassing, niet-aanpassing, onmaatschappelijkheid. (Social adjustment, non-adjustment, dissociality)*, Arnhem, Van Loghum Slaterus.

Mooij, A. (1987), *Interactional multi-level investigation into pupil behavior, achievement, competence and orientation in educational situations (diss.)*, Den Haag, SVO.

Muller, L. (1993), *Directieve Thuisbehandeling. (Directive Hometraining)*, Utrecht, SWP.

Muris, P., Vernaus, A., Hooren, M. van, Merckelbach, H., Heldens, H., Hochstenbach, P., Smeets, M. & Postema, C. (1994), "Effecten van video-hometraining: een pilot-onderzoek. (Effects of Video Hometraining: a pilot study)", *Gedragstherapie*, vol. 27, 51-62.

Napel, H.M.T.D. (1992), *'Een eigen weg': de totstandkoming van het CDA (1952-1980). ('Our own path': the origins of the CDA (1952-1980) (diss.)*), Leiden, drukkerij FSW.

Oosterhof Beugelink, C. (1984), *Hometraining: een pedagogische vorm van hulpverlening aan gezinnen met een geestelijk gehandicapt kind; samen werken aan samen verder leven. (Hometraining: a pedagogical kind of support of families with a mentally handicapped child; working together on living together)*, Groningen, Wolters Noordhoff.

Regt, A. de (1986), "Onmaatschappelijke gezinnen: over het verdwijnen van een categorie. (Maladjusted families: On the disappearance of a category)", in J.W. de Beus & J.A.A. van Doorn, *De geconstrueerde samenleving: vormen en gevolgen van classificerend beleid. (Constructed society: ways and consequences of classifying Policy)*, Amsterdam, Boom Meppel.

Rooy, H. van (1948), *Gezinnen in nood. (Families in distress)*, Amsterdam.

Rosmalen, L. van (1991), *Video Hometraining in breder perspectief. (Video Hometraining in a broader perspective)*, Eindhoven, MKD Tomteboe.

Ruyter, P.A. de (1992), "Hulpverlening aan gezinnen: een waardevol begin. (Family support: a valuable start)", in H. Baartman (ed.), *Praktisch-pedago-gische thuishulp in bewerkelijke gezinnen. (Practical Pedagogical Home Support in families difficult to support)*, Houten/Antwerpen, Bohn Stafleu Van Loghum.

Smits, M.-J. (1992), "Directieve thuisbehandeling. (Directive Hometraining)" in L. Muller (ed.), *Thuisbehandeling en Hometraining. (Hometreatment and Hometraining)*, Utrecht, SWP.

SPIN (1995), *Jaarverslag 1993. (Annual Report 1993)*, Utrecht, SPIN.

Stokman, M. (1995), *Evaluatie en vervolgvoorstel VIB-project in Boddaertcen-trum Katwijk. (Evaluation and proposal for continuation of VIT in Day Care Centre "Boddaert" in Katwijk)*, Leiden, De Mare.

Thierry, E.M. (1985), "Isolatie en heropvoeding: zwak-sociale gezinnen aan het Rotterdamse Zuidplein. (Isolation and reeducation: less-social families at Zuidplein in Rotterdam)", *Tijdschrift voor Agologie*, vol. 14, no. 4, 235-255.

Trevarthen, C. (1979), "Communication and cooperation in early infancy; a description of primary intersubjectivity", in M. Bullowa (ed.), *Before speech. The beginning of interpersonal communication*, Cambridge, Cambridge University Press.

Veldt, M.C.A.E. van der & Bogaart, P.H.M. van den (1995), *Systematic family support in a traditional residential institution. The implementation of VIT in*

"Bergse Bos". Paper presented at the fourth EUSARF congress "There is no place like Home", Leuven, Belgium.

Veldt, M.C.A.E. van der, Bogaart, P.H.M. van den & Mesman Schultz, K. (1992), *Video interactiebegeleiding in een behandelingsgroep. Evaluatie van een gezinsgerichte vernieuwing in de stichting de Mare. (Video Interaction Treatment in a residential treatment group. Evaluation of a family oriented innovation in "de Mare"*), Leiden, COJ.

Veldt, M.C.A.E. van der, Bogaart, P.H.M. van den & Mesman Schultz, K. (1994), *Systematische invoering van Video-interactiebegeleiding. Onderzoek naar de implementatie van VIB op de Stichting de Mare. (Systematic implementation of Video Interaction Treatment. Research on the implementation of VIT in "de Mare"*), Leiden, COJ.

Veldt, M.C.A.E. van der, Weijden, J.A.M. van der & Bogaart, P.H.M. van den (1993), *Video Interaction Treatment. The stepwise implementation of a family-oriented programme in a residential center for youth welfare.* Paper presented at the third EUSARF-congress "Love is not enough", Lüneburg, Germany.

Vogelvang, B.O. (1992), "Definiëring van hometraining. Legitimering van hometraining. (Definition of hometraining. Legitimation of hometraining)", in L. Muller (ed.) *Thuisbehandeling en Hometraining. (Hometreatment and Hometraining*), Utrecht, SWP.

Vogelvang, B.O. (1993), *Video-hometraining 'plus' en het Project aan Huis; verheldering van twee methodieken voor intensieve pedagogische thuisbehandeling. (Video Hometraining 'plus' and Project at Home; clarification of two methods of intensive pedagogical Hometreatment) (diss.*), Amsterdam, Vrije University.

Vogelvang, B.O. (1995), *Leren Opvoeden met Video. Evaluatie van LOV-training vanuit het Boddaert Centrum Apeldoorn. (Learning to Parent with Video*), Amsterdam, Vrije Universiteit.

Wel, F. van (1988), *Gezinnen onder toezicht; de stichting Volkswoningen te Utrecht 1924-1975. (Families in custody; the Foundation for Public Housing in Utrecht 1924-1975*), Amsterdam, SUA.

Wels, P.M.A. & Oortwijn, A.J. (1992), "Video-hometraining; een bijdrage tot wetenschappelijke fundering. (Video Hometraining; a contribution to a scientific foundation)", *Tijdschrift voor Orthopedagogiek*, vol. 31, 3-21.

Wels, P.M.A., Jansen, R.J.A.H. & Pelders, G.E.J.M. (1994), "'Videohometraining bij hyperactiviteit van het kind. (Video Hometraining with the hyperactive child)" *Tijdschrift voor Orthopedagogiek*, vol. 33, 363-379.

Weijden, J.A.M. van der & Veldt, M.C.A.E. van der (1995), Verspreiding en implementatie van Video interactiebegeleiding (VIB). (Dissemination and implementation of Video Interaction Treatment (VIT)) Workshop at the fourth EUSARF-congress "There is no place like Home", Leuven, Belgium.

Wintels, P.M.A.E., Bogaart, P.H.M. van den & Mesman Schultz, K. (1989), *Experimenteel hometrainingsbeleid; belangrijkste resultaten van een programma-evaluatie van tien hometrainingsprojecten. (Experimental Hometraining Policy; Main results of a programme evaluation of ten Hometraining proiects*), Rijswijk, Ministerie van WVC.

Zande, K. van de & Rosmalen, L. van (1994), *Cursusboek voor ouders van MKD "Tomteboe". (Manual for parents of Medical day care centre "Tomteboe"*), Eindhoven, MKD Tomteboe.

7 Home-based services: to each his own?

Herman E.M. BAARTMAN

1. Introduction

Since the 1970s, there has been strong growth in the development and diversity of a new method of helping parents and children in cases where there are problems in child-rearing. This method is 'hometraining', also known as 'in-home services' (Barth, 1991) and as 'home-based family services' (Maybanks and Bryce, 1979).

These terms, however, suggest a certain homogeneity of methodology, which could not be further from the truth. Their only common aspect is that they are concerned with help provided in the home. Beyond this, as we shall see, they include the widest possible range of child-rearing and child-development problems and make use of every conceivable working method.

I intend to cover the following points in this chapter: after a general description of the field itself, in order to identify the area to which the rest of the chapter will be devoted, I shall examine aspects determining the choice between hometraining and traditional ambulant help, while paying some attention to the diversity of methodologies in this area. I shall then concentrate on one type of hometraining: very early, intensive home help in young, 'at-risk' families, a process also termed 'preventive hometraining' as distinct from 'curative hometraining'.

2. Types of hometraining: an overview

Home-based services can be classified into three types: services for families with a developmentally disabled child, educational services, and problem familycentred services.

As regards services for families with a developmentally disabled child, the handicap itself usually forms the basis of the child-rearing problem. Hometraining here aims at acquainting parents with their child's idiosyncrasies and helping them to find the best ways of relating to that specific child in that specific situation. Depending on the child's age, this help can also be strongly directed towards stimulating certain aspects of his or her development - aspects such as communication and self-help skills - and sometimes towards the child's incorporation into the family's daily routines. The Portage Project is a well-known example of this kind of hometraining (Shearer and Shearer, 1972). Specific programmes have been developed for the parents of an autistic child (Kozloff, 1973; Van Berckelaer-Onnes and Kwakkel-Scheffer, 1988) and for the families of a mentally handicapped child (Koch, 1979; Oosterhof-Beugelink, 1984).

A second form of hometraining concerns educational services, sometimes referred to as enrichment programmes, such as the Mother Child Home Program (Levenstein, 1977), CARE (Wasik, Ramey, Bryant and Sparling, 1990) and HIPPY (Lombard, 1981). These are aimed primarily at improving the cognitive potential of children in socio-economically disadvantaged situations. Incidentally, hometraining itself often forms only a part of these programmes.

The third type I have called problem-family-centred services, and it is to this third group that the rest of this chapter will be devoted. This concerns essentially normal children who are in families where the individual, relational, or social problems of other family members threaten the children's own development to a greater or lesser extent. This threat is often such as to involve the risk of placement. Most of these programmes claim to work with 'multi-problem families', though the extent to which this claim is warranted depends on the definitions employed (Ghesquière, Hellinckx and Baartman, 1995): certainly, the group of multi-problem families is distinguished by a heterogeneity of characteristics and problems (Rutter and Madge, 1976). Well-known programmes within this category include Homestart (Van der Eyken, 1982); Families First (Kinney, Haapala and Booth, 1991); Video-hometraining (Biemans and Stroucken, 1992) and *Hulp aan Huis* (Home help) (Garnier and Van Vugt, 1991). Six variants of this kind of hometraining programme are now being employed in the Netherlands (Baartman, 1991; Muller, 1992); five of these originated in the Netherlands and one (Families First) in the United States. Wasik and Roberts (1994) recently described the parameters of a number of American hometraining programmes, concentrating on those programmes in which child abuse and neglect were the most important categories; a total of 224 programmes.

I draw a distinction here between preventive and curative programmes. Preventive programmes aim for the primary prevention of child-rearing problems, curative programmes try to ease existing child-rearing problems or family problems. I shall return to this distinction later.

Every type of hometraining programme I have described here comprises a number of variants whose parameters differ. A comprehensive discussion of all these parameters is impossible here, but as an example I shall mention three of the most important: *focus, intensiveness*, and *professional status of the helper*.

Focus can be broad or narrow, and this is generally linked to the variety of methodologies employed within a programme. De Ruyter (1991) divided six Dutch programmes into two categories: programmes which confine themselves to child management; and programmes which also offer help in other aspects of family life, such as individual welfare, the parents' own relationship, domestic chores, and the family's social position.

Intensiveness is another important parameter, and is determined by three factors: breadth of focus, duration and frequency.

The *professional status of the helper*, whether the helper is a layman or a professional, forms another significant parameter. This is an area in which arguments of principle and economics can occasionally get in each other's way. The economic argument is that non-professionals are cheaper, but this of course depends on their effect: buying something cheaply can turn out to be expensive in the long run. The argument from principle is that knowledgeable non-professionals often find it easier to gain access to certain families and to establish and maintain contact with them.

It has become clear that hometraining is characterised by a high degree of diversity, both in terms of working methods and in terms of clientele. As far as hometraining for problem families is concerned, there is little support for the hypothesis that differences between the various programmes are invariably founded on differences between the families themselves. On the contrary, we may safely assume that homogenous programmes are being applied to a heterogeneous group of families and that homogenous groups of families are being helped by a wide variety of programmes. Ayoub, Willett & Robinson (1992) were able to classify 'at-risk' families - the type of families who are normally the target group for home-based services - into five different homogeneous groups (situationally stressed, chronically stressed, emotionally stressed, multi-risk, and violent multi-risk) on the base of empirical data. Differences in family characteristics appeared to be connected with differences in reaction to treatment.

3. The family as the locus of treatment

Although differences obviously exist between these families, they have at least one thing in common: they all receive hometraining. This is not as fatuous as it sounds: can we not ask how families who receive hometraining differ from families who receive traditional mobile help? In other words, in what ways does their situation differ from that of other families such that a hometraining programme is advised?

This is an important question, for three reasons. First, of course, we want to know whether a hometraining programme really is the most effective help that can be offered for a given set of problems. Second, there is the economic aspect: hometraining is cheaper than residential care, but it is more expensive than mobile help. Third, there is the ethical issue. Hometraining is quite an intrusive form of help: a hometrainer gets to see behind closed doors, literally as well as figuratively. This intrusiveness can be at odds with a family's right to privacy (Levenstein, 1981).

Various reasons are given in the literature as to why the family home is chosen as the locus of treatment. In the following discussion of these explanations I shall confine myself to problem-family-centred services, though certain arguments also apply to other types of hometraining.

The first explanation is a **diagnostic** one: a family's daily problems are best observed on the spot. Several methods assume ecological models of behaviour which imply that people's behaviour is dependent on their living environment, and that insight into a person's environment is indispensable to an understanding of his or her behaviour. This living environment is primarily a social one consisting of the others with whom the person lives. Wherever people coexist there is some sort of rule system, some distribution of jobs, responsibilities and roles, and dissimilarities in the opportunities for altering them. Second, the environment is a physical one: it is large, or small, it is neat and tidy, or chaotic, or even dangerous. Third, there is the question of rhythm; either there is a certain predictability about recurring events, or there is not. Each of these three aspects - the nature of the relationships between family members and their opportunities for making these relationships known, the nature of their physical space and their family rhythms over time - affect the behaviour of parents and children. Conversely, their behaviour also affects these three ecological aspects. This is why observation *in vivo* is held to be more ideal than observation in a separately arranged space such as an interview room. Still, this alone cannot justify offering hometraining help, as an ecological perspective can be brought to bear on every family and on every kind of family problem and child-rearing problem. The overwhelming majority of therapeutic activities to do with family problems and child-rearing problems take place in the professional's domain.

The second explanation is a **therapeutic** one and concerns the assumption that working to change behaviour in certain families is most likely to succeed when it takes place within the ecological context referred to above. This assumption is the result of a number of arguments. The first argument is that an immediate link can be made with the family's daily routines. This implies, for example, that professional advice can be optimally attuned to a situation's specific characteristics. The second argument follows from the fact that certain clients have difficulties with processes such as abstraction, reflection and generalisation. Family life consists of a continuous stream of events and episodes which, taken together, display certain patterns. Professional interviews with a family are aimed not at listing these events, but at isolating their underlying patterns, and identifying aspects of these patterns that would benefit from change. Detecting, describing and discussing these general patterns demands the ability to abstract from the particular; its purpose is to create new general insights and skills which can then be applied to particular instances. This double transfer, from the concrete to the particular and vice versa, and from the interview room to the home and back, generates fewer problems when it takes place in the family's daily living environment.

A third explanation for offering this help within the family context has to do with **the relationship between client and helper**. Two aspects to this relationship may be distinguished. To start with, it is a working alliance. This means that the client must have a genuine desire to change his or her situation together with at least a minimal motivation to do something about it. It also means that the helper has to be able to attune his or her help as closely as possible to the wishes and abilities of the client. A frequent problem here is that a long history of failure has resulted in a pattern described as 'learned helplessness' (Seligman, 1975) or even as an 'apathy-futility syndrome' (Polansky, Borgman and De Saix, 1972). This can mean that a client's motivation to do something about the problem can be so weak that he or she cannot even be bothered to come to the care organisation's offices at agreed times. Another difficulty is that it is sometimes difficult to adequately attune the practices and methodologies of regular mobile care provision with the needs and abilities of the client. This explains the choice of outreach working methods in these cases. A second aspect of the relationship between client and care provider is the therapeutic aspect of the relationship itself, or in other words, the opportunity that the relationship offers for the client to have corrective emotional experiences. Learned helplessness does not only imply that a person lacks self-confidence; having few skills or little worth in one's own eyes soon leads to the conviction that one means just as little in other people's eyes. Outreach work, when resolute and attuned to the client's real needs, can give a person the feeling that he or she is worth the trouble. In this respect, some programmes are not focused only on the accommodating and attuning aspects of care: the frequency and duration of the relationship may be such that the helper spends time within the family itself. Where a family therapist endeavours in the office to bring renewed balance into family relationships by participating in family patterns, a hometrainer can do the same by participating in part of a family's daily life.

To sum up: ecological diagnostics, a practical hands-on method directly focused on daily situations, and improved chances of the development of a relationship between client and helper, together constitute the arguments in favour of providing care to problem families within the home itself. The more a client's family and child-rearing problems are intertwined with the web of ecological factors, the greater the clients' inability to think in abstract terms, and the harder it is likely to be to build up a relationship between client and care provider, the stronger the argument for providing this care in the client's own home environment. This applies especially to the 'problem families' which are the focus of this chapter - families also referred to as 'Child Welfare Clientele' (Bidgood and Van de Sande, 1990) or as 'Protective Services Families' (Tuszynski and Dowd, 1979) - and by no means automatically to families with a handicapped child.

4. Preventive hometraining

In the large majority of cases, home-based help is offered only after child management problems have become critical and complex, after various other forms of help have failed, and very often after a serious crisis means that the child might be placed out of home. Indeed, for several hometraining methods, such as 'Homebuilding' and 'Families First', such a crisis and the threat of placement actually constitute the grounds for this kind of intervention. Several 'Homebuilding'-based programmes therefore have titles such as 'Crisis Intervention Services' and 'Intensive Family-Centred Crisis Services' (Bath and Haapala, 1993). Depending on the age of the child, this crisis can take one of two forms: serious neglect or child abuse by the parents, or serious parental conflicts and antisocial behaviour on the part of the child.

We should be careful here not to lock the stable door after the horse has bolted. A child who is about to be placed out of home has generally already undergone a long period of conflict and of psychological or physical violence. It is by no means unusual to consider hometraining only after one or two children have already been placed.

As I have said, many of these families are characterised by problems which not only date from the birth of the first child but which arose long before. With this in mind, it would be a logical step to apply family help know-how not just at moments of crisis but also well beforehand. This seldom if ever occurs in the Netherlands, a situation which is due in part to the compartmentalisation of care provision in that country. Prenatal and postnatal care are very strongly medically oriented and have little or nothing to do with psychosocial family care. Dutch psychosocial care provision has also traditionally held the view that help should wait until the need for it becomes overwhelming; outreach work is seen by many as overly intrusive.

Nevertheless, in other countries, particularly America, there is an increasing amount of practical experience in the provision of preventive support in the form of home-based services to young at-risk families. These are just the sort of families Dutch care services only usually meet when their problems have matured to the point that they become known to the Child Care and Protection Board.

At policy level, hometraining is promoted for its capacity to prevent placement. In my opinion, the next stage should be that hometraining is developed and employed as a way of preventing child management and family problems. As a first step in this direction, I shall now give an overview of experiences in this field elsewhere. I shall concentrate on four aspects: target groups, objectives, working methods and results.

With respect to the use of the term 'preventive': the term is applicable in so far as all the programmes described intervene at a very early stage and aim to improve child-parent relations, thereby preventing later problems. This intervention is offered at the very beginning of the child-parent relationship. Naturally, this does not rule out the curative aspects of the programme in cases where this intervention is linked with individual and socio-material help for the mothers concerned.

4.1. Target group and objectives

The group of people targeted by these programmes - without exception, mothers - are sometimes referred to as 'risk-mothers' or 'high-risk mothers' and sometimes as mothers with a low socio-economic status. It should be noted here that a low socio-economic status does not, of itself, imply a high-risk group. In practice there is usually a combination of individual and socio-economic risk factors at work. It generally concerns young families or expectant parents in which, to put it briefly, the balance between stress and strength is so precarious that it would be fair to call them 'risk-parents' or 'risk-families'. A good example would be a very young, single mother with almost none of the social or material support normally offered by formal and informal contacts, a partner, education, work and money. Frequently these mothers have disastrous personal histories, and all too often their own family background formed a less than exemplary preparation for their own parenthood.

114

The objectives of these programmes are diverse and may be divided into roughly three categories. There are two types of programmes with a narrow focus: one of these centres on the health of the mother and child by means of prenatal intervention aimed at the high-risk expectant mother (Dawson, Van Doornick and Robinson, 1989) and the promotion of a healthy lifestyle. The indicators considered to measure its effects include the duration of pregnancy and birth weight. The second type focuses primarily on the quality of the parent-child relationship, measured among other things by the quality of the mother's responsiveness and the bonding of the child. The majority of these programmes, which are always postnatal, take place within the framework of attachment research (Barnard, Magyary, Summer, Booth, Mitchell and Spieker, 1988; Jacobson and Frye, 1991; Lieberman, Weston and Pawl, 1991; Lyons-Ruth, Connell, Grunebaum and Botein, 1990). Of course, this does not prevent the results obtained from being of great importance to clinical practice. For an overview of these programmes I refer to Van Ijzendoorn (1994).

Aside from these two types of programmes having a narrow focus, there are also broad- or multi-focus programmes which not only centre on the task of child management but also on other tasks within the family unit, such as individual well-being, social position, domestic chores and the parents' own relationship. Research activities regarding these programmes focus more on the development of care methodology than do unifocal programmes (Barth, 1991; Erickson, Korfmacher and Egeland, 1992; Gray, Cutler, Dean and Kempe, 1977; Larson, 1980; Lealman, Haigh, Philips, Stone and Ord-Smith, 1983; Olds, Henderson, Chamberlain and Tatelbaum, 1986; Siegel, Bauman, Schaefer, Saunders and Ingram, 1980). I will concentrate on these multi-focused programmes.

4.2. Procedure

There is little information available on the methodological aspects of the procedure, but more is known about formal aspects, such as the point at which a programme commences (pre- or postnatal), duration, frequency and the status of the helper (volunteer or professional). A number of the multi-focus programmes begin as early as the final months of pregnancy, and others immediately after birth (for an overview see Fink and McCloskey, 1990). In one of the few programmes in which this variable was experimentally manipulated (Larson, 1980), prenatal intervention turned out to be more beneficial than postnatal. Barth (1991) and Siegel et al. (1980) who, unlike Olds et al. (1986), began intervention postnatally found no differences in effect between the intervention group and the control group. They attributed this to their not having begun prenatally. The overall results, including comparisons of effects, seem to indicate that young mothers with complex problems benefit more from prenatal intervention. It would seem more effective to provide this care to mothers expecting their first child (Olds et al., 1986).

These programmes last anything from three months to two years, although most last from 18 months to two years. In one three-month programme (Siegel et al., 1980) there were a total of nine home visits. In a two-year programme (Olds et al., 1986) some 33 visits were made, initially each week, decreasing in frequency to once every six weeks towards the end. Gabinet (1979) made an interesting discovery in this context. He drew up improvement scores at four points in the intervention period. Interestingly enough, at the third measuring interval, five months into the intervention, a number of scales showed a dip compared with the second measuring interval. Seven months later, however, at the fourth measuring interval, these scores were more favourable than at the second and third intervals. A comparison of assessed programmes led Olds and Kitzman (1990) to conclude that complex problems require a programme of intensive duration and frequency, although the definition of an optimal duration does remain unclear. It should be noted that the correlation between duration and effect need not be linear; a ceiling effect can mean that too long a period of care can result in a curvilinear relationship.

Some programmes incorporate trained lay-helpers, working under supervision, and others use professionals. There appears to be a preference for professionals in cases where there are critical and complex problems.

4.3. Results

Finally, some comments on the most complicated aspect of these programmes: the results. Assessment research using control groups shows that preventive hometraining can have positive effects on a variety of aspects, such as the responsiveness of the mother, the quality of the mother-child relationship, the quality of bonding, the use of physical or verbal violence as a child-management tool, and social contacts (Daro, 1990). On the basis of a comparison of assessment research, Olds and Kitzman (1990) conclude that preventive hometraining can be successful only if:

1. It is based on an ecological model, i.e. with multi-focal objectives and procedures
2. It commences during pregnancy
3. It is intensive with regard to duration and frequency
4. It is carried out by skilled professionals who are able to create a therapeutic relationship with the families
5. It is directed towards families where there is an increased risk for the mother and the child resulting from a lack of personal, social and material resources.

To sum up: preventive hometraining for families at risk should be introduced in the prenatal period, should be multi-focal and intensive and should be carried out by professionals.

This conclusion warrants the following comments:

1. The pleas for an ecological model and for a multi-focused and comprehensive methodology are closely connected. Through the work of Bronfenbrenner (1979), Garbarino (1976) and Belsky (1984) this model is widely used and accepted in the English literature concerning child-rearing problems. However, it strongly resembles the model of the general systems theory which has been used since the 1950s by family therapists. The difference between both models is, that within the general systems theory as used by family therapists, the family is seen more as a system, while it is seen as a subsystem by Bronfenbrenner and others. Both models focus on the clusters of variables and the relations between them which determine the quality of child-rearing, but they both lack a conceptualisation of the child-rearing practices of parents themselves. Therefore, it is not surprising, that the literature about ecologically-oriented, preventive and curative hometraining gives little information about these practices and the concrete ways in which one can try to influence them. This can hinder the transfer of these programmes to other settings.

2. The follow-up period was no longer than two years following termination of the help in virtually any of the assessed programmes. In many instances, the last effect measurement took place at the moment the intervention was concluded. The exceptions are the follow-up studies carried out by Seitz, Rosenbaum and Apfel (1985) and by Wieder et al. (*in* Daro, 1990). In the study carried out by Seitz et al., ten years after the conclusion of the programme an intervention group (n=17) proved to function more favourably with regard to a number of variables than did a control group (n=18). These variables included the level of education of the then very young mothers, unemployment, and the children's' school performance. The follow-up study of Wieder et al. took place five years after the conclusion of the intervention and there was no control group.

3. In the assessment studies, effect criteria are highly diverse in character and number. They may include the child's birthweight, the length of time between successive pregnancies, the use of medical facilities such as vaccination programmes, reports of child abuse, the provision of adequate toys, the degree of informal contacts, and the quality of attachment. Emphasis is frequently laid on the prevention of child abuse. Although child abuse is clearly an indication

of the quality of the parent-child relationship, there are two disadvantages in placing too much emphasis on this in the assessment. First, child abuse is but one way in which family and child-rearing problems may become manifest. The second is more a technical issue. The base-rate of child abuse in the general population is so low that an assessment study into the effects of hometraining programmes has to cover very large experimental and control groups. This does not, of course, apply only to the relatively exceptional phenomenon of child abuse. A comprehensive approach implies measurement of a broad spectrum of variables, and the broader the spectrum the larger the intervention and control groups need to be.

4. The precise relation between a programme's specific methodological characteristics and elements and its specific effects is unclear. For example, it is unclear whether improvement of the mother's responsiveness and sensitivity with regard to bonding should be linked to a therapeutic approach to the mother's own history of attachment. Larson (1980) compared the effects of preventive intervention in a set of three experimental conditions with each other, and with a control group. The variances found in some measured effects, such as acceptance and stimulation of the child, appeared to be more closely linked to the mother's own characteristics (ethnicity, education, age, marital status and parity) rather than to differences in intervention. So which cocktail of interventions is necessary for which effects is determined to an extent by the characteristics of the client. There are indications that the group which benefits most from this form of help are the very young, poor, single mothers (Badger, 1981; Gabinet, 1979; Olds et al., 1986).

5. A broad, comprehensive approach seems the obvious choice where complex problems exist; an argument which, so far, appears to be have been confirmed by the research. Nevertheless, many uncertainties remain. First, the breadth and composition of the intervention should not resemble a shotgun blast, one or two pellets of which can always be counted on to hit their target: care should be taken to incorporate a combination of procedures based on a sound theoretical model regarding the behaviour of child-rearers in general and, in particular, the problems at hand. Second, a comprehensive approach need not imply numerous simultaneous activities, which may not even be practicable; but even then, theory-based priorities must be established. Third, it must be clear to what extent improvements in one area, such as communication with the child, could automatically lead to improvements in other areas, such as communication with neighbours. The extent to which these sorts of generalisations do occur can be said to represent the achievement of a broad approach without having to devote separate attention to each objective.

118

6. By comparing the target groups, working methods and actual effects of evaluated programmes, it is possible to derive conclusions on the most optimal methodology, couched in terms of its duration, frequency, moment of intervention, breadth of focus and so on. However, such conclusions in the literature (see for example, Bidgood and van de Sande, 1990) are often based on discursive comparison, that is, on a systematic review of the literature. Numerous objections can be raised against such a technique, such as selectivity and subjectivity on the part of the reviewer (Hauser-Cram, 1988). A statistical meta-analysis of methodologically comparable programmes based on original group averages and standard deviations would form a significant contribution to such a discursive comparison, but such an analysis has never yet been applied to the area of preventive hometraining.

To conclude, preventive hometraining is demonstrably effective in tackling family problems and child-rearing problems in high-risk families, and there are indications that this effectiveness is increased when more intensive programmes - that is, programmes having a broader focus and a longer duration - are employed. However, little insight has yet been gained into the exact relationships between target group, methodology and effects. This is true not only for preventive hometraining but also for the much more widely applied curative hometraining. This has not prevented curative hometraining from being the subject of a great deal of investment. The time has come for more to be invested in preventive hometraining, together with systematic research into the relationships between target groups, methodologies and effects.

References

Ayoub, C.J., Willett, J.B. and Robinson, D.S. (1992), "Families at risk of child maltreatment: entry-level characteristics and growth in family functioning during treatment", *Child Abuse and Neglect*, vol. 16, 495-511.
Baartman, H.E.M. (ed.) (1991), *Praktisch-Pedagogische Thuishulp in bewerkelijke gezinnen*, Houten, Bohn Stafleu Van Loghum.
Baartman, H.E.M., Garnier, M., Vugt, M. Van and Vogelvang, B. (1989), *Het Project aan Huis; verslag van het onderzoek practisch pedagogische thuishulp in multi-problemgezinnen*, Amsterdam, Vrije Universiteit.
Badger, E. (1981), "Effects of a parent education program on teenage mothers and their offspring", in K.G. Scott, T. Field and E. Robertson (eds), *Teenage parents and their offspring*, New York, Grune & Stratton.

Barnard, K.E., Magyary, D., Summer, G., Booth, C.L., Mitchell, S.K. and Spieker, S. (1988), "Prevention of parenting alterations for women with low social support", *Psychiatry*, vol. 51, 248-253.

Barth, R.P. (1991), "An experimental evaluation of in-home child abuse prevention services", *Child Abuse and Neglect*, vol. 15, 363-375.

Bath, H.I. and Haapala, D.A. (1993), "Intensive family preservation services with abused and neglected children: an examination of group differences", *Child Abuse and Neglect*, vol. 17, 213-225.

Belsky, J. (1984), "The determinants of parenting", *Child Development*, vol. 55, 83-96.

Berckelaer-Onnes, I.A. van and Kwakkel-Scheffer, J.J.C. (1988), *Autisme en thuisbehandeling*, Meppel, Boom.

Bidgood, B.A. and Sande, A. van de (1990), "Home-based programming for a Child Welfare Clientele", in M. Rothery and G. Cameron (eds), *Child maltreatment: expanding our concept of helping*, Hillsdale, Lawrence Erlbaum.

Biemans, H. and Stroucken, T. (1992), "VHT+; videohometraining en trajectbegeleiding", in L. Muller (ed.), *Thuisbehandeling en hometraining*, Utrecht, SWP.

Bronfenbrenner, U. (1979), *The ecology of human development: experiments by nature and design*, Cambridge, Harvard University Press.

Daro, D. (1990), "Prevention of child physical abuse", in R.T. Ammerman and M. Hersen (eds). *Treatment of family violence*, New York, J. Wiley & Sons.

Dawson, P., Doorninck, W.J. van and Robinson, J.L. (1989), "Effects of home based informal social support on child health", *Journal of Developmental and Behavioral Pediatrics*, vol. 10, 63-67.

Erickson, M.F., Korfmacher, J. and Egeland, B.R. (1992), "Attachments past and present: implications for therapeutic intervention with mother-infant dyads", *Development and Psychopathology*, vol. 4, 495-507.

Eyken, W. van der (1982), *Home Start. A four year evaluation*, Leicester, Home Start Consultancy.

Fink, A. and McCloskey, L. (1990), "Moving child abuse and neglect prevention programs forward: improving program evaluations", *Child Abuse and Neglect*, vol. 14, 187-206.

Gabinet, L. (1979), "Prevention of child abuse and neglect in an inner-city population: II. The program and the results", *Child Abuse and Neglect*, vol. 3, 809-817.

Garbarino, J. (1976), "A preliminary study of some ecological correlates of child abuse: the impact of socio-economic stress on mothers", *Child Development*, vol. 47, 178-183.

Garnier, M. and Vugt, M. van (1991), "Hometraining in het project aan Huis", in H.E.M. Baartman (ed.). *Praktisch-pedagogische thuishulp in bewerkelijke gezinnen*, Houten, Bohn Stafleu Van Loghum.

Ghesquière, P., Hellinckx, W. and Baartman, H.E.M. (1995), "Multi-problem families: investigating the client's perspective", in M. Colton, W. Hellinckx, P. Ghesquière & M. Williams (eds), *The art and science of child care*, Aldershot, Arena.

Gray, J.D., Cutler, C.A., Dean, J.G. and Kempe, C.H. (1977), "Prediction and prevention of child abuse and neglect", *Child Abuse and neglect*, vol. 1, 45-58.

Hauser-Cram, P. (1988), "The possibilities and limitations of meta-analysis in understanding family program impact", in H.B. Weiss and F.H. Jacobs (eds), *Evaluating family programs*, New York, Aldine de Gruyter.

Infante-Rivard, C., Filion, G. and Baumgarten, M. (1989), "A public health home intervention among families of low socioeconomic status", *Child Health Care*, vol. 18, 102-107.

Ijzendoorn, M.H. van (1994), *Gehechtheid van ouders en kinderen*, Houten, Bohn Stafleu Van Loghum.

Jacobson, S.W. and Frye, K.F. (1991), "Effect of maternal social support on attachment: experimental evidence", *Child Development*, vol. 62, 572-582.

Kinney, J, Haapala, D.A. and Booth, C. (1991), *Keeping families together: the Homebuilders model*, New York, Aldine de Gruyter.

Koch, G. (1979), "Home-based support services: an alternative to residential placement for the developmentally disabled", in S. Maybanks and M. Bryce (eds), *Home-based services for children and families*, Springfield, Thomas.

Kozloff, M.A. (1973), *Reaching the autistic child; a parent training program*, Champaign.

Larson, C.P. (1980), "Efficacy of prenatal and postpartum home visits on child health and development", *Pediatrics*, vol. 66, 191-197.

Lealman, G.T., Haigh, D., Philips, J.M., Stone, J. and Ord-Smith, C. (1983), "Prediction and prevention of child abuse; an empty hope?", *Lancet*, vol. 1, 1423-1424.

Levenstein, P. (1977), "The mother-child home program", in M.C. Day and R.K. Parker (eds), *The preschool in action*, Boston, Allyn.

Levenstein, E. (1981), "Ethical considerations in home-based programs", in M. Bryce and J. C. Lloyd (eds), *Treating families in the home; an alternative to placement*, Springfield, Thomas.

Lieberman, A.F., Weston, D.R. and Pawl, J.H. (1991), "Preventive intervention and outcome with anxiously attached dyads", *Child Development*, vol. 62, 199-209.

Lombard, A.D. (1981), *Success begins at home: educational foundations of preschoolers*, Toronto, Lexington Books.

Lyons-Ruth, K., Connell, D.B., Grunebaum, H.U. and Botein, S. (1990), "Infants at Social Risk: Maternal Depression and Family Support Services as Mediators of Infant Development and Security of Attachment", *Child Development*, vol. 61, 85-98.

Madden, J., O'Hara, J. and Levenstein, P. (1984) "Home again: effects of the Mother-Child Home Programs on mother and child", *Child Development*, vol. 55, 636-647.

Maybanks, S. and Bryce, M. (eds) (1979), *Home-based services for children and families*, Springfield, Thomas.

Muller, L. (ed.) (1992), *Thuisbehandeling & hometraining*, Utrecht, SWP.

Olds, D.L., Henderson, C.R., Chamberlain, R. and Tatelbaum, R. (1986), "Preventing child abuse and neglect: a randomized trial of nurse home visitation", *Pediatrics*, vol. 78, 65-78.

Olds, D. and Kitzman, H. (1990), "Can home visitation improve the health of women and children at environmental risks?" *Pediatrics*, vol. 86, 108-115.

Oosterhof-Beugelink, C. (1984), *Hometraining: een pedagogische vorm van hulpverlening aan gezinnen met een geestelijk gehandicapt kind*, Gronginen, Wolters-Noordhoff.

Polansky, N., Borgman, R. and Saix, C. de (1972), *Roots of futility*, San Francisco, Jossey-Bass.

Rutter, M. and Madge, N. (1976), *Cycles of disadvantage*, London, Heinemann.

Ruyter, P.A. de (1991), "Hulpverlening in gezinnen: een waardevol begin", in H.E.M. Baartman (ed.), *Praktisch-pedagogische thuishulp in bewerkelijke gezinnen*, Houten, Bohn Stafleu Van Loghum.

Scarr, S. and McCartney, K. (1988), "Far from home: an experimental evaluation of the Mother-Child Home Program in Bermuda", *Child Development*, vol. 59, 531-543.

Seitz, V., Rosenbaum, L.K. and Apfel, N.H. (1985), "Effects of family support prevention: a ten year follow-up", *Child Development*, vol. 56, 376-391.

Seligman, M.E.P. (1975), *Helplessness; on development, depression and death*, San Francisco, Freeman.

Shearer, M. and Shearer, D. (1972), "The Portage Project: a model for early childhood education", *Exceptional Children*, vol. 36, 172-178.

Siegel, E., Bauman, K.E., Schafer, E.S., Saunders, M.M. and Ingram, D.D. (1980), "Hospital and home support during infancy: impact on maternal attachment, child abuse and neglect, and health care utilization", *Pediatrics*, vol. 66, 183-190.

Tuszynski, A. and Dowd, J. (1979), "Home-based services to protective service families", in S. Maybanks & M. Bryce (eds), *Home-based services for children and families*, Springfield, Thomas.

Wasik, B.H., Ramey, C.T., Bryant, D.M. and Sparling, J.J. (1990), "A longitudinal study of two early intervention strategies: project CARE", *Child Development*, vol. 61, 1682-1696.

Wasik, B.H. and Roberts, R.N. (1994), "Survey of home visiting programs for abused and neglected children and their families", *Child Abuse and Neglect*, vol. 18, 271-283.

8 Intensive family preservation work with high-risk families: Critical challenges for research, clinical intervention and policy

James K. WHITTAKER

Introduction

The material in this chapter draws on several earlier presentations and conference proceedings including, most recently, the Second National Australian Family Preservation Conference in Melbourne (February, 1995), the Kinark Family Services First National Families First Symposium, Toronto, Canada (February, 1995), and the Fedele Fauri Memorial Lecture in Child Welfare, the University of Michigan, School of Social Work (1 March 1994).

The purposes of the chapter are:

1. To review the value base, objectives and essential components of a major service initiative in the United States known as Intensive Family Preservation Services.
2. To identify critical challenges this initiative has posed in three interrelated domains: evaluation research; the development of clinical practice protocols; and the refinement of public policy.

Of necessity, this review is limited in scope and the interested reader is referred to the section on Additional Sources for a fuller treatment of the subject. In many ways, the challenges posed by intensive family preservation are not unique. They reflect a rapidly shifting social service scene characterised by ever more modest objectives in the face of declining resources, a predisposition for goal-oriented, short-term services, a focus on measurable outcomes, and a preference for consumer (in this case 'familial') involvement.

When one considers child and family services broadly, several sets of related ideas emerge which have influenced the course of public policy and professional practice in the States in recent years. These include:

- the idea of the family as the ideal developmental context for the child.
- the notion of services as first and foremost family supportive and family strengthening.
- a primary focus on meeting basic developmental needs of children in culturally acceptable ways, as opposed to identifying and treating child/family psychopathology.
- more focus on what might be termed an ecological perspective - looking at the effects of both proximate and distal environments on child outcomes - and moving from changing children and families from the 'inside-out' to the 'outside-in': for example, by working to create more supportive environments as well as by improving individual coping skills.

Consensus on these ideas is by no means complete, and indeed, a revisionist sentiment is increasingly heard, as witness the recent frenzy of debate about the call from some to bring back orphanages. Such sentiment, strongly 'child saving' in its value base, often greatly underestimates the fiscal costs associated with such long-term care. (For example, if one third of all children presently receiving Aid to Families with Dependent Children were placed in minimum standard group care, the cost would be $100 billion versus $8 billion for maintenance payments and food stamps for these children.) As well, we must consider the fact that our present placement capacity in the United States (foster or residential) can often not guarantee basic safety and freedom from abuse to its wards.

At the moment, the move towards family-centred practice is sufficiently strong to exert effects on existing services, but a good deal of where things go in future will depend on the outcomes of the next wave of practice demonstrations and research studies, as well as on how much authority is devolved to individual states to make key programme decisions once firmly set at the federal level. At the time of writing, these decisions are presently being considered in congressional debate in the context of major programme realignments and reductions following our recent (November 1994) elections. Because this chapter will focus on one small but important corner of the social welfare world, it is important to note that programmes and policies beyond the scope of what is generally thought of as 'family preservation' may have a great deal to do with the efficacy of these specialised services. I speak of the critical importance of a minimal social provision for families, including the basics of income, health care, housing, education, employment and public safety - without which family preservation services cannot succeed and for which they are, in no sense, a substitute. Suffice it to say here, that all of these provisions - the basic and the more specialised services - are subject to major change in the immediate political future. With that as a general caution, let us turn briefly to an analysis of how some of these new ideas I have enumerated are being carried out in the development of family-centred social services.

My colleague, Professor Sheila Kamerman of Columbia University, speaks of 'family support' and 'family preservation' services as the two dominant expressions of a move from child-centred to 'family-focused' service. What do these terms mean?

Family support services

The 'Family Support Movement' is at this point more loosely defined than the more narrow 'Family Preservation' initiative. Indeed, there is some considerable debate in my state and others as to whether it ought at all to be associated with *specific* programmatic initiatives, or left as a set of guiding principles. On the programmatic side, family support typically includes: prenatal and infant development programmes; many child abuse and neglect prevention programmes; early childhood education; parent education and support; home and school community linkage programmes; family-oriented day care and many neighbourhood-based mutual help and informal support programmes. Key federal initiatives, such as the Family Preservation and Support legislation, and key private foundation initiatives, such as those from the Annie E. Casey Foundation and key voluntary associations such as the Family Resource Coalition - a national federation of family support programmes with headquarters in Chicago - have given impetus and sustenance to the family support movement.

A recent report to Congress from our General Accounting Office defines Family Support Services thus:

Family support services are primarily community-based activities designed to promote the well-being of vulnerable children and their families. The goals of family support services are to increase the strength and stability of families, increase parents' confidence and confidence in their parenting abilities, afford children a stable and supportive family environment and otherwise enhance child development. Examples include: respite care for parents and care givers, early developmental screening of children; mentoring, tutoring and health education for youth; and a range of home visiting programmes and centre-based activities, such as drop-in centres and parent support groups (General Accounting Office Report, 1995, p. 4).

At this point, I would argue that 'family support' reflects more a set of values than a clearly defined programme strategy. Chief amongst these values is a deep respect for the complex tasks involved in family care giving, particularly in parenting. The relationship between parent and professional is defined as essentially collegial: to paraphrase my colleague, Heather Weiss at Harvard, we no longer view parents as 'empty vessels' waiting to be filled up with professionally-derived child development knowledge, but as active partners in a search for the formal and informal supports necessary to carry out the difficult tasks of parenting.

The following list of value statements from our Family Resource Coalition is illustrative:

* Parenting is not instinctive; it is a tough and demanding job.
* Parents desire and try to do the best for their children.
* Parents want and need support, information and reinforcement in the parenting role.
* Parents are also people with their own needs as adults.
* Programmes should focus on and work with family strengths, not deficits.
* Programmes should empower families, not create dependence on professionals. (Family Resource Coalition, 1983).

Such value shifts shape the ways in which we think and act as professionals and, if put into practice, assure that things will never be the same again.

Suffice it to say that a broad spectrum of opinion exists on how to achieve more 'family support' - from arguments for provision of more entitlements and greater access to various and sundry support services, to arguments for a *de-emphasis* on formal programmes and professional involvement so that the 'mediating structures' of society (church, extended family, neighbours, informal associations and so on) can reclaim their 'natural function' as agents of (non-monetised) family support. The debate on how best to support families is, needless to say, scarcely settled. In addition to basic definitional issues, I believe a key question in family support revolves around the degree to which such services or helpful exchanges should be monetised versus provided voluntarily with minimal involvement of public dollars.

Family preservation services

Intensive family preservation services, by contrast, are brief, highly intensive services generally delivered in the client's home with the overarching goal of preventing unnecessary out-of-home placement.

There has been considerable federal, state and local interest in these services, partly as a response to the escalating cost of out-of-home care, and, partly, because placement services were often offered before less dramatic services were made available to families. Family preservation has been a central focus of federal child welfare reform legislation in 1980 and 1993, as well as the focus of many state legislative initiatives and efforts by national associations and voluntary foundations to promote these services. Perhaps, not since the inauguration of Project Head Start, an early intervention programme begun in the mid-1960s, has so much national attention been focused on a single service strategy.

A recent federal report offers the following and somewhat expanded definition of family preservation:

Family preservation services are typically designed to help families alleviate crises that, left unaddressed, might lead to the out-of-home placement of children. Although more commonly used to prevent the need to remove children from their homes, family preservation services may also be a means to reunite children in foster care with their families. The goals of such services are to maintain the safety of children in their own homes, when appropriate, and to assist families in obtaining services and other support necessary to address the family's needs. (General Accounting Office Report, 1995, p. 4)

What are the defining characteristics/components of intensive family preservation services?

The first is a set of values and beliefs. Variously stated and as referenced earlier, they all speak to the notion of 'family' as the ideal locus for child rearing and family support. Parents are viewed collegially, crises are viewed as opportunities for change, families are presumed to be doing the best they can under difficult circumstances, and so on.

It is well known that debates have raged over the defining characteristics of family preservation services. I would argue that broad consensus exists on the following set of characteristics: (1) imminent risk of placement; (2) immediate response; (3) highly flexible scheduling; (4) intensive intervention; (5) home-based services; (6) time-limited and brief; (7) concrete and clinical services; (8) ecological approach; (9) goal-oriented/limited objectives.

What specific challenges can we identify for family preservation: research, clinical practice and policy?

Here I must quickly restate my ignorance of the European social service scene and hew closely to the patch I know best, which is the United States. I am struck with the abundance of thoughtful commentators at this Congress who are much more helpful than I will be on the particular implications for the future of family and children's services in their respective countries. Let me turn now to some challenges posed by the rapid expansion of family preservation services in the United States.

Challenges for family preservation practice

While the major debate over family preservation at the moment concerns whether or not we have pursued the policy goal of 'preserving families' at the expense of child safety, some fairly fundamental questions remain about the nature of the service itself. For example, which of the components just enumerated should be thought of as *necessary* elements and which as *sufficient* elements to meet the test of 'reasonable efforts' which is our present policy objective? This is more than simply a matter of clinical preferences, because what is deemed as critical ought to be reflected in statutory language as well as regulation. Otherwise, we get the rhetorical wash of 'family values' without the substance to back it up.

As some states choose to move down this prescriptive path, however, we see some resistance building from provider agencies and individual practitioners who view a practice model as being imposed from above. Other questions include: the importance of the locus of service (client's home vs. agency); the length of service; the relative merits of service teams over lone workers and the theoretical focus of the intervention (environment-centred / person-centred / cognitive-behavioural / structural family therapy).

Much of what we are learning about family preservation conflicts with what is still taken to be 'professional' behaviour: with respect to things such as self-disclosure, dependence, carrying out mundane tasks (like cleaning ovens) and working with extended family, friends and community networks. In any event, whether theoretical differences exist, practice is carried out quite differently in family preservation and conventional practice. For example, as my colleague, Jill Kinney (a founder of Homebuilders) says of 'assessment': 'We are there long enough the first time to hear the whole story and back soon enough so that it hasn't changed significantly.' At quite another level, family preservation has challenged the very notion of what is 'professional' as contrasted with 'paraprofessional' activity, with family preservation workers assisting client families with basic household tasks and providing transport to allied services such as drug treatment. Some have questioned the utility of current clinical models of social work practice which tend towards the psychotherapeutic for work with at-risk families in public sector urban social service settings. Whatever the truth of this assertion, I believe we are still relying far too heavily on interpersonal ('therapy') approaches at the expense of environmental intervention - at the individual, family, group, and I would add, neighbourhood, level - which could make a substantial difference in a family's ability to care for its children.

For example, in our own social network research work with care givers in high-risk families, we realise how infrequently and unsystematically care givers are asked such basic questions as: Who is there to help? What type of help is provided? How adequate does the care giver perceive the help to be and what strings are attached? (Whittaker, Tracy, Overstreet, Mooradian and Kapp, 1994). One very practical consequence of this lack of information on social networks and social support is that workers have a paucity of information to draw on in planning for follow-up work with informal helpers (such as mutual aid), an often critical component for families where substance abuse and/or maltreatment is an issue. Other practice dichotomies such as coercive versus empowering models, and culturally-specific versus culturally-blind approaches demand further attention and careful research. We have a great debate going generally in the United States right now (in social services and welfare) about the 'one-size-fits-all' approach.

Once we have identified the critical elements of family preservation, what knowledge and skills are necessary to prepare someone to deliver them consistently? What will training look like in terms of length; skill criterion; entry level criteria for staff; and conceptual/practice base? These are the kinds of questions planners and senior managers are grappling with as they struggle to implement family preservation legislation in many of our states. In general, I believe we have paid far too little attention to the infrastructure necessary to support and sustain family preservation work: the training, the clinical supervision, and so on. This is particularly true once the first wave of enthusiasm subsides.

To return to training, for example, it exists as a kind of 'black hole' in most social service departments, all too often determined by consumer preference as opposed to programme objectives. Moreover, one needs to ask how much of the training offered is experiential and skill based, as opposed to didactic and knowledge based? Is there, for example, a competency criterion for workers in those service components deemed to be the key to success? Too often, I believe, in the United States we operate on a 'train and hope' model.

Similarly, what are the organisational requisites for quality family preservation practice? Can they be found equally in public and voluntary settings? This last is a critical issue, because if family preservation cannot be shown to work save in the most rarefied and specialised of contract agency environments, how can it be promoted as a general social service policy solution? Many of these 'practice issues', in fact, can be reduced to empirical questions, and they constitute a second critical discussion presently taking place on evaluation research in family preservation.

Evaluation research

The results of what is by now a considerable corpus of family preservation research in the United States are decidedly mixed. Some studies show a modest advantage to intensive family preservation for preventing placements over regular services. Others do not. Methodological questions abound.

The first of these goes to the very heart of the logic for family preservation: the notion that we can define a population of families with a child or children at 'imminent risk of placement' and offer some intensive help in a timely manner to prevent many unnecessary placements while maintaining child safety.

It turns out from some of our largest and best designed studies, our ability to predict imminent risk (sometimes referred to as the 'targeting problem') is very limited. For example, in the statewide evaluation of family preservation in Illinois conducted by John Schuerman and Associates, at Chapin Hall/University of Chicago (Schuerman, Rzepnicki and Littell, 1994), less than 7 per cent of cases in the comparison group were placed within four weeks of a case opening, and barely in excess of 20 per cent had been placed a year later: 18 per cent of cases in the comparison group were never opened for service. The problem of accurate targeting has plagued other controlled studies as well, and raises questions about what one can learn about programme effects given the criterion of prevention of unnecessary placements. More fundamentally, such findings raise questions about the very definition of 'success' in family preservation.

We might ask whether placement prevention is a sufficient criterion? Is it even a necessary one? As noted, it turns out that placement is a rather low-probability event and is not that easy to predict. For example, a recent preliminary research report on decision-making from the same research team at the University of Chicago's Chapin Hall - responsible for the most thorough statewide evaluation to date - shows a disappointingly low level of consensus amongst national experts on which 'at-risk' children should and should not go into care (Rossi, Schuerman and Budde, 1995). Given such expert variability and the actual data on imminent risk from Illinois cited above, it will be difficult under all but the most controlled conditions to talk about the efficacy of family preservation in relation to its primary outcome of interest. Moreover, we know that sometimes, placement can be a positive outcome, reflecting the provision of needed services, say, in residential treatment, for a disturbed child. How then do we distinguish between the two in public policy? I shall return to the issue of 'placement per se' in my remarks on challenges for public policy.

The targeting problem, complex as it is, does not exhaust the list of challenges for evaluation researchers. Others include:

1. How do we define and operationalise programme 'intensity'? This takes us back to the issue of treatment components: what are the critical elements in family preservation service and how do we measure them?

2. A related challenge might be thought of as the 'research readiness' question: How do we balance the need for rigorous designs with the reality of nascent and immature practice technologies so that we only move to do summative outcome evaluation when programmes are, in the words of Donald Campbell, an eminent research methodologist, 'PROUD' and ready to be subjected to summative evaluation? Must it be all or nothing in evaluation research, or can we fit together anthropological (qualitative) methods - (what Curtis had in mind when he talked about 'thick description' of emerging early intervention programmes) - with sophisticated multivariate statistical techniques (such as hazard rate analysis), which other investigators have used to provide a more fine-grained picture of what factors predispose towards certain outcomes in different family preservation programmes? Dr. Fran Jacobs (Weiss and Jacobs, 1988) has made a major theoretical contribution to this discussion by providing a typology of research methods appropriate for differential levels of program maturity.

3. On the practical level: How do we foster co-ownership of the research strategy so that practitioners feel like partners in a knowledge-development project, not subjects in an experiment? This is no small issue when the direction of the results can be directly linked to the programme's continued funding.

4. How do we carry out research in a politically charged context where our major 'selling point' for new services may be exactly the reverse of what politicians want: We say: 'Invest now and you will see positive results later.' They say: 'Show us positive results now and we'll pay the bills later!!'

It is clear to me that the public policy debate and the research debate on family preservation are proceeding on two different tracks at the moment, and the question of how and even whether research will influence policy initiatives in this area is very much an open question.

Policy

Ultimately, research and practice should inform public policy, and here again family preservation services have occasioned some spirited debate in the halls of Congress as well as in many of our state legislatures.

Post our November 1994 elections, the central question for family support and family preservation, as with all other social programmes, is how much of the focus, incentives and mandates will be retained at the federal level, versus devolution of decision-making to the state and local level. Presently, legislation is being drafted in our new Congress which would essentially block grant family-preservation and family-support initiatives, and would offer wide latitude to individual states to determine their relative profile amongst all social services and the particulars of their implementation. A national evaluation of family-preservation efforts has been mandated, but the participation of individual states is optional, and to date, several key states have declined to participate for a variety of reasons.

Whether at federal or state level, certain key policy issues remain:

1. What compelling rationales (cost, quality, and so forth) are there for family preservation initiatives? As a corollary: What are reasonable outcome expectations for short-term placement-prevention services in an overall continuum of services extending from prevention/early intervention through residential care?

2. To return to 'placement' for a moment, I believe we need to re-examine the centrality of this concept to our overall child welfare policy. That is, we have built an edifice of public policy around what is, in fact, a relatively low-frequency dichotomous outcome. To a certain extent, we have created a false dichotomy with goodness and light on one side ('family') and evil on the other ('placement'): though recently we have seen some serious revisionist thinking encapsulated in the orphanage debate.

We have organised service efforts around the locus of the child: one is either in or out of care - prevented from going in - or ready to be re-unified. If we look at 'success' more broadly, we see that it may or may not equate with low placement rates or the physical locus of the child, but rather it turns on things like the child's developmental trajectory, including attachment, and the functioning of the family, including its stability. Perhaps - with respect exclusively to the United States - we have been spending far too much time trying to assess the 'imminent risk' of an outcome ('placement') that is subject in the real world to a host of factors independent of the child or family's status or the quality of services offered: for example, administrative policies, judicial discretion, and

133

availability of placement resources. The result of this is that the services we finally do offer (separate from investigation) are episodic, truncated and crisis-oriented, rather than offering continuous support.

There are alternatives:

First, we must recognise that concerns with some placements are legitimate and have merit: egregious conditions do exist in some out-of-home settings; some children are placed unnecessarily and prematurely. The safety of the child remains a concern. Initial placement often leads to future placements and begins a cycle of impermanence all would wish to avoid.

Second, perhaps we need to design a service continuum that softens the differences and blurs the boundaries between in-home and out-of-home options such as shared care, respite care, partial placements, and 'wrap around' services. We might also develop more creative uses for short-term residential care (including whole-family care) and work to personalise care settings, including more reinforcement for direct care givers, such as residential workers/foster carers. Whether or not we reassess 'placement' as a defining concept for policy, there are still numerous implementation issues surrounding family support and family preservation:

* What creative coalitions can be formed to advance family preservation in an already crowded arena? What is the linkage between these short-term service strategies and basic structural remedies like improvement in unemployment benefits and improvements in our basic incomes strategies?
* What particular strategies for creative funding offer most promise?
* What particular mix of services ought to exist in an overall continuum? Increasingly, we are being cautioned against glossing over the need for some high-quality placement resources of the group and foster-family variety.
* On the political level: how are resistances to be dealt with from those who polarise family preservation and child protection, and from a certain segment of residential agencies for whom these services are a direct threat?
* Can we identify a proper metric for assessing the relative costs and benefits of introducing family-preservation services in a service system? What are reasonable expectations for these short-term services with respect to: placement rates; child and family functioning; cost savings; and child safety?

Several highly publicised child deaths of youngsters returned home from foster care, or left at home in an unsafe situation, have intensified the calls for a shift away from a policy perceived to be overly weighted towards 'preserving families' at the expense of protecting individual children.

Finally, as we build a new system of family-preservation services and include it in our overall continuum of service, what 'vaccine' will immunise the new 'family-focused' approach from the very same 'viruses' that affected the old 'child-centred' approach?

Despite many of the questions raised above, I believe the presumption of family preservation - to deliver intensive, focused, culturally sensitive service to families prior to out-of-home placement - is still meritorious. But we must proceed with caution.

Some final thoughts

What I wish to share in conclusion are some 'rules of the road'. Think of these as a kind of EuroGuide to family preservation with some 'routes' and obstacles to steer clear of as well as some potential 'short cuts' to make the journey easier. All are directed towards the overall goal of developing an alternative to either (1) leaving a child exposed to an unacceptable level of risk, or (2) prematurely placing a child for reasons of safety, and thereby severing the family bond, as well as towards the more general goal of developing a more family-supportive service response to families in need.

First, let me identify some potential 'roadblocks' to steer clear of:

1. **Resist mistaken concreteness.** There are no panaceas for the complex problems which confront child and family practitioners. Services, however innovative and powerful, are no substitute for the basics of income, housing, medical care and education which are the building blocks upon which any personal social-service system must rest. Many of us know particularly well the cruel irony involved in severely limiting general welfare budgets while at the same time promoting specific and highly-prescribed service interventions. Within child and family welfare services, we need to think of a fully integrated continuum - including high-quality placement resources for those children and families who require them.

2. **Avoid discounting.** It is past time to end the professional equivalent of the 'War of the Worlds'. We can disagree without personalising. Alternate theoretical models and practice strategies have a place in contributing solutions to the complex problems which define child welfare practice.

3. **Avoid excessive regional pride.** There is, after all, serious intellectual life and creative energy in more than one place. In family preservation, while many good ideas emanate from North-American innovations such as Homebuilders, these are neither static nor place-bound. We need to actively seek out programmes that work in other regions and countries and seriously address

the issue of what modifications might be necessary to adapt them to meet local needs. Evidence abounds in child and family welfare of regional chauvinism getting in the way of good programming for children and families.

4. **Avoid the temptation to seize the moral high ground.** There are *risks* as well as *benefits* to a family-preservation strategy as well as to one which favours placement: How do we identify them? How might we work to minimise them? How can we then present them in such a way that citizens and their representatives can make an informed policy choice. I conclude there are no 'risk-free' approaches when we are trying simultaneously to maximise the values of child safety and family support and preservation.

5. **We need, finally, to move beyond 'train and hope' as a strategy for service reform.** I believe there is a great need for specification of the organisational infrastructure for effective family-centred practice: mechanisms for training, worker supports, funding mechanisms, and citizen support. Similarly, there is an enormous task of 'translation' of empirical findings from basic and applied research in ways that are useful to line practitioners: development of protocols, practice principles and the like. Our National Institute of Medicine has just done this with respect to certain prevention programmes for high-risk children. More such efforts are needed. Once 'best practices' are identified, we need to clearly mark those pathways and 'lay flowers' along them to encourage widespread adoption. The dissemination of model interventions deserves much higher attention on our practice/research agenda as well as in our professional curricula.

So much for the obstacles. Let us now move to the 'short cuts: some routes which, if we followed them, would enhance our chances of success in defining a more effective and humane family-centred service:

1. **Operate on the 'helper principle'.** Frank Riessman, Professor at City University of New York and a leading chronicler and champion of self help, offers an interesting observation on helping (Riessman, 1990):
   ....*help receiving is problematic, as it tends to underline inadequacy - casts the helpee in a dependent role made more asymmetrical because of the higher status of the professional help giver. And the helpee is automatically deprived of the benefits accruing to the helper: increased self esteem, being helped by helping others. If help giving is so beneficial and help receiving is so problematic, the task would seem to be to restructure the helping process so that more people could play the helping role.*

136

We might ask: how would operationalisation of this principle work in family-based services? How might it alter services and professional education? I was surprised to learn recently that a Family Policy Council in my own state, situated at the highest levels in the executive branch, did not include a single parent among its members. Lack of consumerism in child welfare is a major impediment to change in my judgement. It exists for a variety of reasons. We *can* learn much from related fields of service like developmental disabilities and mental health about how to redress this imbalance.

2. **Practise coalition politics.** I think it imperative that we seek out broad bases of support for specific programmes and think creatively about how we can join different programme initiatives in a common agenda. For example, how might we join the 'family-support' and 'family-preservation' initiatives in ways that are mutually reinforcing? How can we address the real needs for expansion of services designed to prevent unnecessary out-of-home care, while at the same time making a clear case for specialised foster-care and group-care services for those children and families who require them. More fundamentally: how do we tie child-welfare service reform to welfare reform such that we minimise the risk of trying to solve what are essentially resource problems (income, housing, medical care) with social-service solutions?

3. **Encourage 'blank-slate' analyses.** In case planning, as well as policy, we need to wipe the slate clean and encourage creativity. Otherwise we run the risk of elevating what is presently feasible with what is desirable: the 'law of the instrument' which says that 'if the only tool you have is a hammer, each problem becomes a nail'. As an example: are there viable *non-service* solutions to the problems which family preservation services seek to correct? I believe that extreme client risk, as in child-related community violence, require us to 'push the envelope' on existing solutions. Such analysis should extend to total system design as well.

4. **Seek out models of affirming practice, agency administration, and research.** Can we practise family empowerment/family support in an organisational structure that is top-down, non-reinforcing, uncommunicative, and sexist? The answer is clearly NO. Therefore, what models of organisation support and nurture the kind of values embodied in a family-support philosophy? What new structures need to be created? Can the old ones (agencies) be successfully 'retro-fitted'?

5. **Finally, let us not lose sight of intangibles.** My colleague, Jill Kinney, one of the founders of Homebuilders, talks about the fact that it is the job of the

Homebuilder therapist to 'instill hope'. Interestingly, the late psychologist, Nicholas Hobbs, said essentially the same thing 30 years earlier in formulating an innovative community-based treatment model for severely emotionally disturbed children (Project Re-ED), when he spoke of the experience and anticipation of 'joy' as a key programme principle. *Moral: don't shy away from objectives that are difficult to measure, simply because they are difficult to quantify and particularly when they reflect a fundamentally human aspiration or expression.*

Some years ago, the great British policy analyst, Richard Titmuss, suggested that public policy in a compassionate society ought not to be concerned simply with relieving individual needs, but with furthering a sense of common citizenship. He said that the 'social growth' engendered by such a model goes to the very texture of the relationship between human beings by illustrating what a compassionate society can achieve when a philosophy of social justice and public accountability is translated into what he termed, '*a hundred and one detailed acts of imagination and tolerance*'.

I suggest that our work with and for children and families - in its whole as well as its parts - is about those 'detailed acts of imagination and tolerance'. If successful, it will support and honour all families in society through our specific intervention, or through example.

In the final analysis, a vibrant and flourishing family-service system echoes for each individual family in pain or despair the hope, comfort and shared strength of others not presently afflicted. If we think about it, save for the vagaries of birth, errant biology, class and status, or simply circumstance, we are all but a half step away from the 'other' families we describe as in need of service, or 'at risk'. In the final analysis, it is not 'us' and 'them'.

It is all of us. Together.

References

General Accounting Office (1995), *Child welfare: Opportunities to further enhance family preservation and support activities*, Washington D.C., U.S. General Accounting Office: GAO/HEHS 95-112.

Riessman, F. (1990), "Restructuring help: A human services paradigm", *American Journal of Community Psychology*, vol. 18, 221-231.

Rossi, P.H., Schuerman, J. & Budde, S. (1995), *Decision making in child maltreatment cases*, Chicago, Chapin Hall Center for Children, University of Chicago.

Schuerman, J.R., Rzepnicki, T.L. & Littell, J.H. (1994), *Putting families first: An experiment in family preservation*, New York, Aldine de Gruyter.

Weiss, H.B. & Jacobs, F.H. (1988), *Evaluating family programs*, New York, Aldine de Gruyter.

Whittaker, J.K., Tracy, E.M., Overstreet, E., Mooradian, J. & Kapp, S. (1994), "Intervention design for practice: Enhancing social supports for high risk youth and families", in J. Rothman & E. Thomas (eds), *Intervention research* (pp. 195-208), New York, Haworth Press.

Additional Sources

Bath, H.I. & Haapala, D.A. (1955), "Evaluation outcomes of family preservation services and the way ahead: A reply to Littell", *Social Service Review*, vol. 69, no. 2, 351-358.

Kinney, J., Haapala, D. & Booth, C. (1991), *Keeping families together: The homebuilders model*, New York, Aldine de Gruyter.

Littell, J. (1955), "Evidence or assertions? The outcomes of family preservation services", *Social Service Review*, vol. 6, no. 2, 338-351.

Pecora, P.J., Whittaker, J.K. & Maluccio, A.N. (1992), *The child welfare challenge: Policy, practice and research*, New York, Aldine de Gruyter.

Whittaker, J.K., Kinney, J., Tracy, E.M. & Booth, C. (eds) (1990), *Reaching high risk families: Intensive family preservation in human services*, New York, Aldine de Gruyter.

9 Supporting children in need and their families through a change in legislation: A case study based on the impact of the Children Act in England and Wales

Matthew COLTON
Margaret WILLIAMS

Introduction

In England and Wales, the idea that children are best brought up by their own families was given legislative expression in the Children Act 1989, which is widely seen as the most important child care law passed by the British Parliament this century. The new concept of family support contained in the Act is said to represent ' ...a quantum leap from the old restricted notions of "prevention" to a more positive outreaching duty of support for children and families...' (Packman and Jordan, 1991, p.323).

We will begin this chapter by tracing the historical antecedents of the Act. Next, we will outline its immediate origins, principles and provisions in relation to family support. This will be followed by an account, based on research, of the progress made in implementing the legislation. We will then examine factors which have impeded progress as a prelude to a discussion of possible ways by which to increase the effectiveness of family support.

The Children Act 1989

Historical antecedents

The narrow conception of prevention replaced by the 1989 Act had its origins in the Victorian welfare system of the 19th century. This system emphasised 'rescue' and 'fresh start', rather than prevention and rehabilitation. Parents were regarded as the cause of the problem, which meant that the solution necessitated permanently separating them from their off-spring. Indeed, the concept of rehabilitation did not reach the statute book until the Children Act 1948 was passed following the Second World War. Together with the social welfare legislation of the 1940s, which reduced poverty and contributed towards full employment, decent housing and improved health, the Children's Departments established by the 1948 Act also provided impetus for preventive work. The Children and Young Persons Act 1963 extended the work of the Children's Departments from a curative rescue service to one whose role was to promote the welfare of children by working with the whole family. This goal was further pursued through the creation of unified local authority social services departments at the beginning of the 1970s.

However, the highly publicised, tragic death in 1973 of the child, Maria Colwell - killed by her step-father shortly after being returned to the care of her mother from foster parents - and research evidence suggesting that substantial numbers of children were being allowed to 'drift' in care (Rowe and Lambert, 1973), fuelled calls for renewed stress on removing children permanently from their parents. The Children Act 1975 appeared to reverse child care policy and practice in the direction of removing children rather than addressing the social disadvantages which put them at risk in the first place.

Immediate origins

However, an inquiry by the Social Services Committee of the House of Commons, published in 1984, argued that the stress on permanency had resulted in neglect of preventive policies and practices. The report also called for '...a major review of the legal framework of child care...' (House of Commons, 1984).

In response, the government set up an interdepartmental committee which, in 1985, published a *Review of Child Care Law* (Department of Health and Social Security, 1985a). The review concentrated on the need to enable parents to keep or receive back their children; and, together with the Government White Paper which followed (House of Commons, 1987), paved the way for the Children Act 1989.

The case for increased emphasis on family support was reinforced by the findings of a series of research projects commissioned by the Department of Health (Department of Health and Social Security, 1985b). Moreover, an inquiry into arrangements for dealing with child abuse in the County of Cleveland, supported the view that measures were needed to safeguard the rights of parents (Department of Health, 1988).

Principles and provisions

A number of key principles underpin the Children Act 1989. For example, the concept of 'parental responsibility' has replaced the traditional emphasis on parental rights and duties. Thus, parents, rather than the state, are responsible for their children, and they cannot divest themselves of this responsibility (although others can exercise it for them in certain circumstances) except through legal adoption. Parents can be seen as 'consumers' who obtain a 'service' from the local authorities in time of need to 'look after' the child for a limited period. In this context, it may be argued that the new focus upon parental responsibility reflects a reinforcement of Right-wing market values.

The focus on parental responsibility is confirmed by emphasis on a second concept: legalism in child care. One important factor in child welfare from the late 1960s on has been a number of criticisms, from both the Left and the Right, that social workers were authoritarian and, indeed, almost beyond the law. The Act has dealt with this by making social workers more accountable to the law, particularly where the exercise of parental responsibility by the local authority is concerned.

Recognition that parents may need a service from the local authority in order to fulfil their responsibilities has led to an emphasis on a third key concept: partnership. The concept of partnership is not actually mentioned in the Act but derives from the *Review of Child Care Law* (Department of Health and Social Security, 1985a). The *Review* argued that the focus should be on maintaining family links 'in order to care for the child in partnership with rather than in opposition to his parents, and to work towards his return to them'. Hence, partnership between parents and local authorities is promoted in the Act, previously restricted notions of 'prevention' are superseded by the much broader concept of 'family support', and local authorities have a general duty to safeguard and promote the upbringing of 'children in need'.

Under the Act, children are deemed to be 'in need' if they require local authority services to achieve or maintain a reasonable standard of health or development, or to prevent significant or further impairment of their health and development, or if they are disabled (s.17, Children Act 1989; Department of Health, 1991). The terms 'health', 'development' and 'disabled' are further defined, but the Act gives no clear indication of what is to be understood by a reasonable standard of health and development, or by significant or further impairment.

Thus, it is evident that the definition of need contained in the Children Act is wide enough, potentially, to embrace all children who could be helped by the provision of services. This, along with the qualified language in which local authorities' duties are generally expressed, means in practice that local authorities have wide discretion in deciding what range and level of services will be provided to whom, by whom, and in what particular way.

The implementation of the Act

Research shows that uneven progress has been made by local authority Social Services Departments in implementing the family support provisions contained in the Children Act. Some Departments have made notable advances, while others have made considerably less progress, failing to make even modest headway in the face of the difficulties encountered.

Agency Policy

Operational policies are obviously a vital component in the process of implementing any piece of legislation. There is wide variation in the length, quality and content of the policy documents of local authority Social Services Departments. The fact that some departments do not have written policies on key areas of the Act naturally raises questions about how the Act is being implemented. Although Departments may be attempting to comply with the requirements of the Act through unwritten and informal policies, service goals are frequently not documented. A lack of formal goals will inevitably lead to inconsistency of service, an absence of effective monitoring procedures, and the possibility that goals will alter in an unplanned way (Colton, Drury and Williams, 1995a; 1995b).

Needs assessment

If policies are to be effectively translated into practice, it is essential that guidance is provided for practitioners. However, such guidance is frequently lacking with regard to key areas pertaining to the assessment of need (Colton et al., 1995a; 1995b; Department of Health, 1994a). As noted earlier, the Act does not say exactly how its definition of need should be interpreted. For their part, social services departments generally appear content to leave the definition of need, and hence the identification of children 'in need', to individual practitioners (Colton et al., 1995a; 1995b). As might be expected, inconsistent service provision has resulted, and has led to dissension in the social network of the families being served.

Moreover, in the absence of appropriate guidance, social workers have resorted to material formulated for use in child protection work. This has reinforced the imbalance between family support and protection (Colton et al., 1995a; 1995b), whereby child protection is given universal priority. Children at risk of abuse or neglect and those being accommodated receive highest priority. Children whose needs are already manifest receive priority above those whose problems are less critical but whose difficulties may worsen if ignored (Department of Health, 1994a; Colton et al., 1995a; 1995b).

Social workers tend to define a child as 'in need' only if there are resources available to meet that need. In other words, the only children identified as being 'in need' are those who can presently be served. To complete the vicious circle, data on the number of children being served are used to estimate the number of children 'in need'. The Act does require that new assessment studies be undertaken, but such studies have rarely been implemented on the grounds that it is not worth while to identify children whose needs cannot be met. Estimates of the cost of meeting needs are rarely produced for similar reasons (Colton et al., 1995a; 1995b).

Interagency co-operation

In the United Kingdom, services for children and families are fragmented between several different local authority agencies, including social services, education, health, the police and probation services, youth services, and the department of social security. Progress towards an interagency strategic approach to the full range of children's services has been disappointing except where it is mandatory. Various reasons have been cited for this: changes in agency structures and personnel, a lack of skills and resources, and agencies remaining fairly insular and wary of joint ventures (Audit Commission, 1994; Department of Health, 1994a).

Although relationships between practitioners from different agencies seem to be generally good, conflicts tend to occur where joint work is most common; for example, between social services, education and health (Colton et al., 1995a; 1995b; Department of Health, 1994a). Difficulties centre around referral procedures, attitudes, lack of understanding of each other's roles, and disagreements over who should take responsibility for particular clients, especially where lack of resources encourages agencies to pass responsibility for clients to someone else. In the present economic climate, the cost associated with reaching agreement and implementing co-operative endeavours has also been a factor.

The principle of partnership has been generally accepted, but specific policies are frequently lacking and the level of implementation varies markedly (Audit Commission, 1994; Colton et al., 1995a; 1995b).

Although parents and older children in the study by Colton et al. (1995a; 1995b) generally felt consulted about decisions made regarding them, they drew a distinction between being consulted and actively participating in decision-making. For example, some felt that they were being used as 'rubber stamps' to give formal consent to decisions made by others in their absence.

An inspection of services to disabled children and their parents found that practitioners generally did not ask (disabled) children how they felt about decisions made about them, and their views were not routinely recorded on case files. This inspection did find some positive practice where social workers recognised parents' unique knowledge of their children, and involved them in decision-making (Department of Health, 1994b).

The partnership element most lacking is undoubtedly information. This may reflect concern that disseminating information about services might lead to increased demand, which would outstrip resources. Parallel anxieties exist regarding complaints procedures about which service users usually know very little (Colton et al., 1995a; 1995b). Social service departments are encountering difficulties regarding the following: using complaints data to review service delivery; selecting suitable independent investigators; and acting within the required timescales for complaints and reviews (Colton et al., 1995a; 1995b; Department of Health, 1993).

Colton (1995a; 1995b) and his colleagues found that in spite of generally positive relationships with social workers, parents often felt that practitioners were ineffective at solving problems, particularly in areas of major concern such as truancy and drug abuse. Parents also felt stigmatised by receiving services. Isolation, which is an aspect of stigma, was a common theme. Parents and children typically considered that both the emotional support and the material help they received were inadequate. Children with siblings or friends in foster care frequently wanted to be accommodated themselves because of the perceived material benefits.

Another difficulty centred around the placement of children in foster homes close to their parents' home. Although this is obviously of benefit in the maintenance of family links, some parents felt that it enabled children to continue to demonstrate problematic behaviour, in the local school, in the family home and in the community. A related problem was the return home of accommodated children to parents who felt that they were still not ready to cope.

Cultural issues

Social Services Departments are attempting to comply with the requirements of the Act by formulating general policies to the effect that a child's ethnic, cultural, linguistic and religious needs will be considered when providing services. However, as with other areas of the Act, written policies of a more detailed nature are frequently lacking. No data are routinely collected on the linguistic, ethnic or religious background of service users. Indeed, little is known about the demography of local populations other than what is available from the Census (Colton et al., 1995a; 1995b).

Other identified problems include: language, exacerbated by a lack of translators; too few practitioners from ethnic minority groups; lack of awareness of ethnic needs; lack of resources for ethnic minority children; and problems in working with children from travelling families, whose unique lifestyle is rarely considered (Colton et al., 1995a; 1995b). Attitudes on the part of some service providers reflect the belief that culturally-specific policies, and indeed services, need not be a priority when the cultural group that will benefit is relatively small.

Impediments to progress

Many of the problems that social welfare practitioners have encountered in operationalising the Act appear to arise from the incongruity between the all-embracing spirit of the Children Act and current political, economic and social realities. Therefore, we will now consider the context of family support, beginning with the organisation of services.

The organisation of services

A positive approach to family support entails the promotion of policies and practices aimed at helping children to enjoy in their own homes, the kind of parenting, the freedom from suffering, the standards of living, and the quality of community life which is considered reasonable for children in our society (Holman, 1988).

We are far from achieving such proactive policies and practices, largely due to the fact that the basic contextual requirements for an effective system of family support are lacking.

According to Holman (1988), the localisation of services into small geographical units would increase the capacity of social workers to help families at an early stage of their difficulties and to enlist local resources. However, on the whole, social services departments have not adopted this approach. Rather, they have tended to pursue a reactive stance with an associated focus on child protection. This has contributed to the fact that need is still defined in terms of individual pathology rather than as a matter of social justice. It is worthy of note that social justice is a more expensive definition than individual pathology since, in terms of social justice, whole communities rather than individual families may be defined as needy.

Family centres should play a pivotal role in community-oriented family support work (Holman, 1988). However, services are not generally decentralised on a local neighbourhood basis, and family centres have so far not been given the pivotal role in the activities of local authorities that effective family support services necessitate (Colton et al., 1995a; 1995b). This is unfortunate, for the evidence suggests that small geographical units of localised services, with a key role for family centres, would make it easier to involve users in decisions about the kinds of services that are offered; they would facilitate participation by users in the actual delivery of services, and would reflect a conception of users which focuses on their strengths as well as on their limitations.

In short, services organised along the lines suggested would be more conducive to establishing a genuine partnership between social workers and services users. The presence of other facilities in the same centre, such as health workers and educational consultants, might also go some way towards providing integrated service and facilitating interagency co-operation.

Reducing inequality and child poverty

A second pre-condition for effective family support services identified by Holman (1988) entails reducing inequality and social deprivation. The broad spirit of proactive family support enshrined in the Children Act 1989 can only be effectively implemented in a society which is moving towards the reduction of its vast inequalities and social deprivations. Yet, it is plain that the United Kingdom of the 1990s does not constitute such a society. Rather than being a society that is moving towards a reduction of inequality, Britain has moved in the opposite direction over the past decade or so. Social polarisation has occurred (Bradshaw, 1990; Halsey, 1988); there is debate about the possible emergence of a distinct underclass (see Murray, 1990); and levels of child poverty have increased (Bradshaw, 1990).

Thus, to an extent unparalleled since 1945, the daily agenda for social welfare practitioners is dominated by the consequences which prolonged and deepening penury produces in the social fabric of society and in the lives of families and individuals (Colton et al., 1995a; 1995b). In this regard, senior officers in social welfare agencies might recognise that they themselves control resources and have

147

the power to improve conditions in impoverished communities through their own spending decisions. With reference to wider anti-poverty strategies, the development of Credit Unions, co-operative buying schemes and Bond banks will also have some impact upon the financial circumstances of disadvantaged groups.

Conflicting models of welfare

The increasing pressure on families has increased the demands placed on local authority Social Services Departments. However, rather than increasing the capacity of social welfare practitioners to meet these demands, it would appear that central government policy has had the opposite effect. The trend towards reducing the role of the state in welfare provision (Johnson, 1990) has contributed to a profound contradiction which social services staff are understandably finding it difficult to resolve.

It is plain that local authority Social Services Departments in England and Wales are faced with a major dilemma. On the one hand, there is the Children Act 1989, which is widely seen as the most progressive reform of child care law this century. On the other hand, there are flourishing social policies, both inside and outside the child care field, which would seem to blatantly contradict the spirit of this reform. One commentator has observed that 'the language of "needs" contained in the 1989 Act, is usually associated with a collectivist model of welfare, and... sits oddly in our new residualist era...' (Hardiker, 1991, p.356). Others have noted that noted that '...concepts...like sharing responsibility between parents and the state, reaching agreements and partnerships...have a surprisingly communitarian or even collectivist ring about them...' (Packman and Jordan, 1991, p.315).

The 'collectivist' philosophy manifested in the Children Act cannot be easily put into practice in an increasingly 'residualist' social policy context. There is an inherent conflict between present resource constraints and the additional resources that are required if a wider definition of need is to be reflected in increased service provision.

Ways forward

It is clear that one of the major challenges facing practitioners and agencies is how to shift the balance of services away from an overwhelming emphasis on child protection towards proactive family support. This requires, first, that social services policy documents reflect the positive outreaching duty of support for children and families contained in the Act; and, second, that the procedures by which this duty is to be fulfilled are specified. Steps to be taken might include the following.

1. Social services agencies should discourage social workers from using protection material to guide them in the assessment of children in need by issuing alternative guidance designed to emphasise family support. This should preferably be done in co-operation with other statutory and voluntary agencies.
2. Budgeting arrangements should be reviewed. For example, in recognition of the Children Act trend towards fewer applications for care proceedings and fewer children in care, it may be possible to recycle resources trapped in capital costs and turn these into available revenue.

However, it is apparent that merely urging agencies to make better use of existing resources is not sufficient. Issues of a more fundamental nature must be addressed. Perhaps more than any other factor, poverty threatens the practical achievement of proactive family support services. Yet, for both policy makers and practitioners, poverty appears to have been relegated to the margin of their concerns and actions. It is as if the only way of coping with the overwhelming fact of hardcore poverty - the product of increasing inequality - is to look the other way and act as though it were not happening. Whilst understandable, perhaps, this response merely leads into a cul-de-sac of inappropriate and ineffective policy and practice. The successful implementation of the Children Act, and indeed, community care policy more widely, necessitates that poverty be placed again at the centre of the policy, practice and research agenda.

This does not imply that individuals and families who live in poverty should be transformed into 'welfare' clients in order to obtain services. Nor is it to suggest that there is any substitute for action at the national level to tackle primary poverty and to ensure that local authorities have the resources necessary to carry out their mandate under the Act. A comprehensive national strategy to tackle need is required involving employment, housing, wages, taxation and social security policies.

Nevertheless, there are four distinct strategies through which, even in these difficult times, social welfare practitioners and agencies in England and Wales can at least seek to make a direct impact upon the financial circumstances of their service users.

1. Policy makers and senior officers within social welfare agencies can recognise their own status as major resource holders and the impact which their own spending decisions might make upon the impoverished communities with whom their organisations have almost all their dealings. Through patterns of

employment, location of offices, choices concerning purchase of goods and materials, organisations have the capacity to invest within the human, physical and social fabric of such communities.

As indicated, the organisation of service delivery appears incompatible with the concept of family support contained in Part III of the Children Act. Family support services should be decentralised on a local neighbourhood basis, and family centres should play a pivotal role in such services.

Currently, however, it is difficult to escape the impression that local authority social services departments tend to operate in ways that are self-defeating, that seem bound to frustrate their efforts to develop effective family support services, and that appear inimical to their attempts to fashion an authentic partnership with parents, children and local communities: workers tend to be drafted in from outside the local area, operations are often directed from remote headquarters, and more appears to be sucked out of deprived communities in terms of simple financial resources than is invested in them.

2. Within social welfare organisations, a reformulation needs to take place in traditional welfare rights activities. To begin with, these strands need reaffirmation as part of mainstream work, rather than being located at the margin of organisational activity. Social workers have long been somewhat ambivalent in their attitudes towards income maximisation. At a time when the social democratic institutions of the welfare state are under wider threat, and the policies of rationing and coercion are in the ascendency, a new style of intervention in this field has to be developed. A technocratic understanding of the labyrinthine ways in which the remnants of the welfare state doles out its remaining benefits is not sufficient. Rather, a more proactive approach is required, which recognises and seeks to redress the unfairness and discriminations within the system.

3. With regard to the wider anti-poverty strategies of local authorities, whilst the development of Credit Unions, co-operative buying schemes and Bond banks are not solutions to primary poverty, they remain capable of producing an impact upon the financial circumstances of groups in poverty. Moreover, they do this in ways which build upon the extensive systems of mutual support which remain remarkably vigorous within the most disadvantaged communities.

Nevertheless, given the reality of limited resources, it is inevitable that difficult choices will have to be made with respect to defining and prioritising the different types and levels of need. The decisions finally reached will not only reflect the current fiscal climate; they will also be influenced by the skills and attitudes of service providers.

It may be argued that resources, attitudes and skills are inter-related factors. New skills, for example, can only be achieved through training, for which resources are needed; and existing skills may only be fully demonstrated if service providers are genuinely committed both to the kinds of services they are required to offer and to the people whose needs they are supposed to meet. In other words, operationalisation of the Children Act will be affected not just by the content of the Act, nor solely by the resources required for its implementation, but by its entire economic, political and social context.

References

Audit Commission (1994), *Seen But Not Heard: Co-ordinating Community Child Health and Social Services for Children in Need*, HMSO, London.

Bradshaw, J. (1990), *Child Poverty and Deprivation in the UK*, National Children's Bureau, London.

Children Act 1948, HMSO, London.

Children and Young Persons Act, 1963, HMSO, London.

Children Act 1975, HMSO, London.

Children Act 1989, HMSO, London.

Colton, M., Drury, C. and Williams, M. (1995a), *Children in Need*, Avebury, Aldershot.

Colton, M., Drury, C. and Williams, M. (1995b), *Staying Together: Supporting Families Under the Children Act*, Avebury, Aldershot.

Department of Health and Social Security (1985a), *A Review of Child Care Law*, HMSO, London.

Department of Health and Social Security (1985b), *Social Work Decisions in Child Care: Recent Research Findings and their Implications*, HMSO, London.

Department of Health (1988), *Report of the Inquiry into Child Abuse in Cleveland*, HMSO, London.

Department of Health (1991), *The Children Act 1989 Guidance and Regulations; Volume 2, Family Support, Day Care and Educational Provision for Young Children*, HMSO, London.

Department of Health (1993), Social Services Inspectorate, *The Inspection of the Complaints Procedures in Local Authority Social Services Departments*, HMSO, London.

Department of Health (1994a), *Children Act Report 1993*, Cm 2584, HMSO, London.

Department of Health (1994b), Social Services Inspectorate, *National Inspection of Services to Disabled Children and their Families*, HMSO, London.

Halsey, A.H., (ed.), (1988), *British Social Trends Since 1900: A Guide to the Changing Structure of Britain*, Macmillan, London.

Hardiker, P., Exton, K. and Barker, M. (1991), "The Social Policy Contexts of Prevention in Child Care", *British Journal of Social Work*, vol. 21, no. 4, August 1991.

Holman, B. (1988), *Putting Families First: Prevention and Child Care*, Macmillan, London.

Home Office, Department of Health, Department of Education and Science, and Welsh Office (1991), *Working Together Under the Children Act 1989: A Guide to Arrangements for Inter-Agency Co-operation for the Protection of Children from Abuse*, HMSO, London.

House of Commons (1984), *Second Report from the Social Services Committee, Session 1983-84, Children in Care*, HMSO, London.

House of Commons (1987), *The Law on Child Care and Family Services*, HMSO, London.

Johnson, N. (1990), *Restructuring the Welfare State: A Decade of Change*, Harvester Wheatsheaf, London.

Murray, C. (1990), *The Emerging British Underclass*, Institute of Economic Affairs, London.

Packman, J. and Jordan, B. (1991), "The Children Act: Looking Forward, Looking Back", *The British Journal of Social Work*, vol. 21, no. 4, August.

Rowe, J. and Lambert, L. (1973), *Children Who Wait*, Association of British Adoption and Fostering Agencies, London.

10 When parenting is in danger: How do we protect children without separating them from their families?

There are multiple forms and severity levels of parental dysfunction. Neglect, with or without violence, is one of the most important forms of parental dysfunction that threatens children's development and adaptation. It is clear that neglect has serious consequences on children's lives and there is reason to believe that neglect plays a central role in the origin of several social problems.

Neglect is a form of maltreatment characterised by the absence of care regarding health, hygiene, nutrition, supervision, education or the emotional needs of the child. Types of neglect are multiple and at least 12 types have been described (Zuravin, 1991). Even if some children are victims of only one type of neglect, as they are in the majority of cases, neglect is multifaceted and several types are often observed together. This lack of care endangers the child's health and development, and sometimes its life. As child-care needs depend on the child's age and developmental level, neglect can only be defined according to the child's degree of dependence/autonomy. This kind of maltreatment is character-ised by omission rather than commission of parental acts. So, young children suffer especially from neglect.

Neglect may be circumstantial or more rooted in family life: that is, chronic. Circumstantial neglect occurs when a particular precipitating event such as divorce or illness occurs. Chronic neglect, on the contrary, can be explained by a diversity of factors.

The incidence of child neglect among the cases of maltreatment reported by protection agencies in various countries is very high. For example, in Quebec, the overall data available from social services in 1990 (12,256 cases) break down as follows: 77 per cent of neglect cases, 10 per cent of physical abuse cases and 13 per cent of sexual abuse cases. In France, an analysis reported by Gabel (1993) shows that out of 334 reported cases of maltreatment received by one service during the year 1990, 56 per cent were cases of neglect. In the United States, among cases of physical abuse and neglect reported in 1988 to the New York State Central Registry for Child Abuse (Green, 1990), 93 per cent were cases of neglect.

Child abuse and neglect intervention programmes

The development of new practices in child protection against violence and sexual abuse has increased during the last decade. However, little progress has been made on neglect. Field work has led to the development of multiple forms of practice. These practices are generally quite subjective and not very systematic, depending more on the personal skills of the worker than on models or programmes. Child placement is one tactic that is used very often in neglect cases (60 per cent of cases). This proportion of foster care placements is the highest among maltreatment cases. The return of the child to the family often leads to recurrences of the neglectful situation that have serious consequences. Few follow-up studies or statistics exist on this subject, but experienced workers have expressed great concern for this phenomenon. We observe a kind of inefficacy in actual interventions with neglect and the results of these interventions are usually repeated placements of a good number of children.

It must be emphasised also that recent research reviews about intervention with abusive and neglectful parents (Azar and Wolfe, 1989; Cohn and Daro, 1987; Fink and McCloskey, 1990; Gaudin, 1993) raise serious questions about actual treatment effectiveness.

Why this failure? A quick look at neglectful families characteristics can help to answer this question.

Neglecting families' characteristics

It is already well documented that neglectful families live in poverty, the parents have very low incomes and are unemployed or in social assistance (Chamberland, Bouchard and Beaudry, 1986; Crittenden, 1988; Kadushin and Martin, 1981). These parents have also very little schooling, even less than non-maltreating parents of the same social and economic level (Ethier et al., 1993). Several studies (Polansky, Gaudin, Ammons & Davis, 1985; Bouchard and Desfossés, 1989; Garbarino and Sherman, 1980) have highlighted the fact that neglectful families had limited social networks and did not know how to use community resources. Neglectful parents make very little use of the natural help network around them and their social participation is lower. To a great extent, it is therefore the lack of ability on the part of these parents to establish contact and entertain mutual and reciprocal social relationships which seems to be responsible for the social isolation, and not only poor social ecology (Polansky et al., 1985). Familial relationships are also troubled (Burgess and Conger, 1978) and a high degree of conjugal violence and family instability can be observed (Palacio-Quintin, 1995). Neglectful mothers have little interaction with their children and do not take pleasure from parent-child relationships (Barth, 1985). On the other hand, young neglected children show disorganised/disoriented attachment to their mothers (Carlson, Ciccheti, Barnett and Braumwald, 1989).

Neglectful mothers and fathers have often had a difficult childhood and youth (family violence, placements...) and experience a lot of stressful situations as adults. These parents have a very high level of stress, and particularly parental stress (Ethier and Palacio-Quintin, 1991; Palacio-Quintin, Couture and Paquet, 1995).

Low self-esteem and depression (Downey and Coyne, 1990), intellectual difficulties (Crittenden, 1988; Martin and Walters, 1982; Palacio-Quintin et al., 1995) and poor ability to solve the problems of daily life (Hansen, Pallotta, Thishelman, Conaway, and MacMillan, 1989) have also been observed in neglectful parents. Finally, our clinical experience has allowed us to observe that distrust and lack of motivation for change are outstanding characteristics of neglectful families.

All these facts allow us to see that the dynamic of the neglect phenomenon cannot be explained by a single psychological, educational, economic or social factor but rather by a series of factors inter-related in a complex network. Intervention will therefore have to be multidimensional to take all these factors into account.

A search for solutions

Our research team has tried to find an answer to these problems. The ecological theory of human development (Bronfenbrenner, 1977, 1979) and its application to maltreatment (Belsky, 1980; Garbarino, 1990; Garbarino and Sherman, 1980) serves us as a theoretical framework.

Neglectful and abusive behaviour by parents towards a child must be considered within the overall context of the family and the environment of which they are part. Changing inadequate parental behaviour must take into account the balancing processes of the family, of each of its members and of the family's social network (i.e. the impact of the marital relationship on the parent-child relationship, the impact of the father-child relationship on the mother-child relationship, the impact of the parent-extended family relationship on the parent-child relationship, and so forth).

The more a family organisation promotes the mutual satisfaction of needs and sharing of physical, psychological and social resources between its members, the more these members will be able to face the daily stressors (such as limited financial resources, inadequate housing, etc.). Neglectful families are especially overloaded by daily stress, due to: 1) the number of stressors to which they are exposed; 2) a type of family organisation which does not allow the mutual satisfaction of needs nor flexibility in the face of change; 3) and the limited repertoire of emotions, behaviours and ways to perceive the environment of each of the members.

An ecosystemic analysis of inadequate parental conduct allows a relativisation of the parent's responsibility (i.e. the mother) by attempting to pinpoint the contribution of other family members and the social network to the appearance and maintenance of the neglect and abuse situation. The ecosystemic analysis also allows the exploration of the resources that exist within the family and its network (i.e. adequate relationship between the mother and one of her sisters, appropriate behaviour by fathers in controlling child behaviour in certain situations, etc.).

In our opinion, this ecosystemic approach must also consider the characteristics of the individuals involved in the phenomenon, i.e. the intrapsychic dimension. This dimension is unfortunately often forgotten by various researchers and workers who say they adhere to the ecological theory while exclusively emphasising the social dimension of intrafamily maltreatment. For instance, how can we ignore the fact that a depressed state of mind and incapacity to reciprocate can affect the organisation of the social network?

Ecosystemic intervention must therefore allow a simultaneous re-balancing of individual aspects (parenting skills, control of impulses, empathy, self-esteem, etc.), of the family organisation (cohesion, adaptability, clear boundaries, etc.) and of the organisation of the social network (strength of ties, quality and reciprocity of social support, social and job market integration, etc.).

These principles have been put into effect in an intervention model called the Personal, Familial and Community-Help programme (PFCHP) (Palacio-Quintin, Éthier, Jourdan-Ionescu and Lacharité, 1995).

The Personal, Familial and Community-Help programme

In the Personal, Familial and Community-Help programme, neglect is particularly targeted as well as the dynamic relation between neglect and family violence. The programme is intended for the whole family: the mother, the father (or mother's present partner) and the children. The needs of each person and the needs of the family as a whole are considered. The programme is also centred on community support. It aims to restore the neglectful family in the community, to teach the parents the means necessary to develop a social network and to enable them to make use of the available community resources. It also aims to improve the relationships not only within the family itself, but also with the environment, and to increase the quality of life for these families.

Since the rehabilitation of a neglectful family is a long process, the programme must continue for at least a year and in some cases several years.

The programme is multifaceted. It intervenes simultaneously on several dimensions of the life experiences (both psychological and social) of the neglecting family. A multidisciplinary team is essential to achieve our proposed goals. Practitioners of various backgrounds co-operate (psychologists, social workers, group therapists...).

The programme includes five dimensions:

1. Group activities for 'the parent as a child and adult' to distance the person from past events that come in the way of the parent-child relationship, put a stop to conjugal violence, increase spousal support, and improve family dynamics and parents' mental health.
2. Group activities for 'the parent as a parent' to acquire parenting skills and problem-solving abilities and to receive information about community resources.
3. Child stimulation through educational group activities.
4. Community support for the entire family. This support is offered through 'support families' who make the link between the family and the community. The people involved in support family intervention are volunteer women and men who are currently raising or have raised children, want to help, know how to listen, make contact easily, are quite available (including weekends) and do not have too many personal problems or problems with their own children, meaning that they should have an overall feeling of success and satisfaction towards their role as parents. It is preferable that these parents be from a socioeconomic environment that is close to that of the neglecting families with whom they will be working. Support families are regularly supervised by a member of the clinical team.
5. Individual case follow-up by the social worker of the protection service.

The co-ordination of the whole programme is assumed by a clinical team. The clinical team is composed of the social worker authorised by the protection agency to assume the family case, the two specialists leading the two parents' groups, one psychologist assuming the supervision of the support families and the co-ordination of the team, and an external supervisor. Following the five dimensions of intervention that are systematically programmed for the entire client population, regular individual follow-up is done by the clinical team every two weeks.

The team must draw up a complete assessment of what happened in each family. From this balance sheet, various recommendations for action are identified and implemented by the person concerned on the team or by the support family, as the case may be. If it has to do with a particular attitude to take towards a parent during group activities, the group facilitator will follow up on it. If it is a personal process to be suggested to the parent (e.g., undertaking professional training, an alcoholism recovery programme, job search, individual psychotherapy, a specific change in the way the family operates, etc.), the social worker, who is officially in charge of the client interface, will advise whether the client is ready to undertake this type of process. If the client is ready for action, the support family can contribute by assisting with the process to be undertaken. The member of the clinical team who supervises support families will explain the direction of the planned process. However, if the client is not ready to undertake the type of process suggested, new strategies will have to be considered at the next meeting of the clinical team. It is especially important to balance ideas about what the team thinks is desirable for family well-being and what the member of the family feels and is ready to undertake. In addition to a multidisciplinary approach, this form of teamwork allows the team to provide major support to the worker directly in charge of the case, as well as a guarantee of some distancing from the client's situation. It is also the central element that provides coherence in the intervention process.

The experience and the results

We have implemented the programme with 31 families referred by the child protection agency of Quebec, Mauricie-Bois-Francs section. These families were identified by the protection agency as being neglectful or neglectful and abusive towards their young child (from 0 to 6 years old). These families have a total of 80 children, 57 of whom are under 6 years of age. They are chronically neglectful families. Some facts about the previous family history and children's situation at the beginning of PFCHC presented in Table 10.1 clearly demonstrate this.

Table 10.1
Previous family history and children's situation at the beginning of PFCHC

Previous history	
Previous protection agency intervention	78.8 %
Children having already been placed	50 %
Families having at least one child already placed	67.7 %
Children's situation at the beginning of PFCHP	
Children already in foster care	17.5%
Children already in part-time foster care	15 %
Children placements anticipated by the protection agency	45 %
At home	22.5 %

Table 10.1 shows that the protection agency has already intervened with most of the families (78.8 per cent), that the children of more than half the families (67.7 per cent) have already been in foster care and that 32.5 per cent of children were in full-time or part-time foster care at the time of being accepted into the PFCHC programme.

The evaluation of the programme was carried out using an experimental model. Families in the experimental and control groups were given pre- and post-tests covering several dimensions and the intervention processes was also evaluated. We will not discuss this further here. The principal issue here is how well we succeeded in keeping children at home after 21 months of intervention. In order to address this issue, we compared the predictions made by the protection agency practitioners with the situation of each of the 80 children at the end of our programme. To be more precise, when each case was accepted into the programme, we asked the practitioner authorised to deal with the case to tell us which decision would be taken regarding the child's situation if our programme were not offered. Each child was classified by practitioners into one of three categories: a) the child would remain or would be placed in full-time foster care; b) the child would need part-time foster care; or c) the child would remain at home with intervention by the practitioner.

The results of our study show that we avoided the full-time placement of 42 children (52.5 per cent of the sample), six of them being children already placed who were returned home (7.5 per cent of the sample). In addition, eight children left part-time foster care to live full time at home. Table 10.2 shows the distribution of children with respect to their situation when the PFCHP experience ended and the situation that was anticipated for them if regular services were used.

Table 10.2
Children's situation at the end of PFCHP compared with predictions made by the protection agency

Child situation	PFCHP		Predictions	
	N	%	N	%
1- Child stays at home	22.5	66	82.5	18
2- Child is in part-time foster care	4	5	12	15
3- Child is in foster care	10	12.5	50	62.5
4- 2 + 3	14	17.5	62	77.5

We can see that most of the PFCHP children (82.5 per cent) were at home and that only 12.5 per cent were in full-time foster care. The expectations were very different had regular services been used. For instance, only 22.5 per cent of the children were expected to be at home and 62.5 per cent were expected to be in full-time foster care. In addition, fewer children of PFCHP families needed to be in part-time foster care (5 per cent) than was expected when using regular services (15 per cent).

Conclusion

The PFCH programme was designed to meet the intervention needs of a client population that poses a serious challenge to youth protection services worldwide. These are families which present a major neglect component towards young children. These chronic parental neglectful behaviours are part of a very disturbed personal and family life situation. Many of the families accepted by protection services for neglect towards a young child also have older children. In these cases, it is observed that these children or adolescents also present major adaptation problems and are often the recipients of various social or rehabilitation services. The client population is therefore one with multiple problems which the current selective interventions, centred around child protection, are not solving adequately, frequently resulting in child placement.

Our experience suggests that the PAPFC has helped to avoid a great number of child placements and has enabled young, neglected children to stay with their families while their safety is monitored and better conditions for their development are provided. PAPFC also permitted the reintegration into their families of several children already placed in foster homes, some of whom had been away for quite some time.

If these children have been able to remain with or return to their families, it is because concrete and dynamic changes have been brought about in these families - changes that have been evaluated by pre-test post-test analysis, as well as by the clinical study of cases. The parents' remarks at the end of the programme were very revealing. They declared that they were distrustful at the beginning, but they gradually gained confidence because they felt understood and respected: also, they had received the help they needed to stand on their own feet.

Finally, I would like to say that child placement should not be completely banned. In some extremely problematic cases, it is the only answer. In such cases, the placement must be made in a timely and stable way. The placement should not be considered as a therapeutic intervention, but as a lesser evil in certain circumstances. We must do most of the work within the family, in a global, concerted and durable manner. The intervention must be carried out as early as possible, and in some cases continued support should be provided to the family throughout the fostering period. If we want to produce lasting changes in families, we must first change the intervention system. Practitioners and decision-makers must resolve to effect a radical change in field work before asking families with major parenting problems to change themselves.

References

Azar, S.T. & Wolfe, D.A. (1989), "Child abuse and neglect", in E.J. Mash & R.A. Barkley (Eds), *Treatment of childhood disorders* (pp. 451-493), Guilford, New York.

Barth, R.P. (1985), "Beating the blues: cognitive-behavioral treatment for depression in child-maltreating young mothers", *Clinical Social Work Journal*, vol. 13, no. 4, 317-328.

Belsky, J. (1980), "Child Maltreatment: An Ecological Integration", *American Psychologist*, vol. 35, no. 4, 320-335.

Bouchard, C. & Desfossés, E. (1989), "Utilisation des comportements coercitifs envers les enfants: stress, conflits et manque de soutien dans la vie des mères", *Apprentissage et Socialisation*, vol. 12, no. 1, 19-28.

Bronfenbrenner, U. (1977), "Toward an experimental ecology of human development", *American Psychologist*, vol. 32, 513-531.

Bronfenbrenner, U. (1979), *The Ecology of Human Development: Experiments by nature and design*, Havard University Press, Cambridge, Mass.

Burgess, R.L. & Conger, R.D. (1978), "Family interaction in abusing, neglectful, and normal families", *Child Development*, vol. 49, 1163-1173.

Carlson, V., Ciccheti, D., Barnett, D. & Braumwald, K. (1989), "Disorganized/disoriented attachment relationships in maltreated infants", *Developmental Psychology*, vol. 25, 525-531.

Chamberland, C., Bouchard, C. & Beaudry, J. (1986), "Conduites abusives et négligentes envers les enfants: réalités canadiennes et américaines", *Revue canadienne des sciences du comportement*, vol. 18, 391-412.

Cohn, A.H. & Daro, D. (1987), "Is treatment too late: What ten years of evaluative research tell us", *Child Abuse and Neglect*, vol. 11, 433-442.

Crittenden, P. (1988), "Family and dyadic patterns of functioning in maltreating families", in K. Browne, C. Davies & P. Stratton (eds), *Early Prediction of Child Abuse*, Wiley, New York.

Downey, G. & Coyne, J. (1990), "Children of depressed parents: An integrative review", *Psychological Bulletin*, vol. 108, 50-76.

Ethier, L.S. & Palacio-Quintin, E. (1991), "Abused children and their families", in G. Kaiser, H. Kury & Albrecht (eds), *Particular Groups of Victims. Victims and Criminal Justice*, Vol. 52, 394-414. Max Planck Institute Series, Freiburg.

Éthier, L.S. , Palacio-Quintin, E., Couture, G., Jourdan-Ionescu, C. & Lacharité C. (1993), *Évaluation psychosociale des mères négligentes. Rapport présenté au Conseil de la santé et des services sociaux du centre du Québec (CRSSS 04)*, 47 pp.

Fink, A. & McCloskey, L. (1990), "Moving child abuse and neglect prevention programs forward: Improving program evaluations", *Child Abuse & Neglect*, vol. 14, 187-206.

Gabel, M. (1993), "Évaluation administrative", in M. Manciaux (sous la direction de), *L'enfant maltraité* (pp. 543-563), Éditions Fleurus, Paris.

Garbarino, J. & Sherman, D. (1980), "High-risk neighbourhoods and high-risk families. The human ecology of child maltreatement", *Child Development*, vol. 51, 188-198.

Garbarino, J. (1990), "The Human Ecology of Early Risk", in S.J. Meisels & J. P. Shonkoff (eds), *Handbook of Early Chidhood Intervention*, Cambridge University Press, Massachussett.

Gaudin, J.M. (1993), "Effective intervention with neglectful families", *Criminal Justice and Behavior*, vol. 20, no. 1, 66-89.

Green, A.H. (1990), "Child Neglect", in R.T. Ammerman & M. Hersen (eds), *Case Studies in Family Violence*, Plenum Press, New York.

Hansen, D.J., Pallotta, G.M., Thishelman, A.C., Conaway, L.P. & MacMillan, V.M. (1989), "Parental Problem-Solving Skills and Child Behavior Problems: A Comparison of Physically Abusive, Neglectful, Clinic and Community Families", *Journal of Family Violence*, vol. 4, no. 4, 353-368.

Kadushin, A. & Martin, J.A. (1981), *Child abuse. An international event*, Columbia University Press, New York.

Martin, M.J. & Walters, J. (1982), "Familial Correlates of Selected Types of Child Abuse and Neglect", *Journal of Marriage and the Family*, May, 267-276.

Palacio-Quintin, E. (1995), *Les mauvais traitements envers les enfants: les facteurs sociaux et la dynamique familiale. Actes du séminaire "Les liens entre la violence physique, psychologique et sexuelle faite aux enfants et aux femmes"* (pp. 5-14), CRI-VIFF, Collection Reflexions, Montréal.

Palacio-Quintin, E., Éthier, L.S., Jourdan-Ionescu, C. & Lacharité, C. (1995), "L'intervention auprès des familles négligentes", in J.P. Pourtois & H. Desmet (eds), *Blessure d'enfant* (pp. 173-212), De Boeck, Bruxelles.

Palacio-Quintin, E., Couture, G. & Paquet, J. (1995), *Projet d'intervention auprès des familles négligentes présentant ou non des comportements violents. Rapport soumis à à la Division de la prévention de la violence familiale*, Santé Canada, 247 pp.

Polansky, N.A., Gaudin, J.M., Ammons, P.W. & Davis, K. (1985), "The psychological ecology of the neglectful mother", *Child Abuse and Neglect*, vol. 9, 265-275.

Zuravin, S.J. (1991), "Research definitions of child abuse and neglect: Current problems", in R.H. Starr, Jr. & D.A. Wolfe (eds), *The effects of child abuse and neglect: Research issues*, Guilford, New York.

11 Evaluation of Portage in the Netherlands: An overview of six intervention studies

Bieuwe F. VAN DER MEULEN
W.G. SIPMA

Introduction

Over the last 20 years quite a number of home-teaching programmes for families with younger and older children have been developed in Holland (see, for example, Van der Meulen and Elzinga, 1994). One of these programmes is the so-called Portage Programme Netherlands (PPN), originally an American programme designed for supporting parents of 0-6 year-old children in cases of problems with child-raising. We talk about child-raising problems when, in the judgement of the persons concerned, parenting is not proceeding as planned or desired. These problems vary for each family as to their nature, seriousness and complexity. The problems may be connected with specific characteristics of the child, of the parents, of the child's environment or of the interactions between child, parent and environment. If the people involved want to solve or reduce the problems, orthopedagogical support can be offered. When this is done in a systematic and goal-oriented way, it may be called an intervention programme. PPN is such an intervention programme. However, the programme is not useful for just any rearing problems. In various Dutch research projects since 1986, attention has been paid to the question of the uses and effects of the programme in Holland. First, we will describe the programme and then focus on the programme's effects, as investigated in six Dutch research projects.

The Portage Programme Netherlands

In the late 1960s, the Portage Programme was developed in the town of Portage, Wisconsin, America (Shearer and Shearer, 1972). The programme was used for supporting families with young children with developmental problems in their homes. The programme was found to be very successful and received official government recognition in 1975. Since that time the programme has been taken up and adapted by many agencies abroad and translated into more than 29 languages. There is an International Portage Association which encourages and co-ordinates further development and research of the programme. National Portage organisations have been founded in several countries, such as Japan, England, the Philippines, India, and lately the Netherlands as well.

Since 1986 the usefulness and the effects of this intervention programme in Holland have been investigated at the Department of Special Education of the University of Groningen (see Bulsink, Van der Meulen and Smrkovsky, 1988; Van der Meulen and Sipma, 1990; Van der Meulen and Sipma, 1991; Sipma and Van der Meulen, 1994; Sipma, Vaniddekinge and Van der Meulen, 1994; Sipma, 1996). In several projects, however, the programme was not only used in the case of families with a child with developmental problems. Research was also carried out into whether the programme, as a form of orthopedagogical home support, could be used with families whose children have association problems. To further these research projects, the programme was translated and adapted for the Dutch situation (Van der Meulen, Sipma and Feenstra, 1993; Van der Meulen and Sipma, 1993a; Van der Meulen, Sipma, Bulsink and Smrkovsky, 1993; Van der Meulen and Sipma, 1993b; Van der Meulen and Sipma, 1993c).

Supporting parents in the solution or reduction of child-rearing problems is one of the most important goals of PPN. Encouraging an optimal parent-child interaction and encouraging the child's development are both central points. In the case of a family with a child with a Down's Syndrome, support may be mainly directed at stimulating the child's development. In cases of families who complain that their child is not eating, sleeping or playing properly, or is short-tempered, or when the parents have poor parenting skills or engage in conflict, support will be mainly directed at stimulating a positive interaction between parent and child. During home teaching, the child's developmental capabilities should be the starting-point. Characteristic of the programme is the active involvement of the children's primary caregivers with the planning and implementation of the support activities. Assessment, planning, recording progress, and constantly adjusting the treatment goals are also characteristic of the programme. The capabilities and strengths of parent and child are taken as the points of departure for support. In particular, behaviour modification techniques drawn from behaviour therapy are used to systematically instruct the parents in how to gradually teach their child new developmental skills and what they themselves can do in order to reduce undesired behaviours.

Another characteristic of the programme is for parents to play games and do exercises with their child on a daily basis. For this purpose, they receive weekly support from the home teacher who, together with the parents, sets goals every week which are expected to be able to be achieved after a week's practice. The parents record the results on Activity Charts, thus making explicit that week's goal. The relationship between the parents and the home teacher is one of co-operation, and the most appropriate goals and activities are chosen by mutual consent. The home teachers are supported by a co-ordinator.

The programme offers a clear structure, supported by an intervention model common to all families, and a set of programme materials. However, the programme should be managed in a flexible way to achieve a fit with the specific child and family.

Before discussing the intervention model and the materials, we will briefly examine the starting-points of the programme.

The programme offers a structured set-up, allowing the activities of the home teacher and the parents to be directed according to the following precepts:

1. Intervention is most successful when carried out as soon as possible after recognising a problem.
2. Intervention is best implemented by the primary caregivers.
3. Intervention should take place in the child's daily environment.
4. Extensive assessment prior to intervention is necessary.
5. Intervention should be directed at the interactions between the child, the parents and the immediate environment (Sameroff and Chandler, 1975; Sameroff and Fiese, 1991).
6. Intervention should take as short a time as possible (six to twelve months).

Model and materials

Identification and screening are followed by the assessment phase, during which data are collected about the child's development and home situation, and about the parents' wishes, complaints and child-rearing problems, resulting in an individualised treatment plan. This plan describes the goals of home support, which are related to the child's development and behaviour and to the parents' attitudes about child-rearing. The Portage Checklist as well as the problem analysis materials are used to make the plan concrete and formulate the short-term goals. Once the programme has been planned, the home-teaching process that takes place during the home visit every week is begun.

Every week the home teacher visits the family on a fixed day for about an hour. Together with the parents, new goals are chosen and practised during the home visit. The home teacher writes down on the Activity Charts how the parents can achieve the chosen aim. The parents practise the activity daily and write down on the chart how the activity worked out. After a week the home teacher pays another visit and a new goal is chosen; the activity is written down on the chart and practised with the child.

During the support process, we constantly monitor how the activities develop and whether the set objectives are reached. Thus, we are able to constantly evaluate progress and adjust our goals. Explicit attention is also paid to generalisation and maintaining the progress already achieved. At the end of the intervention period, another assessment is undertaken in order to show the results of the intervention.

The most characteristic features of PPN are the Portage Checklist (with 580 skills) and the Activity Chart. Before and after the intervention the child's developmental skills in six areas are mapped by means of the Portage Checklist. Together with the home teacher, the parents themselves complete this list. Thus a lot of information about the parents' and child's capabilities and interests is collected. The list functions as a planning tool during the support process. For each behavioural goal an activity is devised which is described and evaluated on the Activity Chart. This chart is the parents' weekly plan of work. Some Activity Charts focus on the child's goals and others on the parents' goals. The task analysis scheme is used to divide goals into subgoals.

The most extensive part of the material consists of the card file. This file provides some suggestions for exercises/activities for each of the 580 skills.

PPN can be applied to families who have child-rearing problems with a child of the developmental age of 0-6 years. These problems may be related to serious developmental problems on the part of the child, or to problematic relationships between parent and child, as a result of which the child's development is stunted or in danger of becoming so.

At present, the best-known target groups in Holland are: families with mentally handicapped children; and families having relational problems not connected with any handicap of the child. The child-rearing problems of these groups are viewed as moderately serious. Parents complain that their children are not willing to listen, are boisterous, aggressive or short-tempered, are not able to play alone or with other children, have problems with eating or sleeping, or the parents do not seem able to form a relationship with the child.

167

Effectiveness research

PPN interventions focus on the interactions between the parents, the child and the immediate environment. It is not easy to conduct scientific research in this area since the high degree of certainty required is difficult to attain when working with families in vulnerable situations and with parents who are eager for help in child-rearing. In addition, the research process cannot be permitted to burden the family; and there are parents and social workers who would prefer to just get on with the support without engaging in research or even sound preparation.

Research into the effectiveness of the interventions is important (see, for example, Baker, 1984; Marfo and Kysela, 1985; Dunst, Snyder and Mankinen, 1989; Guralnick and Bennet, 1987; Farran, 1990) because, in our view, there are only moderate effects in most cases (Guralnick, 1991), or even undesired effects (Van der Meulen and Sipma, 1994). One of the reasons for these rather disappointing results in empirical terms has to do with the problems of matching. The intervention addresses the inter-relationship between the parent, the child and the immediate environment, while the home teacher and the co-ordinator also play an essential part. In the case of optimal matching between the major actors, the intervention will possibly be more effective than our studies showed. However, this must be demonstrated in new evaluative studies.

The choice between different programmes with the same interventive goal is also a matter of achieving an optimal match. Nonetheless, the major difficulty is still a demonstration of the causal relationship between the intervention and the observed change. Why is this so difficult? Some answers are as follows (see also, for example, Sipma, 1996):

- There are problems concerning research design. For example, if the very first contact between social worker and family members is part of the intervention, a research model including pre-measurement will hardly be practicable. In addition, the families concerned are heterogeneous and it is accordingly difficult to achieve pre-experimental equivalence of groups.
- There are problems with the definition of effectiveness (see, among others, Dunst, Snyder and Mankinen, 1989). For example, are there measuring instruments available which will allow the effects to be operationalised in a valid and reliable way?
- There are strong social pressures on the researcher. For example, the future financing of applied research is often dependent on earlier positive test results; dealing with undesired negative results is often a tricky issue in the political arena.

The effectiveness of intervention through PPN can be demonstrated for a large number of variables. Examples are: variables related to the child, such as development, non-compliancy, health, and so forth; variables related to the parents, such as parenting skills and attitudes about parenthood; environmental variables, such as quality of the physical environment, number of social contacts, and so on.

The purpose of the PPN intervention is to equip parents as far as possible for dealing with the child's non-compliant behaviour and stimulating the child's development. In many cases, mental development is delayed and the desired outcome of the intervention is to increase the pace of the child's mental development. As mental and motor developmental progress is measured in a special way, we will explain the procedure here.

We have several tests at our disposal to measure mental and motor development. However, with mentally handicapped children the delays often invalidate the age-norms of the tests. All the researcher can do is to measure the child's score in age-equivalents, but these scores are relatively useless since their distributional characteristics are not known. Researchers have tried to solve this problem in different ways (Wolory, 1983; Rosenberg, Robinson, Finkler and Rose, 1987; Vriesema, 1990; Lambert, Piret, Scohy and Lambert-Boite, 1993), and a number of measures have been envisaged.

In Groningen we have developed an index based on at least two pre-measurements and at least one post-measurement, relating the child's developmental age to his or her calendar age at the times of measuring. The two pre-measurements are meant to establish the baseline; the post-measurement takes place after intervention. Thus a kink in the line can reflect a positive effect. The baseline makes an angle with the vertical axis. The tangent of that angle is considered a measure of the developmental progress before intervention. The tangent of the angle which the line connecting the second and the third times of measuring makes with the vertical axis is considered a measure of the developmental progress after intervention. The difference between the two tangents is called the Index of Progress. In formula form, the Index of Progress = $[(DA3 - DA2)/(CA3 - CA2)] - [(DA2 - DA1)/(CA2 - CA1)]$, where DA = Developmental Age and CA = Calendar Age.

In the six investigations we will now briefly discuss, this measure will always be mentioned. Its interpretation is unambiguous: a positive IP indicates a relatively increased pace of development, an IP of 0 means standard developmental progress and a negative IP indicates a decreased pace of development.

Design

The research studies discussed here concern six Dutch projects, mainly financed by sponsors. For the first time, these six investigations are compared with one another, as shown in Table 11.1.

Table 11.1
The six Dutch samples

Location of research	Sample and location of intervention	Number of families	Period
University of Groningen (1)	non-compliant children/ children with developmental problems, 0-6 year, at home	11	1987 Feb - 1988 Aug
University of Groningen (2)	mentally handicapped children * 3-6 years, at home	10	1989 Sept - 1990 Dec
Social Pedagogical Services Gorinchem (3)	mentally handicapped children 0-6 years, at home	11	1989 Dec - 1990 Dec
University of Groningen (4)	non-compliant children/ children with developmental delays 0-6 years, at home	48	1991 Feb - 1994 Jan
Social Pedagogical Services Alkmaar (5)	mentally handicapped children, 3-36 months, at home	30	1991 Aug - 1995 Feb
Services for persons with a mental handicap, at Gorinchem (6)	mentally handicapped children, different groups, in two day-care centres, also at home, 0-6 years, *	95	1992 Sept - 1995 Jan

*Visiting a day-care centre for mentally handicapped children.

Sources:
(1) Bulsink, Van der Meulen and Smrkovsky (1988)
(2) Sipma and Van der Meulen (1991); Van der Meulen and Sipma (1991)
(3) Sipma and Vanmarle-Dekker (1991)
(4) Sipma and Van der Meulen (1994)
(5) Vangennep, Procee, Van der Meulen, Janssen, Vermeer and Degraaf (1995)
(6) Vanoudheusden, Vanmarle-Dekker & Van der Meulen (1995)

The samples are not random; the families/children were included in the samples on the basis of willingness to participate, and in every case ethical principles precluded the formation of a control group. Each of the six projects applied specific inclusion and exclusion criteria to the selection of participants which will possibly complicate generalisation of the results.

Taking into account the aims of PPN, intervention is expected to affect the following variables with respect to the child, the parents and the immediate environment (see Table 11.2):

Table 11.2
Variables by which intervention effects were measured

object of in-tervention	variable	instruments (mainly) *
child	-Index of Progress	-BSID; MSCA 2½--8½; K-ABC
	-seriousness of problem behaviour	-CBCL, 2 versions: 2-3; 4-18
parent	-rearing load -rearing skills -judgement on programme and effect -parental competence	-NVOS (Dutch, part A & B) -NVOS (Dutch, part C) -Questionnaire Child Rear-ing Scale (Dutch question-naire ad hoc) -Child Rearing Scale (CRS, Dutch); Vision on Parent-hood (VOP, Dutch)
direct envi-ronment	quality of home-environ-ment	HOME (0-3 year)

* the references for the instruments are as follows:
BSID: Bayley (1969); Van der Meulen and Smrkovsky (1983, 1984)
MSCA: McCarthy (1972); Van der Meulen and Smrkovsky (1985). It should be noted that the MSCA (McCarthy Scales of Children's Abilities) was translated into a Dutch version, McCarthy Ontwikkelingsschalen (MOS 2½-8½)
K-ABC: Kaufman and Kaufman (1983); Neutel, Van der Meulen and Lutjespel-berg (1995)
CBCL: Achenbach (1991); Verhulst, Koot, Akkerhuis and Veerman (1990)
NVOS: Wels and Robbroekcx (1989)
CRS: Janssen (1982)
VOP: Janssen (1982)
HOME: Caldwell and Bradley (1979); Dejong and Meijer (1985)

The Index of Progress has been computed with the help of test results on BOS 2-30 (Vandermeulen and Smrkovsky, 1983; 1984) - the Dutch version of the BSID; test results on MOS 2½-8½ (Van der Meulen and Smrkovsky, 1985) - the Dutch version of the MSCA; and in some cases test results on GOS (Neutel, Van der Meulen and Lutjespelberg, 1995) - the Dutch version of a part of the K-ABC. The BOS, MOS and GOS scores are expressed in months. It should be noted that the BSID (Bayley Scales of Infant Development (Bayley, 1969)) was translated into a Dutch version, Bayley Ontwikkelingsschalen or BOS 2-30.

The seriousness of the children's problem behaviour was measured using CBCL (Verhulst, Koot, Akkerhuis, & Veerman, 1990; both versions). The CBCL scores (both versions) are expressed in standard scores with an average of $T = 50$ and $s = 10$.

The parents' child-rearing load was established using a Dutch questionnaire called NVOS (Wels and Robbroeckx, 1989). The NVOS scores are expressed in score averages of the number of answers per category (part A, part B, part C).

Parenting skills were operationalised with the aid of two questionnaires (Janssen, 1982). The scores on the Child-Rearing Scale and Attitudes about Parenthood are rough sum scores of items.

The characteristics of the immediate environment were measured using HOME 0-3 (Caldwell and Bradley, 1979), an instrument that bases the scores on a form of structured interview. The HOME scores are rough sum scores of items that contribute to a good quality home environment. We used the Dutch version, called MOK (Dejong and Meijer, 1985).

The parents' opinion of the effectiveness of the intervention was drawn from a structured interview conducted after the intervention.

Naturally, the six research projects measured many more variables than can be discussed in this chapter. Here, we limit ourselves to the most important variables which we term 'external variables', in contrast to the large number of variables yielded by the programme itself, such as scores on Activity Charts, ordinal position on the Checklist, number of learned or spontaneously acquired skills, and so forth.

In all six projects, the mental and motor development of the children was determined by means of two pre-measurements and at least one post-measurement, thus allowing the Index of Progress to be computed. The change in the value of the remaining variables was rated by means of before and after measurements.

In virtually all cases, there was a pre-measurement phase, lasting from 1 to 3 months, followed by an intervention phase, lasting approximately 6 months, followed by a post-measurement phase and follow-up. Follow-up will not be discussed here.

Results

The most important empirical results, divided according to the research project and the types of variables, are shown in Table 11.3. The Table is structured to provide results on variables pertaining to children, parents and the immediate environment in that order. In most cases three measurements have been carried out. The following symbols are used:

\# Results only pertain to children aged 2-3 years. For older children CBCL 4-16 was used, with practically the same results (after intervention 59.0, before intervention 62.6; $p = .0351^*$ one-tailed).

% Only the mothers' opinions were solicited. Fathers' opinions were scored separately in a similar way.

\$ Both these variables represent the concept of 'child-rearing competence'.

Positive, statistically significant test results are indicated with * or **, .05 and .01 one-tailed levels of significance respectively.

Table 11.3
Outcomes of six studies

	Groningen-1	Groningen-2	Gorinchem-3	Groningen-4	Alkmaar-5	Gorinchem-6
N	11	10	11	48	30	95
Mental development after intervention	1.12	.63	.46	.99	.38	.47
Mental development before intervention	.71	-.09	.70	3.04	.34	.18
Mental Index of Progress	.41	.72*	-.24	-2.04	.04	.29**
Motor development after intervention	1.26	.82	.56	1.27	.65	.44
Motor development before intervention	.42	.33	.69	2.21	.47	.23
Motor Index of Progress	.84**	.49	-.13	-.94	-.32	.21
Seriousness of problem behaviour after intervention				55.4		
Seriousness problem behaviour before intervention				63.2		
Change in problem behaviour (#)				-7.8**		
Rearing load of parents after intervention				19.2		
Rearing load of parents before intervention				22.1		
Change in rearing load of parents				-2.9**		
Educational skills after intervention				2.35		
Educational skills before intervention				2.52		
Change in educational skills (%)				-.17*		
Judgement of parents on PPN and effect	pos	pos	pos	pos	pos	pos
Parental competence after intervention					116.5	
Parental competence before intervention					113.0	
Change in parental competence (%) ($)					2.5*	
Vision on parenthood after intervention					52.1	
Vision on parenthood before intervention					54.0	
Change in vison on parenthood ($)					1.9*	
Quality of home environment after intervention	40.9	40.8		37.8		
Quality of home environment before intervention	38.6	38.1		35.9		
Change in quality of home environment	2.3*	2.7*		1.9**		

University of Groningen, project 1, non-compliant children, N=11

Some very young children are difficult to get along with from their parents' perspective and the parents have questions about how to approach them. There is no reason to consider developmental problems. PPN has been used with these families. One of the aims was to find out whether improved parent-child relationships would affect the children's development.

Conclusion: it is quite possible to tackle the problems of non-compliance with PPN.

University of Groningen, project 2, children with developmental problems, N = 10

The chief purpose of the study was to give the mental and motor development of mentally handicapped children a significant push. The question here was whether the quality of the home environment would also benefit.

Conclusion: the rate of mental development increased strongly and there was a positive effect on the quality of the home environment.

Social Pedagogical Services Groningen, project 3, children mainly with developmental problems, N = 11

Do children develop faster when they are systematically empowered to influence their environment?

Conclusion: no positive effect could be shown in Gorinchem. The question of whether the parent-child relationship improved was not explicitly examined. Like all parents, the Gorinchem parents were enthusiastic about the programme. This is not surprising since improvement in the child's development usually occurs, and the parents, if not the researchers, ascribe this improvement to help with child-rearing problems.

University of Groningen, project 4, mainly non-compliant children, N = 48

The primary aim of the project was to reduce the relationship problems between parents and child in families with moderate child-rearing problems. In this project, the hypothesis was that when relationship problems decreased, the rate of the child's developmental progress would increase.

Conclusion: the parents' child-rearing load decreased as a result of PPN intervention; the seriousness of the problem behaviour decreased as well. Parenting skills increased. However, no positive effect on the child's development could be demonstrated. In fact, some children developed more rapidly than expected before intervention. When the children were divided into two subgroups, one with a relatively high and the other with a relatively low rate of development, it appeared that those who developed fast gained most from the intervention; a somewhat tragic effect that has been observed before in enrichment programmes.

Social Pedagogical Services Alkmaar, project 5, children with serious developmental delays, N = 30

This project was part of a much larger study on the relative effectiveness of three intervention programmes.

Conclusion: the rate of the child's development was not increased in a statistically significant way. Nevertheless, parenting skills improved and so did attitudes about parenthood with respect to rearing a handicapped child: consequently, there was an improvement in parental competence overall. This result indicates that perhaps it is not necessary to achieve the primary aim (increasing the rate of the child's development) in order to legitimise the use of the programme.

Services for persons with a mental handicap at Gorinchem, project 6, children with serious developmental delays, N = 95

In this study an effort was made, for the first time, to adapt PPN to a day-care centre, in combination with home help. The research yielded a new variant of PPN, viz. the Portage Group Programme.

Conclusion: PPN can provide impetus to children's mental development. The introduction of the programme in day-care centres for mentally handicapped children is recommended.

Evaluation

In a number of cases it can be demonstrated that PPN support has a significant influence on children's development. In all cases the quality of the home environment increases demonstrably. In all cases the parents' parenting style is shown to change significantly. All in all, it may be stated that something always changes for the better and the child-rearing process is more positive overall after the intervention. In addition, it was demonstrated, especially in the fourth study, that relationship problems between parent and child can be successfully tackled.

The variable of 'parental satisfaction' is a necessary but not a sufficient condition for support to be effective. The results in this respect were constant over the six research projects.

With respect to increase in the rate of the children's development, it is not easy to distinguish effects explicitly caused by the intervention from effects due to the parents' maturation, growth and spontaneous increase in skill (see Boezeman and Willems, 1995).

To what extent, then, can our moderate and varying research results be stated in general terms with respect to other programmes? Given the design, we have tried to subject the hypothesis - that intervention does have an effect - to as severe a test as possible. It is our assumption that, when tested in the same way, other programmes will also show moderate and varying results. We look forward with interest to empirical research in this connection.

Are there any theoretical notions to support or explain the fact that we found moderate results? There are indeed. One might think of behavioural genetics (see, among others, Scarr, 1992, 1993; and Baumrind's (1993) and Jackson's (1993) sharp reactions to them; and Scarr's (1993) vehement retort). This trend in developmental psychology advances the proposition that, for children whose development is on a predictable but undesirable trajectory, interventions have only temporary and limited effects (see also Heymans, 1992; 1993).

Is there any possibility of making the observed changes more stable and the outcome more solid? We hope so; the following suggestions come to mind:

- improve the design: more testees, more randomisation of the groups (Campbell and Stanley, 1966), and more longitudinal measurements of more variables;
- take great care with the (further) training of professional home teachers and co-ordinators; that is to say, do not settle for 'train and hope'.

References

Achenbach, T.M. (1991). *Manual for the Child Behaviour Checklist and 1991 Profile*. Burlington: University of Vermont, Department of Psychiatry.

Baker, B.L. (1984), "Intervention with Families with Young, Severely Handicapped Children", in J. Blacher (ed.), *Severely Handicapped Young Children and Their Families*, Academic Press, Orlando.

Baumrind, D. (1993), "The Average Expectable Enironment is Not Good Enough: A Response to Scarr", *Child Development*, vol. 64, 1299-1317.

Bayley, N. (1969). *Manual for the Bayley Scales of Infant Development*. New York: The Psychological Corportion.

Boezeman, L. and Willems, A. (1995), "Placebo of panacee? Onderzoek naar de effecten van Vroeghulp geven verrassende resultaten", *Fiad Forum*, 16-18.

Bulsink, H.H., Vandermeulen, B.F. and Smrkovsky, M. (1988), *Eindrapport Portage-project Groningen (unpublished)*, Vakgroep Orthopedagogiek, Groningen.

Caldwell, B.M. and Bradley, R.H. (1979), *Home Observation for Measurement of the Environment*, University of Arkansas, Little Rock.

Campbell, D.T. and Stanley, J.C. (1966), *Experimental and quasi-experimental designs for research*. Rand McNally College Publishing Company, Chicago.

Dejong, A. and Meijer, Th. (1985), *Meten van Omgevingskenmerken van Kinderen (unpublished doctoral thesis)*, Afdeling Orthopedagogiek, Groningen.

Dunst, C.J., Snyder, S.W. and Mankinen, M. (1989), "Efficacy of early intervention", in M.C. Wang, M.C. Reynolds and H.J. Walberg (eds), *Handbook of special education. Research and practice*. vol. 3, Pergamon Press, Oxford.

Farran, D.C. (1990), "Effects of intervention with disadvantaged and disabled children", in S.J. Meisels and J.P. Shonkhoff (eds), *Handbook of early child-hood intervention*, Cambridge University Press, New York.

Guralnick, M.J. (1991). The Next Decade of Research on the Effectiveness of Early Intervention. *Exceptional Children*, 58, 174-183.

Guralnick, M.J. and Bennet, F.C. (eds) (1987), *The Effectiveness of Early Intervention for At-Risk and Handicapped Children*, Academic Press, Orlando, Florida.

Heymans, P.G. (1992), "Heeft opvoeding wel invloed op de (morele) ontwik-keling?" in Hox, J.J., Terlaak, J.J.F. and Van der Meulen, B.F., *Beïnvloeding van de ontwikkeling door opvoeding?* Stichting Kinderstudies, Groningen.

Heymans, P.G. (1993), "Developmental tasks: a cultural analysis of human development", in Terlaak, J.J.F. et al. (eds), *Developmental Tasks: towards a cultural analysis of human development*, Kluwer Academic Publishing, Dordrecht.

Jackson, J.F. (1993), "Human Behavioral Genetics, Scarr's Theory, and her Views on Interventions: A Critical Review and Commentary on Their Implications for African American Children", *Child Development*, vol. 64, 1318-1332.

Janssen, C.G.C. (1982), *Ouders van geestelijk gehandicapte kinderen. Naar een vollediger gezinsonderzoek*, Swets and Zeitlinger, Lisse.

Kaufman, A.S. and Kaufman, N.L. (1983), *Kaufman Assessment Battery for Children. Intepretative manual*, American Guidance Service, Circle Pines, MN.

Lambert, J., Piret, M., Scohy, C. and Lambert-Boite, F. (1993), "Wirkungen der Früherziehung auf die Entwicklung der Kinder", *VHN*, vol. 1, 29-40.

Marfo, K. and Kysela, G. (1985), "Early intervention with mentally handicapped children. A critical appraisal of applied research", *Journal of Pediatric Psychology*, vol. 10, 305-324.

McCarthy, D. (1972). *Manual of McCarthy Scales of Children's Abilities*. New York: The Psychological Corporation.

Meisels, S.J. and Wasik, B.A. (1990), "Who should be served? Identifying children in need of early intervention", in S.J. Meisels and J.P. Shonkhoff (eds), *Handbook of early childhood intervention*, Cambridge University Press, New York.

Neutel, R.J., Van der Meulen, B.F. and Lutjespelberg, H.C. (1995), *Groningse Ontwikkelingsschalen GOS*, Swets and Zeitlinger, Lisse/Amsterdam.

Rosenberg, S.A., Robinson, C.C., Finkler, D. and Rose, J.S. (1987), "An empirical comparison of formulas evaluating early intervention program impact on development", *Exceptional Children*, 213-219.

Sameroff, A.J. and Fiese, B.H. (1991), "Transactional regulations and early intervention", in Shonkhoff, J.P. and Meisels, S.J., *Handbook of early childhood intervention*, University Press, Cambridge.

Sameroff, A.J. amd Chandler, M.J. (1975), "Reproductive risk and the continuum of caretaking casualty", in F.D. Horowitz et al. (eds), *Review of Child Development Research*, vol. 4, University of Chicago Press, Chicago.

Scarr, S. (1992), "Developmental Theories for the 1990s: Development and Individual Differences", *Child Development*, vol. 63, 1-19.

Scarr, S. (1993), "Biological and Cultural Diversity: The Legacy of Darwin for Development", *Child Development*, vol. 64, 1333-1353.

Seitz, V. and Provence, S. (1990), "Caregiver-focused models of early intervention", in S.J. Meisels and J.P. Shonkhoff (eds), *Handbook of early childhood intervention*, Cambridge University Press, New York.

Shearer, M.S. and Shearer, D.E. (1972), The Portage Project: a model for early childhood education. *Exceptional Children*, vol. 38, 210-217.

Shearer, M.S. and Shearer, D.E. (1974), *The Portage Project*. Paper presented at the Conference on Early Intervention of High Risk Infants and Young Children. Chapel Hill, North Carolina.

Sipma, W.G. (1996), *Orthopedagogische thuisbegeleiding met het Portage Programma (dissertation)*, Stichting Kinderstudies, Groningen.

Sipma, W.G. and Vanmarle-Dekker, M.J. (1991), "Het Portage Programma Nederland toegepast in Gorinchem", in Van der Meulen, B.F. ans Terlaak, J.J.F. (eds), *Empirisch Gezinsonderzoek*, Stichting Kinderstudies, Groningen.

Sipma, W.G. and Van der Meulen, B.F. (1991), *Portage Programma Nederland: een onderzoek bij en hulpverlening aan geestelijk gehandicapte kinderen*, Stichting Kinderstudies, Groningen.

Sipma, W.G. and Van der Meulen, B.F. (1994), *Orthopedagogische thuisbegeleiding met behulp van het Portage Programma Nederland bij gezinnen met matige opvoedingsproblemen. Deel I: Eindrapport*, Stichting Kinderstudies, Groningen.

Sipma, W.G., Vaniddekinge, J. and Van der Meulen, B.F. (1994), *Orthopedagogische thuisbegeleiding met behulp van het Portage Programma*

Nederland bij gezinnen met matige opvoedingsproblemen. Deel II: Casuïstiek en bibliografie, Stichting Kinderstudies, Groningen.

Tavormina, J.B. (1974), "Basic models of parent counseling. A critical review", *Psychological Bulletin*, vol. 81, 827-835.

Van der Meulen, B.F. and Smrkovsky, M. (1983), *Bayley Ontwikkelingsschalen BOS 2-30*, Swets and Zeitlinger, Lisse.

Van der Meulen, B.F. and Smrkovsky, M. (1984), *Bayley Ontwikkelingsschalen*, Stichting Kinderstudies, Groningen.

Van der Meulen, B.F. and Smrkovsky, M. (1985), *McCarthy Ontwikkelings-schalen MOS 2½-8½*, Swets and Zeitlinger, Lisse.

Van der Meulen, B.F. and Sipma, W.G. (1990), "Het Portage-project Groningen. Onderzoek naar de effecten van een programma voor vroegtijdige thuis-interventie", *Nederlands Tijdschrift voor Zwakzinnigenzorg*, vol. 16, no. 8, 167-182.

Van der Meulen, B.F. amd Sipma, W.G. (1991), "The Portage Project Groningen. Measurement Procedures and Results", in J. Herwig and M. Stine (eds), *Proceedings from the Third International Portage Conference*, CESA#5, Portage.

Van der Meulen, B.F. and Sipma, W.G. (1993a), *Portage Programma Nederland. Portage Checklist. Wessex Taalactiviteitenlijst*, Swets and Zeitlinger, Lisse.

Van der Meulen, B.F. and Sipma, W.G. (1993b), *Portage Programma Nederland. Wessex taalvaardighedenlijst*, Swets and Zeitlinger, Lisse.

Van der Meulen, B.F. and Sipma, W.G. (1993c), *5 Portage Programma Nederland. Formulieren behorende bij het Portage Programma Nederland (Activiteitenkaarten op basis van het Probleemanalyseschema; Activiteiten-kaarten op basis van de Vaardighedenlijst; Ouderactiviteitenkaarten; Taakanalyse-schema's; Probleemanalyseschema's, Slaapschema's & Probleemprioriteitelijsten)*, Swets and Zeitlinger, Lisse.

Van der Meulen, B.F. and Sipma, W.G. (1994), Scarr, Clarke and Clarke and the Portage Programma Nederland. 'Is there a limit to the effectiveness of early intervention?' in J.E. Rink, R.C. Vos, K.P. van den Bos, R. van Wijck and P.L. Vriesema (eds), *The limits of Orthopedagogy: changing perspectives. Part 2*. Leuven: Garant, 102-111.

Van der Meulen, B.F., Sipma, W.G. and Feenstra, C.E.J. (1993), *Portage Programma Nederland. Handleiding voor thuisbegeleiders*, Swets & Zeitlinger, Lisse.

Van der Meulen, B.F., Sipma, W.G., Bulsink, H.H. and Smrkovsky, M. (1993), *Portage Programma Nederland. Vaardighedenlijst*, Swets and Zeitlinger, Lisse.

Van der Meulen, B.F. and Elzinga-Westerveld, H.J., (1994), *Pedagogische thuishulp voor gezinnen met jonge kinderen in Nederland Pedagogische thuishulp voor gezinnen met jonge kinderen in Nederland*, Garant, Leuven-Apeldoorn.

Van Gennep, A.T.G., Procee, A.I., Van der Meulen, B.F., Janssen, C.G.C., Vermeer, A. and Degraaf, E.A.B. (1995), *Evaluatie van vroeghulp in Nederland*, VU Uitgeverij, Amsterdam.

Vanoudheusden, M.A., Vanmarle-Dekker, M.J. and Van der Meulen, B.F. (1995), *Vroege ontwikkelinsstimulering met behulp van Portage in en vanuit een Kinderdagverblijf. Eindrapport, Regionale Stichting Dienstverlening aan Verstandelijk Gehandicapten, Gorinchem (unpublished)*.

Verhulst, F.C., Koot, J.M., Akkerhuis, G.W. and Veerman, J.W. (1990), *Praktische handleiding bij de CBCL*, Van Gorcum, Assen.

Vriesema, P.L. (1990), *Vroegtijdige orthopedagogische hulpverlening*, Stichting Kinderstudies, Groningen (dissertation).

Vriesema, P.L. and Nakken, H. (1993), "Drie vormen van vroegtijdige pedagogische thuisbegeleiding voor ouders en kind", in Vangemert, G.H. and R.B. Minderaa, *Zorg voor verstandelijk gehandicapten*, Van Gorcum, Assen/ Maastricht.

Wels, P.M.A. and Robbroeckx, L.M.H. (1989), *Handleiding bij de Nijmeegse Vragenlijst voor de Opvoedingssituatie (NVOS, versie 3.2)*, Instituut voor Orthopedagogiek, KU Nijmegen, Nijmegen (unpublished).

Wolery, M. (1983), "Proportional Change Index: An Alternative for Comparing Child Change Data", *Exceptional Children*, vol. 50, 167-170.

Zigler, E.F. (1990), "Foreword", in S.J. Meisels and J.P. Shonkhoff (eds), *Handbook of early childhood intervention*, Cambridge University Press, New York.

12 Process-oriented research into home-based treatment programmes

Bas VOGELVANG

1. Introduction

This chapter will discuss evaluation research into home-based treatment programmes. It will focus on the process of change in families. How do changes take place during treatment, and how can home-visitors encourage this process of change by using the right strategies and interventions?

To begin with, two examples of a successful intervention are presented. Both interventions were applied by home-visitors working for the Project at Home, a treatment programme for multi-problem families in Amsterdam.

1. The house of the Jones' family is very dirty. Also, the children get sick too often. The home-visitor to the Joneses explains to the parents that this is caused by dust and bacteria. He advises them to clean the house, and offers his assistance if necessary. The parents do nothing about it. The house becomes dirtier than ever. On one visit, the home-visitor arrives at the house with a plastic bag. The parents always await his arrival while looking out the window. In front of the house, observed by the parents, the home-visitor takes a dirty overall out of his bag and puts it on over his clean clothes. After this, he rings the bell as if he had not seen the parents looking out of the window, and enters the house. In the weeks that follow, the parents make efforts to clean their house.
2. After five months of home-based treatment, Mrs Smith has made remarkable progress. Nevertheless, her oldest son of four years old is diagnosed as

developmentally delayed, and needs to be placed in a day-care centre. Mrs Smith was raised in institutions herself, and has very bad memories of them. Therefore, she is very reluctant to place her son, even in a day-care centre. In order to motivate Mrs Smith, the home-visitor arranges an informal first visit of mother and child to the day-care centre. She prepares this visit with Mrs Smith in a very detailed manner, ranging from getting the right bus tickets, to letting Mrs Smith explain the purpose of this visit to her son, to preparing her for handling her anger and sorrow when she enters an institution again for the first time since childhood. The visit is very successful: although she gets emotional, Mrs Smith is able to explain her side of the story to the staff of the day-care centre. The visit is also successful for her son, because his mother is a relaxed role-model. After this visit, Mrs. Smith accepts placement of her son.

We have seen two successful interventions. The strategy in the first was confronting: it disrupted an old pattern, after which the parents changed independently. The second intervention not only included the disruption of an old pattern, but the creation and nurturance of a new pattern in close co-operation as well. These two kinds of interventions, the disrupting and nurturing of patterns, will be important themes in this chapter. They will be discussed in detail later, when a model of change in families will be presented.

This chapter is based on the author's findings on several home-visiting programmes, and on a literature survey: covering the period 1978-1995, only those programme evaluations were selected which took treatment features and/or treatment processes into account. As will be explained in more detail later, this is called the throughput of a programme. Furthermore, only those articles were selected in which explicit attempts were made to specify effective contributions to the process of change. These criteria were fulfilled in only a few articles. For instance, intervention A appeared to contribute to success when applied in family type 2, or strategy B appeared to be very useful in all families.

However, despite these efforts, none of the authors of these articles tried to *integrate* these findings into a *model of change*. None of them even mentioned a model of change. This is surprising, because the lack of such a model has far-reaching consequences: home-visitors typically say things as 'in some families, change is slow but gradual, and in others it is unpredictable, rapid and chaotic'. Without research aiming to clarify, structure, and validate this knowledge, and incorporate it into a model of change, home-visitors do not know how to fully make use of the circumstances of family life to promote or elicit change.

Following this introduction, the range of home-visiting programmes which will be discussed is presented, and some important concepts regarding evaluation research of home-based treatment programmes are examined. This is followed by a short description of the most important models of family functioning used in home-based treatment programmes, and their implications for process-oriented research.

After this, the main part of this chapter will concern a synthesis of theoretical notions and research findings on effective contributions to the process of change in families. This synthesis is presented in the form of a model of change. In this model, interventions can be applied to families by their home-visitor, or to home-visitors by their supervisors.

2. Typology of home-visiting programmes

In 1990, Nelson, Landsman and Deutelbaum proposed a typology of home-visiting programmes. They combined the intensity and duration of programmes and theoretical approaches. Their synthesis looked like this:

Primary prevention:
These programmes are typically designed for populations at-risk for parenting problems, especially child-abuse and neglect, and social isolation. They are preferably applied during pregnancy or in families with young children. Examples are:
- parent training
- social support services, including volunteer aid.

Preservation (secondary and tertiary prevention):
These programmes are intended for high-risk populations. Preservation includes both secondary and tertiary prevention of out-of-home placement and reunification of families, or the return from placement of children:

A.   Prevention of out-of-home placement-programmes.
B.   Reunification or return from placement-programmes.
1 - home-based treatment modules in residential and day-care centres.
2 - crisis-oriented programmes (IFPPs)
3 - home-visiting programmes (FPPs)
4 - family treatment models (FPPs)

1. Home-based treatment modules in residential and day-care centres. The application of home-treatment modules in day-care or residential centres has only recently been developed. During these home-based treatments, families are being prepared for independent functioning, or for a move to more

184

intensive home-based treatment. An example is LOV-training in the Netherlands, which makes use of video (Vogelvang 1995).

2. *Crisis-oriented programmes (IFPPs)*. Families First is, of course, the 'flagship programme' of crisis-oriented programmes. These programmes are called Intensive in order to emphasise the short treatment duration in combination with the very high visiting frequency and structured approach.

3. *Home-visiting programmes (FPPs)*. Home-visiting programmes are the most prevalent amongst FPPs. They resemble IFPPs, but the treatment duration is longer, and home-visitors use long-term interventions based on a systems approach. Examples of these projects can be found throughout Western Europe and the United States.

4. *Family treatment models (FPPs)*. Family Treatment Programmes differ from the other programmes in their emphasis on therapeutic interventions and lesser involvement in the provision of direct and concrete services. These services combine principles of systemic and structural family therapy. An example is the recent development of a home-based family treatment programme by Zarski and Harry Aponte, pioneer of structural family therapy (1992). Elements of this approach can be found in some European home-visiting programmes.

This chapter will be restricted to evaluation research of crisis-oriented programmes and home-visiting programmes.

3. Input, throughput and output

To prepare a display of research findings in the following sections, three well-known facets of treatment will be described: input, throughput, and output. These facets are helpful in bringing some order into research findings.

3.1. Input-research into home-based treatment programmes

Input refers to the questions *'Who is getting help, why do they need help, and what kind of help do they need?'* Answering these questions leads to continuous modification of the throughput or processes during treatment. First, continuous research is conducted in order to sort out and describe types of families, types of problems and problem-constellations, healthy aspects in families, and types of background variables such as the type of referring agency, or the family's career in the social services. Unfortunately, this massive amount of unco-ordinated research comes from studies which cannot be compared and often show severe methodological flaws.

Second, some research is being done to introduce some order into these findings by formulating models of family functioning or by testing ecological or systems theories. It can be argued that four models of family functioning have proved to be a valid, useful contribution to the evolution of home-based treatment programmes. These are:

1. Bronfenbrenner's ecological model of human development.
2. Minuchin's structural family therapy, based on systems theory.
3. Nagy's contextual therapy, based on a model of intra- and intergenerational loyalty.
4. Learning theory and social learning theory.

1. *Bronfenbrenner's ecological model of human development.* The ecological model has been very important. Not only has it shown us that problems or symptoms can be related to different bio-psycho-social levels, but it also impels us not to intervene automatically at the micro-level of parent-child interaction. For instance, in a comparison by Lutzker and Rice of home-based treatment programmes intended to treat child abuse and neglect, it was found that broad, so-called multi-faceted programmes proved to be most successful. These are *ecologically valid* programmes. As Barry Dym (1988) concludes: 'Bronfenbrenner has broadened our perspective'. However, Dym also concludes that Bronfenbrenner, up to now, has given no clear indications on *how to use* the ecological model in order to bring about changes in families. This has left home-visitors somewhat bewildered and confused. Where are they to start, given the 'a priori multi-level complexity' of even one single problem. Dym quotes an American movie: 'Do we have to change the world first in order to learn this kid to read?'

2. *Minuchin's structural family therapy, based on systems theory.* Minuchin's structural family therapy, based on the systems theory, suffers from a lack which is the opposite of Bronfenbrenners model. Minuchin gives us several strategies and interventions but the model is *stuck on an intra-familial level.* A family's social network is hardly ever included in his writings. Nevertheless, structural family therapy has proven to be a tremendous starting point for home-visitors. Systems theory not only gives us tools to understand family patterns, but it also points out that home-visitors become part of a newly created, temporary system with all family members. Because this is inevitable, this temporary system must be monitored and corrected if necessary. Alexander Korittko, supervisor of a home-based treatment programme based in Hanover, Germany, puts it like this: 'In-home family treatment results in a very close physical and psychological relationship between the family and the family helper as compared to other forms of professional interventions. For

186

both, it is essential to put a tremendous effort into this process in order to let this closeness develop.' (1994)

3. *Nagy's contextual therapy, based on a model of intra- and intergenerational loyalty.* If Bronfenbrenner broadened our view in space, Boszormeny-Nagy's contextual family therapy broadened our view in time. Nagy pointed out to us that, as well as horizontal relationships between family members of the same generations, such as grandparents, parents and siblings, vertical relationships between parents and grandparents, and children and parents, are equally important to understanding family problems. He showed us that 'innocent' next generations can become corrupted by old family ledgers of credits and debts, for example because parents are paralysed through being loyal to the grandparents. Nagy's model suffers from a slightly different lack compared with Minuchin's model: it does incorporate extra-familial ties, namely with the grandparents, but it does not take full account of other relationships in the family's social network, nor of the family members' relationship with the home-visitor.

4. *Learning theory and social learning theory.* Finally, learning theory and social learning have proved to be valuable for home-based treatment programmes. Especially on a micro-level of parent-child interaction, the mapping of behaviour sequences and contingencies is a valuable tool for understanding and modifying functional relationships. This functional approach is also its weak point. In multi-problem families, it is very difficult to work on a functional, almost technical level. This is due to commonly observed practices of multi-problem families which oppose change, such as denial of family problems, exchanging one problem for another, the shifting of symptoms, and an apathetic or defiant attitude. The behavioural approach 'needs' willing clients. This is probably why Families First is quite successful in most families, because it only accepts families in acute crisis, which generates a stronger motivation to change.

These four models of family functioning, when applied in input-research, have taught us the following:

1. Both an intra- and extrafamilial approach to diagnosis are possible, and often both are necessary.
2. Both intra- and extrafamilial patterns, boundaries and hierarchies underlie family symptoms.
3. Three types of classification of families (input) are possible, and valid:
   a. *Types of families* can be found by looking at the etiology or developmental history of family problems (Bath and Haapala, 1993).

b. A *continuum of the severity or problems* can be formulated by looking at the balance of stress and competence in family life (Ayoub and Willett, 1992).

c. Interacting with b., a *continuum of amount of subsystems and systems responsible for regulating internal family processes* can be formulated. At one end of the continuum, families function independently and are only looking for some advice. At the other end of this continuum, a dilution takes place. This refers to the gradual taking over of the responsibility for internal family processes by the larger dynamics of social services. This happens in severely disorganised families (Colapinto 1995, Maluccio, Fein and Davis 1994, Fein and Staff 1993). At the midpoint of this continuum, we find families oscillating between independency and dependency.

When we shift our attention to a model of change, these lessons have to be taken into account.

3.2. *Throughput-research into home-based treatment programmes*

With respect to **throughput**, we find the same different types of research as in input-research.

First, we see descriptive research. On this level we can distinguish the *form and content* of treatments. *Treatment-form* refers to the questions:

1. 'where, when, how often, for how long, and with whom does treatment take place?', and

2. 'in what way do treatment features change over time during treatment, and why?'

In most research, only the first question is being addressed. For example, at what moment and why it is decided to increase or decrease the frequency of home-visits, is hardly ever a research question.

Treatment-content refers to the description of treatment goals and treatment means: that is, interventions and strategies, and changes in these during the treatment process.

Second, research is possible on models or theories of change. This type of research attempts to identify essential interventions, strategies, and forms of treatment, and to come up with prescriptions for future treatment. It attempts to formulate blueprints, or cookbooks, for successful treatments in different families with different problems. In their ideal form, blueprints are formulated as relational or even causal models of change.

3.3. Output-research into home-based treatment programmes

Finally, output refers to the question 'What changes take place in families, and do we have the right to treat these changes as the results of treatment?' In other words, 'did *we* help a bit?'.

Also on the output-level, both descriptive and relational-causal research can be distinguished.

1. Programme-evaluation is descriptive, and refers to the achievement of general programme goals or specific family goals
2. Impact research or effectiveness research is relational-causal, and refers to attempts to pin down programme-effectiveness in terms of a substantial contribution of the programme to the observed changes. This kind of research is very rare.

The three facets (input, throughput and output) interact. As Powell (1988) puts it, in his definition of process-oriented research: 'When, how, and on the basis of what kind of information and decisions, do assessments, goals and interventions change during treatments, and how are these changes related to success, which is the overall change or improvement in family functioning.'

Thus, finding successful ingredients or 'essential elements' of programme-throughput requires a comparison of input, throughput and output findings, as depicted in Figure 12.1.

- By comparing input and output, both the selection of families and prognosis can be improved. This should increase the effectiveness of a programme.
- By comparing input and throughput, different processes during treatment can be predicted and even encouraged. This should increase the adaptability of a programme.
- By comparing throughput and output, forms, strategies and interventions leading to success, can be identified. This should increase the efficiency of a programme.
- Finally by integrating all three comparisons, routes for successful selection of clients and successful treatment can be found. These routes can be presented to home-visitors as blueprints for treatment. These blueprints, or cookbooks, consist of do's and don't's for home-visitors.

However, as Francine Jacobs (1988) emphasises, this kind of research is only possible if programmes have gone through a development process from pioneering attempts into documented, clarified, exportable and socially embedded programmes.

189

4. Intermezzo: how to build a model of change

There are two options in proposing a model of change: The first is to integrate the research findings in the selected articles, and inductively try to build a model from these results. However, using this method, there is a chance that the resulting model will be of limited value because a model of change was not even mentioned in any of the selected articles. In other words, did these authors select an appropriate set of variables in the first place, in order to describe the through-put of the programme?

The second option, which we will follow now, is to look into more general (abstract, theoretical) models of change first. Then, deductively, we will try to find research findings which validate or disprove these models. Support for this approach can be found in a quote by Anthony Maluccio:

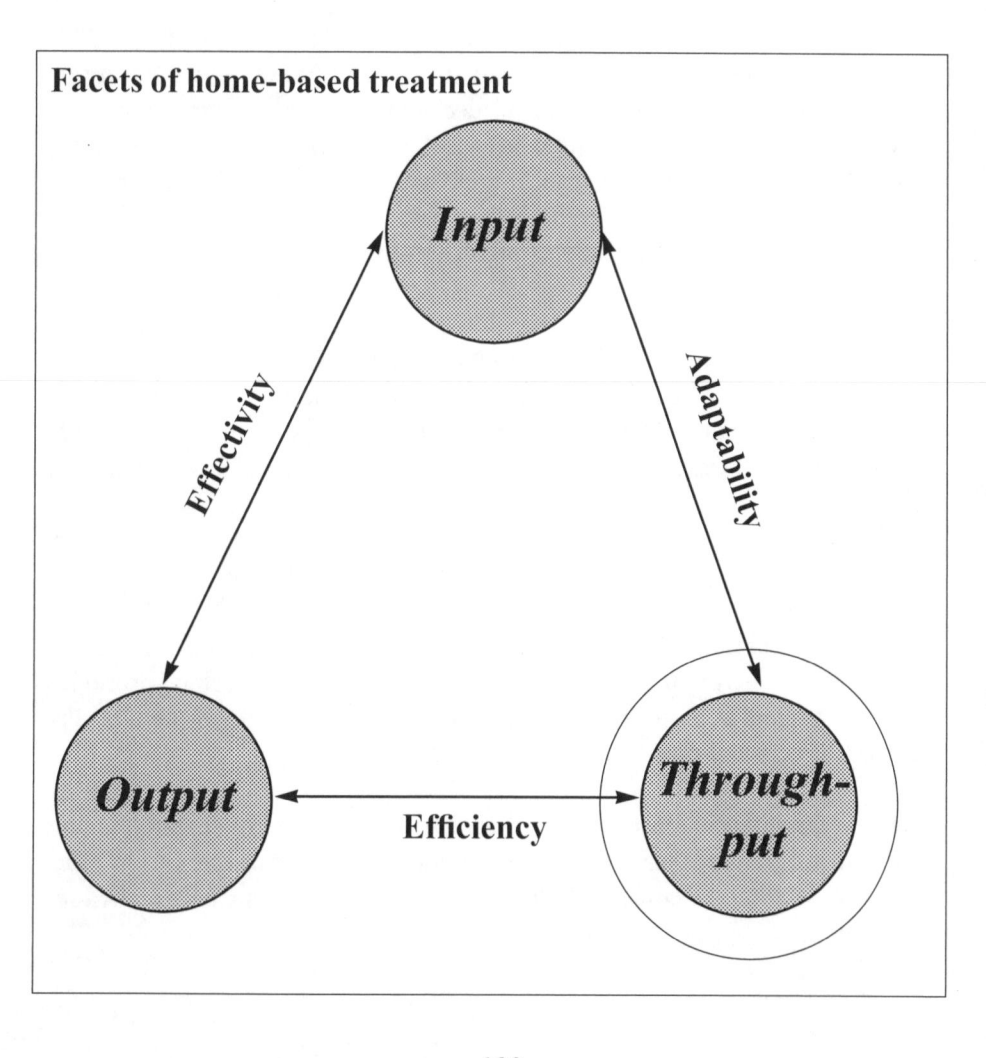

Future research should emphasize methodology in order to develop knowledge appropriate to the human services, and not mimic the procedures in the physical sciences.(...) The rigorous method of isolating and connecting specific input and outcome variables may not be as productive or appropriate as interactive investigation of the complex processes that affect children and families. This interplay of causal and interpretative perspectives has been proposed as the most promising direction for research in the human services (1994).

5. Model of change

5.1. Concepts and research findings

The model that will be presented contains several important concepts, which were derived from more general models of change, and from the lessons on input research which were discussed earlier. These elements will be discussed in this section. Furthermore, the validity of using each of these concepts in clarifying the process of change in families during home-based treatment will be illustrated with research findings.

1. *First, all systems in question, ranging from the parent-child system to a family's broad social network, make use of maps: A map refers to transactional patterns to guarantee internal smooth functioning, to give system members a sense of belonging, and to carry out adjustments to external pressures/demands. These patterns can also include the interaction between a family and a home-visitor.*

These maps can be functional, or dysfunctional. Furthermore, maps can be stable or unstable. A stable dysfunctional pattern, for instance, is scapegoating. Another stable dysfunctional pattern, is the home-visitor acting as mediator between parents and children, and being unable to escape this role. If pressure increases, maps need to be adjusted (change). For instance, if the problem-behaviour of the scapegoated child deteriorates, the pattern can become unstable. The parents might look for advice. This is an example of internal pressure. Pressure can also be of external origin. For instance, the supervisor may tell the home-visitor that his or her role needs to change, thereby making the pattern unstable by using external pressure.

2. Second, *parallel processes take place:* The interactional processes between the family and home-visitor are reflected in a parallel interactional process between the home-visitor and his or her supervisor, other team-members, and even the other services or institutions involved. Treatment must be considered

as a temporary extension of the family system with the addition of a home-visitor (or vice versa, as the temporary addition of a family to a team of home-visitors). It is also possible to intervene at this level.

3. *The ecological concept of reciprocity* (Bronfenbrenner, 1979) resembles the notion of parallel processes. Reciprocity refers to the progressive, mutual accommodation inside and between subsystems. When we take an aerial view, we see all subsystems co-evolving. These subsystems are children and parents, siblings, and partners, but also families and their home-visitor, and even the larger system of the family and all the services involved. Reciprocity denotes the process by which the *connections between* systems change because of internal or external pressures. After a system changes, it stabilises, until new pressures come up. Changes can be small, like trying out some new advice, or very large, like the adjustment of the parent-child relationship after divorce, or the adjustment of the family and home-visitor relationship during treatment termination.

The concept of reciprocity is especially visible in the progressive intertwining of problems in multi-problem families. This is because dysfunctional patterns function as both internal and external pressures.

* A research-illustration of this principle is the following: Bidgood and Van de Sande (1990) reviewed two types of home-based treatment programmes for the prevention of child abuse and neglect: parent training, focusing on parent-child interaction; and multi-faceted programmes, which address all family problems. It was quite evident that the latter type was more successful in preventing child-abuse and neglect. In other words, reciprocity must be acknowledged in both diagnosis and treatment.
* A second illustration is this: In research concerning Project at Home, a multi-faceted FPP for multi-problem families in Amsterdam, it was found that the degree of reciprocity of family members and home-visitors was predictive of the degree of improvement in parenting. Home-visits comprised a mixture of planned subjects and daily life events, which clearly proves the validity of the use of reciprocity and mutual adaptation of families and home-visitors (Vogelvang 1993).

Within families, and also in the interaction between the family, the home-visitor, and all the other institutions involved, all parties display a process of mutual adaptation. All parties, or systems, lay out their transactional patterns. In some cases this adaptation is very smooth, resulting in a swift start. In other cases, things go wrong. The following is an example of this:

Ayoub & Willett (1992) categorised over 100 families in an FPP by using factor analysis. All families were referred for incidents of child abuse and neglect. A typology with five types of families resulted. These types will be discussed, but an interpretation of them is also offered, using the concept of reciprocity.

1. **Situationally stressed** families suffered from transient problems in adjusting to life events. Treatment was short and very successful.
2. In **chronically stressed** families, there was a history of more than one problem, leading to recurrent crises. Treatment was of longer duration, but was quite successful in most cases, because in all families healthy aspects in family functioning could be identified and used as building blocks.
3. Families with **parental-emotional distress** were usually multi-problem families in which one or both parents suffered from post-traumatic stress, depression or other psychiatric problems. In these families, specific parent-child conflicts were not prevalent. Treatments tended to have the longest duration of all, thereby being very expensive. No improvements in family functioning were observed, but no deterioration either. Therefore, these families were referred to as 'zero-growth families'. Thus, treatment was very necessary, relatively quiet (there were no bad conflicts), and no changes occurred. What happened here, was that the responsibility for internal family processes was shared between the family and the institution offering treatment in a very balanced way. These treatments were cases of stable mutual accommodation between the family and the institution.
4. **Multirisk** families resembled families with parental emotional distress, but here, bad parent-child conflicts were present. Treatment in these families was not very successful and of moderate duration. What we see here is that mutual accommodation did not result in a long-standing stable pattern between family and institution. This is because the bad parent-child conflicts tended to destabilise the efforts of the home-visitor to adjust to the family. Also, the home-visitor's supervisor probably urged him or her to confront the ongoing abuse, thereby adding external pressure as well.
5. Finally, in **violent multirisk** families, treatment was very short and not successful at all. Because of the ongoing violence, child protective services increasingly emphasised the need for out-of-home placement of the child. Both internal and external pressure were very high, making it impossible for the home-visitor to create a stable and functional temporary system.

Ayoub and Willett's 'zero-growth families' are also the subject of Colapinto's writings (1995). He calls these families 'diluted families': these internally fragile families stabilise themselves by establishing firm bonds with social services. In the long run, their internal processes are taken over by the helping services. This pattern can fluctuate also, as was found by Mallucio, Fein and Davis (1994) in their recent evaluation of reunification programmes; *a child is removed from the home, the parents comply to treatment demands in order to be reunited with their child, reunification follows, and after a honeymoon-period, the situation deteriorates again, ending in removal of the child from the parents' home.* This is an example of what Mallucio calls an 'extrafamilial loop'. In times of instability, a family looks for stabilisation outside. In violent multirisk families, the home-visitor and family form a very unstable system. The home-visitor asks the supervisor for advice and, in this way, the unstable system is extended. As the supervisor becomes increasingly alarmed by the ongoing abuse, child protective services are called in, thus extending the system even further. The system responsible for internal family processes is being inflated, to ensure the functioning of the family, or even its existence.

Some research findings on this are as follows:

1. In 1988, Reid, Kagan and Schlosberg differentiated families for which FPP was successful, resulting in prevention of out-of-home placement of the referred child, from families in which the child was placed outside the home. It appeared that not only were the children and the families different, but so were their referring agencies.

Both the parents and the referring agencies in the placement-outside-the-home group appeared to be better connected to the FPP at the outset of treatment: everyone attended the first meeting and there were lots of telephone calls. In other words, everyone regarded the situation around the problem child as more problematic.

It appeared that both the family and the referring agency in the placement-outside-the-home group, found each other in a period of instability. In order to stabilise their mutual system, everyone worked together: the referring agency did its very best to get the family in treatment and took over some of the families responsibilities, the family did not abuse the child but didn't seem to be very interested either, and the problem child displayed more severe problem behaviour. In the group where out-of-home placement was prevented, parents were less dependent and more autonomous.

2. Mallucio, Fein and Davis (1994) evaluated research findings on several family reunification programmes. Three factors emerged as being predictive of re-entry into placement.

   a. The child had been placed out of the home more than once.
   b. Parents were more ambivalent about reunification with their child.
   c. Home-visitors and their supervisors were more ambivalent about reunification.

Mallucio states: 'It was found that service delivery variables can affect outcomes (re-entry into placement) as profoundly as child and family characteristics.

Ambivalence about reunification on the part of parents, practitioners, and administrators are unexpected correlates of re-entry into placement.'

Maluccio et al. refer to research conducted by Cheung, who found that difficulty in formulating workable goals with clients was directly related to re-entry into placement. Of course, this difficulty is a result of the ambivalence of the parties involved: *because this mutual system intends to stabilise itself, no fundamental changes are possible, leading to an inability to formulate workable goals.*

We must conclude that conducting process-oriented research which restricts itself to family variables only, can lead to partially valid results. If Mallucio and his colleagues had studied internal family variables only, they would have concluded that working with the ambivalence of parents can contribute to success. Of course, this is only partially true because external ambivalence played a very important part as well. Interventions aimed at the home-visitor, or even at child protection services, might also contribute to success. Maluccio, Fein and Davis studied the whole story and recommended that other researchers do the same: 'The whole story must be studied, not just the client's side'.

The above findings point out to us that a consistent use of the concept of reciprocity is warranted: in some cases the complexity of problems can extend to the referring agency system and to other helping services involved as well. In these cases, as Colapinto points out, the problems are not idiosyncratic interactional processes any longer. The problems are not located and workable only within the independent family system because 'the system is open, not just in the sense of being influenced by the social environment, but in the very specific sense of being managed by it'. It must be taken into account, then, in process-oriented research, that all parties are equally responsible for these merry-go-rounds (cycles) to keep on turning. We see these cycles within families as well as in the interplay of families and social services, although not in every case. Some families do not need to co-evolve with agencies, because they are able to maintain their independent functioning. Others need recurrent contact with social services in order to stabilise themselves.

5.2. *Nurturance versus disruption*

In this section we come to 'changing the whole story', to the subject of bringing about fundamental change in families. The model of change which is presented here is based on writings of Barry Dym (1988) and Jorge Colapinto (1995). These authors have published material on change in families. They rely on systems theory and the ecological theory.

This model of change, in a nutshell, consists of

- finding stable patterns and unstable patterns (*both within families and in their relationships with other systems*)
- locating their connections
- selecting one or more unstable patterns, and
- intervening at the right moment. There are two kinds of interventions to do this: disruption of dysfunctional patterns and nurturance of functional patterns (see Figure 12.2).

1. **Disruption.** Barry Dym quotes Salvador Minuchin, who advises the home-visitor, in order to bring about change, to do the following: disrupt *dysfunctional* patterns in times of instability, then retreat, and wait for change. What does this mean? In times of instability, habitual patterns emerge which bring the system back to its old and stable but dysfunctional state. For instance, in our scapegoating family, the parents might start to argue about something. This destabilises the scapegoating pattern, causing the problem-child to behave more badly. His or her actions stabilise the dysfunctional pattern again, and this state *disengages the family from the home-visitor*. The home-visitor needs to:
   a. block these habitual patterns, for instance by shifting the family's attention, prescribing 'no change', or circular questioning, etc., and
   b. retreat and *wait for the family to change on its own*.
   If we use the concept of reciprocity in a consistent way, we have to conclude that disrupting interventions can also be applied towards stable dysfunctional patterns of which *home-visitors* are part. Because of the parallel processes at work, this kind of intervention can lead to change in families as well.
2. **Nurturance:** Jorge Colapinto tells us that nurturance might be necessary, referring to the improvement of existing but *weak functional patterns*. This is especially the case in very disorganised and neglectful families in which stable but functional patterns are disrupted constantly, for instance by ambivalence about reunification (as we have seen). In this case, the opposite of resistance and disengagement is at work: the family gives up its independence. There is change, but it is professionalised change, which has no value

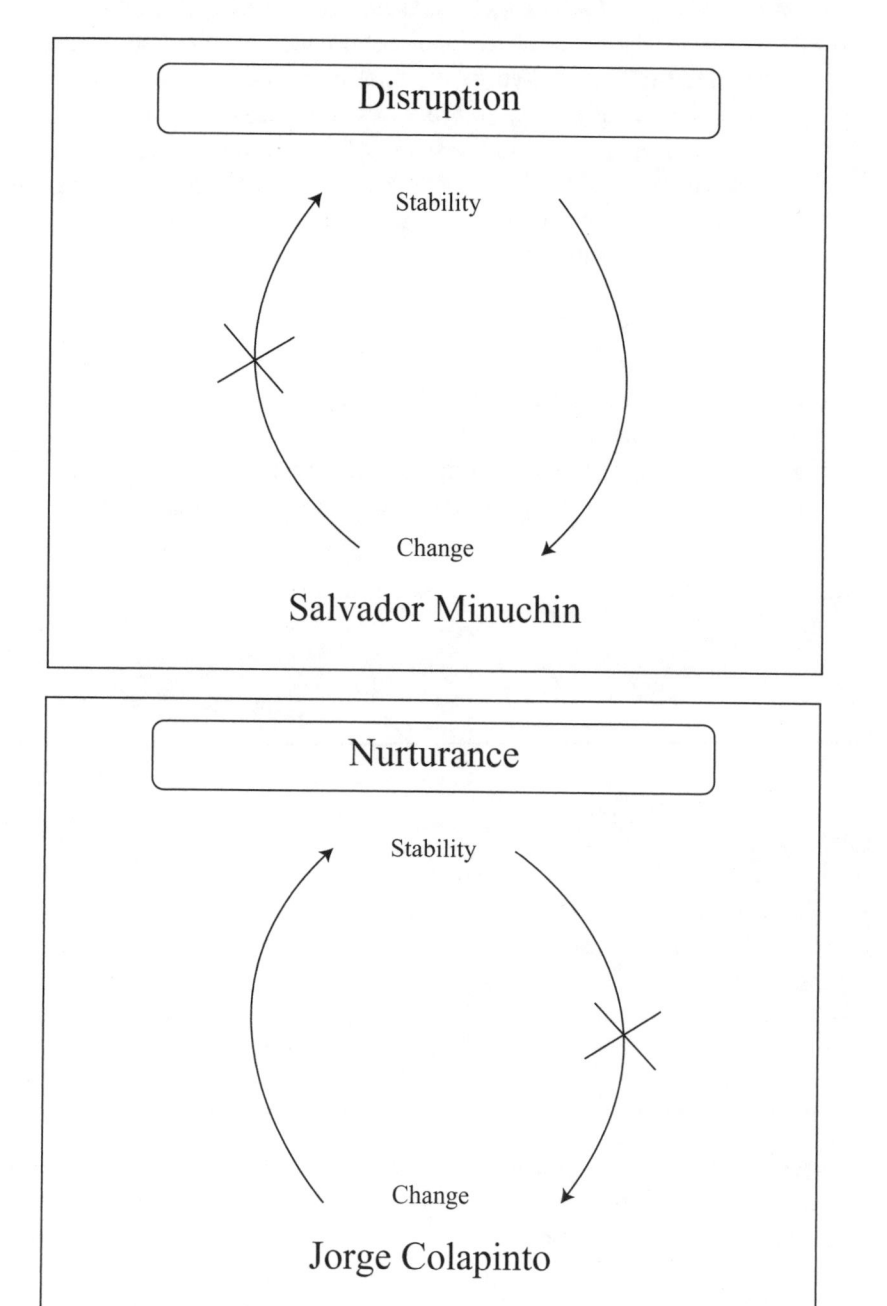

Disruption

Stability

Change

Salvador Minuchin

Nurturance

Stability

Change

Jorge Colapinto

for the family. In order to address these reactions to instability, Colapinto advises us to create and arrange situations in which problem-solving is carried out, and decisions are taken as much as possible by parents and children together. Colapinto advises us to *bring family-interactions back to the family.* The same arguments to extend the scope of disrupting interventions in Minuchin's case, apply to Colapinto's type of intervention: nurturance can also be used as external pressure for family change. It can be directed at the home-visitor, or even at team functioning.

5.3. A model of change

In order to bring about change, both the home-visitor and his or her back-ups - the supervisor and other team-members - have to choose between nurturance of functional patterns and disruption of dysfunctional patterns during treatment. To *choose between both,* we need to look at the ingredients of every cell first.

Reaction to instability/stress (family or trainer)	Family-intervention	Home-visitor/team – intervention
Dilution (enmeshment)	Family Nurturance –*planned* –*daily life*	Trainer Disruption
Disengagement	Family Disruption –*planned* –*daily life*	Trainer Nurturance

1. *Family nurturance.* Systems theory, applied to home-based treatment, tells us that an *alliance between family members and the home-visitor has to be formed.* Such an alliance can be formed by focusing on symptoms family members regard as acute. Pointing out these symptoms is an independent act of the family. These kinds of acts need to be nurtured. In most cases, treatment has to start with an emphasis on nurturance. This is an ingredient of home-based treatment programmes which appears as a successful element in many publications. In particular, the offering of concrete services is a good strategy to form this alliance. *This was found to be the case in both Intensive*

and regular Family Preservation Programmes, such as Families First (NIZW 1992), the Project at Home (Vogelvang 1993), and the SCOH reunification programme (Lawder and Poulin 1983). A second useful strategy is to take the family's side in all contacts and negotiations with the 'outside world'. This is what happened in the second successful intervention, in which the home-visitor accompanied Mrs Smith and her son to the day-care centre.

Later on during treatment, when an alliance has been formed, the nurturing of functional family processes remains just as important. Research findings support this. For example:

* In 1993 a process-oriented evaluation study was conducted on the Project at Home, a multi-faceted FPP for multi-problem families in Amsterdam. One of the results was that arranging situations in which parents and children were brought together around explicit games or tasks appeared to be predictive of parenting improvement. The more the home-visitor suc-ceeded in arranging this, the more parenting improved. During these situations, the home-visitor helped the parents to speak out, to formulate their thoughts, emotions, strategies and decisions out loud. The home-visitor did not take over. This is a clear example of the value of nurturing primary processes in family life.
* In the same research project, it was found that the parents' willingness to accept help significantly increased if the home-visitor paid **less** attention to the problem-child on his or her own. If this was done **together** with the parents, their willingness to accept help increased.

Another example of nurturance is the encouragement of positive communi-cation in Video-hometraining.

2. *Trainer/team disruption.* Disruption of patterns which include the home-visitor is the counterpart of nurturing family processes. This type of interven-tion generates external pressure for families. As treatment proceeds, there is a chance of home-visitors becoming too involved in the family system. The kind of problems the family present can be overwhelming. Many home-visitors respond to this by feeling responsible for change. This can easily lead to a stable pattern which is counterproductive to change. What is needed is a disruption of this pattern, thereby nurturing the family's primary responsibility and freeing the home-visitor. An example of this is the following:

In 1995, a process-oriented research study into LOV-training was conducted. This is a short and intensive home-based treatment conducted in combination with day-care. Parent-child contacts around arranged games and activities are videotaped and discussed with family members. The emphasis in these discussions is on family-members formulating their own opinions. Clearly, this is an example of nurturing. The supervisors of this programme make explicit use of a model of change. When elements of supervision which contributed to change in families were looked for, the following results were found (Vogelvang 1995):

1. In successful treatments, there was a constant search for dysfunctional interaction-patterns between the family and home-visitor which primarily originated in the home-visitor. These patterns consisted of the taking over of internal family-processes by the home-visitor. For instance, by asking questions in a suggestive manner, or by being too directive, the home-visitor blocked any opportunity on the part of the family to formulate their own opinions.
2. After such a pattern had been detected, the supervisor did not take over either! If he had done, he would have been responsible for even further dilution of the family. Instead, the home-visitor was asked during supervision to formulate a solution. In order to safeguard nurturance in the family, a disrupting intervention was used towards the home-visitor. This was much more prevalent in successful treatments.

Korittko (1994) gives us the same advice: Because most families have experienced and created fast changes in their relationships, loss of contact, and interpersonal instability within and outside their system, slow building of trust is necessary: 'I feel strongly that it is a mistake to take over functions in the family too quickly (...). This can send a message of incompetence to the parents, which can either lead to feelings of competition and rejection or to high expectations and a process of infantilisation.'

3. *Family disruption.* The case of the home-visitor bringing his overall in a plastic bag is an example of a disrupting intervention. The family's disengagement, in the form of an increasingly dirty house, was answered by prescribing no change in a very visual manner. The home-visitor showed the family, by putting on his overall, that he had given up. The only thing he could think of now, was to prevent becoming dirty or sick himself. Most of the time, because home-visitors feel responsible, it is very hard for them to apply disrupting interventions. It feels like they are abandoning the family after an alliance has been formed. But in many cases disruption is necessary. It just takes too long for crippling symptoms to disappear when only functional patterns are nurtured. The following is an example of this: One of the results of research into the Project at Home was that there was a significantly lower

improvement in parenting when more attention was given to the parents' marital problems. Of course, this was no surprise: Time and energy were not used for solving parenting problems, but were consumed by the partners. However, parenting problems **did** improve if the home-visitor showed his or her disappointment about not being able to work on parenting: 'All this talking about your relationship did not help your child up to now, which is too bad'. By reacting in this way, the home-visitor blocked a habitual pattern. (Vogelvang 1993).

4. *Trainer/team nurturance.* Nurturing interventions towards the home-visitor are very much needed in order to ensure 'clean' family disruptions. To support the home-visitor in using disrupting interventions, the supervisor has to make sure that the decision to apply such an intervention is independently taken by the home-visitor. He himself has to know why and decide how to apply it. The home-visitor should not disrupt a family pattern because he feels angry, disappointed, frustrated, or afraid. When this happens, the home-visitor has taken over the family's problems. This refers to *counter-transference* by home-visitors. This in itself is not a bad sign, because these emotions can function as very important cues for both understanding the family's problems and discovering the home-visitor's more personal dilemmas. They are the key to getting closer to the family. Kagan and Schlosberg, in their book 'Families in perpetual crisis' (1989) give us very useful tools for both disrupting the family's resistance and nurturing the home-visitor's cognitive and emotional household at the same time. 'It is what the family helper has experienced in life herself or himself, what emotionally touches him or her in the beginning, that allows him or her to make contact to the family's inner circle.' (Goldbrunner 1989). 'The family worker who is able to address painful issues in his or her family will be better able to work with the extreme pain and despair in chronic crisis-oriented families.' (Kagan & Schlosberg 1989).

5. A last important point refers to the subjects or themes during home-visits. A valid distinction is possible between *planned and arranged* activities during home-visits, versus *unpredictable or even chaotic* daily-life occasions for disruption and nurturance. In many programme-descriptions it is mentioned that working together with the family around normal, daily life-subjects is equally important as working in a planned, structured way. In other words, being totally dependent on planned activities impoverishes the potential impact of home-based treatment, as does using primarily daily life as working material. Balancing both is very important. Two research findings to illustrate this are:

* In the research of the Project at Home mentioned before, it was found that reciprocity between family members and home-visitors was predictive of the improvement of parenting. Successful treatments, in terms of the improvement of parenting and problem-behaviour of the referred child, included a mixture of planned subjects and daily life events during visits. In particular, daily-life events in the form of small crises were very important occasions in this respect. When these incidents occur, for instance a washing machine breaking down or a child coming home after being bullied at school, chances of taking over by the home-visitor are multiplied by a factor of ten. Holding on to nurturance of the family's own process on these occasions also proved to be predictive of treatment success. The home-visitor tried to make sure that the decision on how to solve the crisis at hand was made by the family members themselves. The home-visitor only offered some small assistance, such as suggesting a good repair-person for the washing machine or even dialing the number, but not making the telephone call. On the other hand, treatments were also more successful when parents were willing to engage in planned and arranged activities. This clearly proves the validity of **mutual** adaptation of the family's daily lives and the home-visitor's plans (Vogelvang 1993).
* This finding was also reported by Families First. After the offering of concrete services, the number of interruptions and suggestions made by parents during visits was the second strongest predictive factor of successful treatment, in terms of preventing out-of-home placement (NIZW 1992).
* In research, conducted into both LOV-training and Video-hometraining, it was found that both parenting and the children's behaviour problems showed more improvement if the home-visitor succeeded in holding on to his or her methodical principles (Vogelvang 1993; 1995). In other words, there were relatively few 'surprises' (critical incidents) during treatment. Interestingly, both methods focus completely on nurturance of family processes, and both methods use a structured approach to encourage these. In other words, if planned nurturance by home-visitors was 'attacked' by chaotic disrupting events, the home-visitor was left behind speechless. This clearly shows the importance of balancing. Multi-problem families will disengage themselves from home-based treatment programmes which fail to prepare home-visitors to have flexible answers to daily-life events.

6. Recommendations

In order to conduct process-oriented research which takes both factors into account, the following is recommended:

First: Decide to follow Maluccio's advice: *The whole story must be studied.* Before you start to hand out questionnaires, take an aerial view and look at all parties involved, yourself included.

Second: Select a set of appropriate variables:

Input:
- etiology
- severity of problems / healthy aspects
- helping history / dilution in dynamics of social services
- role of involved institutions
- stable versus unstable patterns

Throughput/family:
- treatment goals
- treatment form
- interventions: nurturing / disrupting
- planned activities and daily-life events
- critical incidents

Throughput/worker:
- stable versus unstable patterns
- holding on to methodical principles
- co-ordination of involved institutions

Output:
- treatment success in terms of achieving programme goals
- treatment success in terms of client autonomy
- treatment success in terms of client satisfaction

And finally: Choose to work with a model of change. Without discussing and finally adopting a model of change and evaluating it, researchers implicitly still adopt an instrumental, medical model of linear causality. This means identifying effective ingredients in terms of one-to-one relationships between the home-visitors' actions and the changes in families. Of course, reality will never fit in. Looking for contributions to change without using a model of change will eventually frustrate home-visitors because they are implicitly promised cook-books. In this way, a full ecological and systemic approach is lost. It is like admitting the fact that there is a solar system, but still putting the earth and moon (family and home-visitor) in the centre of it.

References

Ayoub, C.C. and Willett, J.B. (1992), Families at risk of child maltreatment: entry-level characteristics and growth in family function during treatment. *Child Abuse and Neglect*, vol. 16, 495-511.

Bronfenbrenner, U. (1979), *The ecology of human development*, Cambridge, Mass., Harvard University Press.

Bath, H.I. and Haapala, D.A. (1993), Intensive family preservation services with abused and neglected children: an examination of group differences, *Child Abuse and Neglect*, vol. 17, 213-225.

Bidgood, B.A. and Van de Sande, A. (1990), Home-based programming for a child welfare clientele, in M. Rothery and G. Cameron (eds), *Child Maltreatment: Expanding our concept of helping*, Hillsdale, New Jersey, Lawrence Erlbaum Associates.

Coenegracht, A., De hulpverlener als gezinslid, *Welzijnsmaandblad*, vol. 39, no. 3, 24-29.

Colapinto, J.A. (1995), Dilution of family process in social services: implications for treatment of neglectful families, *Family Process*, vol. 34, no. 3, 59-74.

Dym, B. (1988), Ecological perspectives on change in families, in H.B. Weiss & F.H. Jacobs, *Evaluating family programs?* New York, Aldine de Gruyter.

Fein, E. and Staff, I. (1993), Last best chance: findings from a reunification services program, *Child Welfare*, vol. 72, no. 1, 25-40.

Goldbrunner, H. (1989), *Arbeit mit Problemfamilien*, Mainz, Mathias Grunewald Verlag.

Jacobs, F.H. (1988), The five-tiered approach to evaluation: Context and implementation, in H.B. Weiss and F.H. Jacobs, *Evaluating family programs*, New York, Aldine de Gruyter.

Kagan, R.M. and Schlosberg, S.B. (1989), *Families in perpetual crisis*, New York, Norton.

Korittko, A. (1994), In-home treatment for families in crisis and its supervision: a systemic multi-level approach, *Contemporary Family Therapy*, vol. 16, no. 3, 231-243.

Lawder, E.A. and Poulin, J.E. (1983), *Helping the multi-problem family: a study of services to children in their own homes* (SCOH), Philadelphia, Children's Aid Society of Pennsylvania.

Maluccio, A.N., Fein, E. and Davis, I.P. (1994), Family Reunification: Research findings, issues, and directions, *Child Welfare*, vol. 53, no. 5, 489-504.

Nelson, K.E., Landsman, M.J. and Deutelbaum, W. (1990), Three models of family-centered placement prevention services, *Child Welfare*, vol. 69, no. 1, 3-21.

NIZW (1992), *Families First, een verslag*, Utrecht, NIZW.

Powell, D.R. (1988), Towards an understanding of the program variable in comprehensive parent support programs, in, H.B. Weiss and F.H. Jacobs, *Evaluating family programs*, New York, Aldine de Gruyter.

Reid, W.J., Kagan, R.M. and Schlosberg, S.B. (1988), Prevention of placement: critical factors in program success, *Child Welfare*, vol. 67, no. 1, 25-36

Vogelvang, B.O. (1993), *Video-hometraining "Plus" en het Project aan Huis; verheldering van twee methodieken voor intensieve pedagogische thuisbehandeling.* Academisch proefschrift Vrije Universiteit Amsterdam, Enschede, CopyPrint 2000. *(Video-hometraining "Plus" and the Project at Home; clarification of two methods for intensive home-based pedagogical treatment.)*

Vogelvang, B.O. (1995), *Leren Opvoeden met Video. Evaluatie van LOV-training vanuit het Boddaert Centrum Apeldoorn*, Amsterdam, Vakgroep Pedagogiek Vrije Universiteit / Apeldoorn, Boddaert Centrum.

Zarski, J.J., Aponte, H.J., Bixenstine, C. and Cibik, P. (1992), Beyond home-based family intervention: a multi-family approach toward change, *Contemporary Family Therapy*, vol. 14, no. 1, 3-15.

13 Evaluating family preservation services: Asking the right questions[1]

Francine H. JACOBS
Patricia H. WILLIAMS
Jennifer L. KAPUSCIK

Family preservation programmes are intensive, home-based services of relatively short duration that are offered to families at imminent risk of having a child placed out-of-home; families in which the child is in acute danger are not considered eligible. The central goal of family preservation is to improve the family's child-rearing abilities to the point where the family unit may be maintained without endangering the child. Unnecessary out-of-home placements should be reduced as a result. Many programme participants, providers and supporters are convinced of the effectiveness of this approach, though relatively few of these efforts have been evaluated successfully by conventional methods.

Over the past several years, and particularly in the past year, family preservation services in the United States have taken centre stage in a national debate about child welfare, and they have come to be seen as the first step in attempts to reform the child protective services (CPS) system. All this visibility has raised increasingly frequent questions about FPS' effectiveness - how well do they work? What goals do they accomplish? Almost 20 years of evaluation research have not yielded definitive answers, and it is not clear that we will ever be able to respond with certitude to these questions. Nonetheless, it is important to consider what we **have** learned, both about the impact of family preservation and about our ability to discern it, in order to improve services to these vulnerable families.

This chapter is divided into two sections: in the first, I will briefly describe three 'waves' of family preservation evaluation research that have been undertaken in the United States, identify the strengths and limitations to past approaches, and summarise the findings from these studies. In the second portion, mindful of the challenges family preservation poses to evaluators, I will recommend promising evaluation activities for the future.

The first wave of evaluations

The first set of FPS evaluations were carried out from the late 1970s through the early 1990s. These evaluations began as small-scale efforts, focused on individual programmes; later, several programmes within particular states were combined for study. A substantial percentage of these evaluations were of the Homebuilders model in Washington and Utah. Placement rates and other system-based indicators (for example, length of stay in out-of-home care, if placed) were selected as the central outcome measures; post-test only or pre- and post-test designs generally were employed. For those studies relying on placement rates the post-test only designs were seen to be stringent enough because, given the 'imminent risk' eligibility criterion for entry into family preservation, the assumption was that without the programme the placement rate would be close to 100 per cent. Thus, for example, any forestalling or elimination of the need to place a child could be legitimately claimed as a success.

This group of evaluations boasted wildly positive findings, suggesting that FPS was successful in avoiding placement for at least two-thirds of all families involved. These rates ranged from 75-93 per cent of families immediately after treatment (Callister, Mitchell, and Tolley, 1986; Nelson, 1991; Pecora, Fraser and Haapala, 1992; Spaid and Fraser, 1991; Thieman and Dail, 1993); 86-100 per cent of families 3-months post-intervention (Bartsch, Kawamura and Seely, 1993; Kinney, Haapala, Booth and Leavitt, 1990); and 69-96 per cent of families at one year after the cessation of services (Bartsch, Kawamura, and Seely, 1993; Bath and Haapala, 1993; Bath, Richey and Haapala, 1992; Cunningham, Homer, Bass and Brown, 1993; Haapala and Kinney, 1988; Kinney, Haapala, Booth and Leavitt, 1990; Nelson, 1990; Thieman and Dail, 1992a; 1992b). FPS was also found to be less costly when compared to providing foster care and other types of out-of-home placement (Bartsch, Kawamura and Seely, 1993; Cunningham, Homer, Bass and Brown, 1993; Kinney, Haapala, Booth and Leavitt, 1990; Kinney, Madsen, Fleming and Booth, 1977; Nelson, 1990; New York City Department of Juvenile Justice, 1992; 1993).

Child welfare reformers were heartened by these results, and it appears that they added fuel to the growing movement in the United States towards retaining seriously abused and neglected children in their own homes. However, the studies were criticised roundly, and largely appropriately, on numerous methodological grounds. Two related concerns - the lack of any, or of any reliable, comparison data, and the reliance on placement rates as principal outcome measures - were among the most frequently cited criticisms (Frankel, 1988; Rossi, 1992b). To the first, the usually-noted limitations of non-experimental design were applied. Claims of causal effects were disputed by those familiar with the exigencies of child protective service practice: they posited that not all families 'at imminent risk' actually experienced placement, so how was one to gauge the net effect, if any, of the programme? (Rossi, 1992b). Clearly many other factors could have accounted for the impacts observed.

The popularity of placement rates as the measure of success was also seen as especially problematic. Peter Rossi (1991; 1992a; 1992b), among others, argued that these rates are not independent measures of programme effectiveness because of the many influences 'outside the programme', including political and judicial forces, that affect policy and placement decisions (Rossi, 1991, 1992a, 1992b). For example, they may more accurately reflect top-down agency directives ('we are going to reduce placements') than 'true' improvements in family life that obviate the need for child removal (Berlin, 1992; Kirk, 1993). In addition, the focus on reduced placement rates neglects the fact that placement can sometimes be in the best interest of the child (Berlin, 1992), and that increased contact between workers and clients during the course of FPS may actually make family problems more evident and placement more likely (Bath and Haapala, 1994). Furthermore, even if these indicators were to be considered appropriate, the studies did not measure them consistently or comprehensively. Some considered placement with a family member an 'out-of-home' arrangement while others did not; many concerned themselves with foster care placement only, failing to consider placements in other systems of care (i.e. mental health) or those placement decisions made outside public systems altogether (i.e. child runaways) (Blythe, Salley, and Jayaratne, 1994).

The programme goal to reduce placement rates was expected to have direct effects on child welfare costs, and several studies reported these positive results (see, for example, Kinney, Haapala, Booth and Leavitt, 1990). However, many of these cost studies were relatively primitive in design: for example, they assumed that all comparable cases would have experienced placement had they not been enrolled in FPS (Nelson, 1990); they only considered typical FPS programme and out-of-home placement costs, not the other services and resources that may have been utilised by the family (particularly after termination from the programme); and because they generally only tracked families for a short period after programme termination, they could not account for the costs incurred by families in which placement was delayed but not eliminated (Frankel, 1988).

Because most of the programmes in these early years claimed reduced out-of-home placements and CPS costs as their pre-eminent goals, this choice of outcome indicators is understandable from the evaluator's perspective. On the other hand, both evaluators and programme personnel missed opportunities to refine programme intervention theory and to uncover other programme effects - on child and family functioning, for example - by not being more thoughtful and deliberate in generating a diverse set of goals and attempting to measure progress towards attaining them.

In summary, then, this first wave of evaluations produced conditions ripe for what researchers would call Type I errors (false positives). They demonstrated significant programme effects, but the designs were relatively weak and the choice of outcome measures overly constrained. While it is likely that FPS did affect placement rates, based on these data, it is not possible to determine accurately the extent of that effect.

The second wave of evaluations

The second wave of evaluations profited from lessons learned in the earlier generation. During the 1990s, larger scale, controlled studies were undertaken, usually by state agencies or groups of programmes. These evaluations generally utilised quasi-experimental or experimental designs, and diversified the outcomes to be measured.

A range of approaches to controls was taken in these studies. Some used enhanced non-experimental designs combining pre- and post-testing of subjects with small comparison groups (Fraser, Pecora and Haapala, 1991). More studies used a quasi-experimental method studying several types of control groups (see Rossi, 1991; 1992a; 1992b), including unserved families (Fraser, Pecora and Haapala, 1991; Yuan, McDonald, Wheeler, Struckman-Johnson and Rivest, 1990), matched or constructed comparison groups (Schwartz, AuClaire and Harris, 1991; University Associates, 1993), and retrospective 'randomly selected' groups of programme graduates and others (Collier and Hill, 1993). Experimental designs with randomised control groups were attempted by several evaluators (Feldman, 1991; Henggeler, Melton and Smith, 1992; Schuerman, Rzepnicki, Littell and Chak, 1993; Schuerman, Rzepnicki and Littell, 1994); the largest being the state-wide experiment with Illinois' Families First conducted by John Schuerman et al. (1993; 1994).

These studies also broadened the range of outcomes examined to include measures of child, parent, and family functioning. For example, various standardised measures were utilised to assess child outcomes such as well-being (Berry, 1993; Feldman, 1991; Yuan et al., 1990), behaviour problems (Henggeler et al., 1992; Hornick, Phillips and Kerr, 1989; Wells and Whittington, 1993), and social competence and peer relations (Hengegler et al., 1992). Functional measures such as juvenile rearrest, reconviction, and reincarceration rates (Collier and Hill, 1993; Hengegler et al., 1992) were also used. In addition, evaluations began including parent and family measures, tapping domains such as parent-child conflict (Wells and Whittington, 1993), overall parental functioning (Feldman, 1991; Schuerman et al., 1993; Schuerman et al., 1994), stress and support (Feldman, 1991; Fraser et al., 1991; Schuerman et al., 1994; Wells and Whittington, 1993), and family relations (Berry, 1993; Feldman, 1991; Fraser et al., 1991; Henggeler et al., 1992; Scannapieco, 1993; Thieman and Dail, 1992a; 1992b; Wells and Whittington, 1993).

The findings were disappointing to programme proponents. Indeed, even though these studies searched for effects across many more domains of child, parent, family and agency functioning than did the previous generation, they turned up few statistically significant results. Furthermore, even when effects were identified in a number of studies, they were contested by the results of others. For example, several studies showed significant differences in placement rates between treatment and control groups (Henggeler et al., 1992; Schwartz et al., 1991), while others did not (Schuerman et al., 1994; Schuerman et al., 1993; University Associates, 1993; Yuan et al., 1990). Others such as Feldman (1991) found initial differences in placement rates but the strength of the effect dissipated over time. The only somewhat consistent statistically significant positive results were modest improvements in certain discrete aspects of child and family functioning.

This wave of evaluations addressed some of the more glaring methodological shortcomings of the earlier evaluations. Nonetheless, these evaluations also were criticised, appropriately, on methodological grounds (see Rossi 1992a; 1992b; 1993). These included, for example, the lack of attention to treatment integrity and control group activity, sample sizes too small to detect significant effects, and the differential attrition from treatment and control groups. The resistance of caseworkers to make random assignments also was noted.

There are at least two important aspects to the issue of treatment integrity. First, expectations of effects from family preservation initially were based on the Homebuilders model. To the extent that evaluators sought to measure effects from different, usually less intensive, programme models, they were, in essence, changing the terms of the bargain. Yet several, including the often-noted recent experiment evaluating Illinois' Families First, were based on programme models that departed substantially from that of Homebuilders (see Schuerman et al., 1993; Schuerman et al., 1994; Henggeler et al., 1992). Second, even in those studies of programmes that purported to be implementing Homebuilders or another specific model of family preservation, there was insufficient attention to documenting the extent to which the model was implemented faithfully; wide variations across sites in multisite studies were common.

Documentation of the services comparison groups families received also was lacking. While all children with substantiated maltreatment are served in some way by the public protective service system, several studies in this wave failed to specify which child protective, and other, services were being used by clients in the control groups (Rossi 1991; 1992a; 1992b). These services were simply described, for example, as 'traditional services' (Blythe et al., 1994), 'existing community services' (Feldman, 1991), 'usual services' (Henggeler et al., 1992), or as out-of-home placements such as 'foster care' (Collier and Hill, 1993; Schwartz et al., 1991; University Associates, 1993). It may be, in fact, that the treatment and control groups were receiving similar services, particularly if the model of family preservation being promoted by the child welfare agency was a less intensive one, and other similar support programmes were available within the community (Yuan et al., 1990).

Regarding the resistance of workers to random assignment, Schuerman et al. (1993) ultimately had to drop one of the seven sites from their analyses because of the workers' failure to follow random assignment protocols. In summarising some of the problems in implementing random assignment, Kaye and Bell (1993b) noted that early attempts were often thwarted because caseworkers felt it was unethical to risk a child's safety by randomly assigning her or him to treatment versus control groups or were hesitant about referring families to FPS if they had a chance of ending up not being served at all.

However interesting the methodological lessons from this wave of evaluations, perhaps the more critical one to learn concerned an aspect of programme operations - the targeting of services.

The original intent of programmes such as Homebuilders was to serve those families at 'imminent risk' for having their children removed from the home. However straightforward the intent, this criterion has proven difficult, in fact virtually impossible, to apply consistently across cases and workers. On the one hand, workers appear reluctant to use it for many families they perceive as needing services often only available through family preservation. On the other hand, families thought to be at imminent risk of placement by one worker often are not ultimately placed. The placement rates of control groups bear out this fact.

One would assume that if treatment and comparison groups were truly at imminent risk of placement at the time of referral, all or nearly all of those children assigned to the control group would be placed shortly after referral (Blythe et al., 1994). However, once studies began to utilise comparison groups, a very different picture emerged. While prior research found that treatment group families had low placement rates, work in this wave found that control group families also tended to remain intact, with placement rates ranging only from 7-24 per cent (Feldman, 1991; Schuerman et al., 1994; Schuerman et al., 1993; University Associates, 1993; Yuan et al., 1990). Even when caseworkers paid special attention to the level of imminent risk of placement of families included

211

in evaluation studies, assuring a high level of risk for all entrants, and equivalence of risk between treatment and control groups, proved extremely challenging. For example, while caseworkers in the study of Michigan's Families First claimed that 96 per cent of families in treatment and control groups were at risk, only 24 per cent of matched comparison children were placed during a one-year period following the intervention (University Associates, 1993). This programme implementation problem has held serious consequences for evaluations seeking to establish the effectiveness of FPS.

The findings from the second wave of evaluations suggest that family preservation does not have broad, significant effects on children, families, or child protective service system behaviours. However, given the inability of the programmes to implement the targeting component faithfully, and the additional methodological problems that emerged, these results may represent Type II errors ('false negatives'). That is, there may well have been many significant effects from the programmes, but the research has been unable to capture them. This is thought to be a common situation for complex social programmes (Posavac and Carey, 1989).

The third wave of evaluations

Current evaluation efforts have brought further refinements in evaluation questions, research design, and outcome measurement. (See Pecora, Fraser, Nelson, McCroskey, and Meezan, 1995.) Among the most ambitious is a US Department of Health and Human Services project, the National Evaluation of Family Preservation Services. This study is an attempt to describe six selected family preservation programmes and to evaluate their impact on children and families using an experimental design. At the present time, four sites have been tentatively selected: three placement prevention-oriented FPS programmes and one family reunification programme. The evaluation intends to answer a broad array of questions, including the following:

1 Does FPS prevent placement and placement re-entry?
2 Does it alter children's placement careers (length of stay, length of reunification, etc.)?
3 Are outcomes for children and families improved?
4 For which subgroups does the programme work well? What are the characteristics of 'successful families'?
5 Which combinations of services produce which outcomes?
6 Which combinations of services are most cost-effective?

Because this study is still in its planning phase, it is difficult to be more specific about its design. The evaluators involved with it include a number of the most eminent family preservation researchers in the United States. Nonetheless, it has caused considerable controversy in policy, programme and research circles, as many debate the possibility of successfully undertaking an experimental evaluation of so complex a programme as family preservation.

Getting to the bottom line: What do we know about the effectiveness of family preservation?

A kind interpretation of the findings available to date is that they are equivocal: It is possible, in fact likely, that family preservation works for many families in a range of situations, but so far the research has provided little guidance in identifying those families and situations. Powerful effects generally have emerged from less 'powerful' designs, but the more powerful designs have their own methodological limitations, and are cumbersome and expensive to implement. FPS does not appear, at this point, to be 'the' solution to the problems besetting the child welfare system or the families within it. On the other hand, family preservation has been 'oversold' by many parties; it probably is not reasonable to expect the full range of effects that have potentially been attributed to this intervention.

This said, here are some tentative conclusions based on the research available to date:

1 It seems likely that FPS affects placement rates, though it is difficult to figure out exactly how and by how much. From their early review of the literature, Wells and Biegel (1991) conclude that FPS prevents or delays the placement of about one half of children, when comparing the placement rates of those in treatment and controls who were placed during the first two months of service delivery (those they defined as truly at imminent risk of placement). Others have drawn similar conclusions. The original criticisms of using placement rates, of course, still apply.

2 Programme effects seem relatively short-lived, with little information currently available to inform us about what happens to families 12 months post-intervention. In general, it has been found that differences in placement rates between treatment and control groups dissipate within 12 months after services are terminated, with families with adolescents being most vulnerable. Nearly one half of teens experience a placement 12-14 months post-referral (Wells and Biegel, 1991).

3 Most families are not 'cured' after FPS, although results from the second wave of evaluations do suggest modest increases in positive child and family

213

functioning. In general, studies have shown families to improve more in certain areas (recognition and motivation to solve problems, residence security, children's behaviour problems, family cohesion, and parental acceptance, discipline and child care), and less in others (changes in the overall family environment, child well-being, and perceived social support) (Berry, 1993; Collier and Hill, 1993; Feldman, 1991; Hengegler et al., 1992; Hornick et al., 1989; Schuerman et al., 1994; Wells and Whittington, 1993; Yuan et al., 1990).

4 There may be significant effects on other potential beneficiaries - the child welfare system, local communities, other public systems serving children - that have not yet been examined empirically. Several researchers (Family Preservation Evaluation Project, in preparation; Kaye and Bell, 1993a; 1993b; Wells and Biegel, 1991) suggest that diversifying the thinking about who can profit from family preservation services, and how they can profit, might render visible some 'effects' that have not yet been measured.

The most obvious explanation of 'no effects' evaluation results is that there is a **theory failure** and, indeed, the programme simply does not work. Regarding family preservation this would mean that our notion of how families change through receipt of these services is incorrect. But there are alternative explanations for the inability to establish programme effects. A second possibility is **implementation failure** - that is, the theory of intervention may be correct, but the programme has not been implemented as it should be. Thus the results are not achievable. Finally, one can explain 'no effects' conclusions as resulting from a **research or evaluation failure**. In this case it would mean that the intervention theory is correct, and the programme may even have been implemented as designed, but the methods available for measuring these effects are unavailable or faulty in some way.

Given the range of both implementation and research failures with family preservation, it appears shortsighted to conclude that there is a theory failure, and that the intervention is ineffective. On the other hand, evidence of its effectiveness based in traditional methodologies is sparse. What are the next steps for evaluators interested in this programme?

A new evaluation agenda

We suggest here a shift in focus for evaluators. With almost two decades of providing family preservation under our belts, we should be more sophisticated about the kinds of evaluation questions we now ask. We have been so focused on answering the 'big' question of 'whether or not it works, once and forever', that we have neglected other important questions along the way. For example, insofar as we are interested in programme impact, it is better to ask questions about who it *appears* to work well for and who not, under which conditions, *to the best of our ability to measure.* These, however, are not satisfying questions for many programme advocates and methodologists - advocates want to believe it serves all 'imminent risk' families equally well, and scientists only credit questions that allow for certain, causal conclusions. Nevertheless, these are critical 'next generation' questions.

In addition, having promoted a particular model of family preservation (in the US, the Homebuilders model), we have not been as open to learning about how and why the model has been modified (and how it needs to be modified), what participants really think about its possible effectiveness, and where its likely limitations are. It is time for these questions as well.

Burning family preservation evaluation issues. When evaluation is done 'right', it provides a detailed picture of what the programme actually is, including the following:

- who it serves
- how it defines and measures success
- the theories of change that undergird it
- the participants for whom it appears to work and those for whom it appears not to work
- what adaptations to the model exist, and how they appear to effect participants
- what participants think of the service - their satisfaction and their perceptions of effects, and
- the effects of its particular context (eg. resources in the community) on the possibilities of success.

In the absence of this information, disappointing impact evaluation results are difficult to interpret or counteract, and data-driven programme improvements impossible to make. Evaluations have paid too little attention to this description. For example, it is hard to imagine many brief interventions with families in serious crises (including FPS) powerful enough to sustain themselves without good, step-down, wrap-around community services ready to move in after the family is stabilised. But evaluations rarely collect information on what services are available, accessible, and then used, after family preservation efforts are finished. This information is critical to understanding why some families remain intact, or remain relatively well-functioning, and others do not.

Similarly, most evaluations, certainly those at the state and county levels, have used social or other service indicators - placement rates and length of placement among the most frequent - as measures of success. These are understandable and necessary choices, and must continue to be collected. But programmes themselves think about success much more broadly, and tailor their definitions of success specifically for each family. This is absolutely as it should be. So, a parent getting to work on time may be a major accomplishment. A great deal of misunderstanding about the programme can ensue when these 'smaller' goals are not credited in an evaluation.

To be more specific, it makes sense to explore the following:

The population in family preservation

Many studies have described family preservation clients using the static variables available in protective service agency MIS's: for example, child age, sex, and disability, if any; family characteristics, such as race, composition, SES, parental problems; and event characteristics, eg. type and severity of maltreatment, number of perpetrators, and the like. There is additional, and more perhaps more illuminating, information to collect and analyse - for example, the number and types of previous family contact with the child welfare system; the type of collateral family involvement with other service systems, the nature and quality of a family's social support network, including kin; and the parent's openness and motivation to change. This information would provide a much fuller profile of family preservation clients, and would begin to help us tease out the differential effects of family preservation based on, perhaps, more meaningful or influential characteristics.

The threshold for inclusion in family preservation

Many child welfare administrators and programme founders have attempted a series of actions to correct the targeting problem. Our guess is that because referral for family preservation is so context dependent - influenced dramatically by the range and depth of other services available to caseworkers within the CPS and outside it, and by the caseworker's skills, experience and beliefs - we will never achieve the optimal approach to targeting, applied uniformly across states and programmes. That said, there is something important to learn about what criteria which workers use to enrol families in FPS, especially if we can gain an understanding of what else is available for families in each CPS office locale. This investigation would begin to illuminate the complement of services workers feel are necessary to address adequately a variety of family crises, some of which legitimately belong in FPS and some of which do not. This issue relates in a central way to CPS reform.

Family preservation programmes generally require the worker and family to develop a list of goals for the period of the intervention. While maintaining family integrity is always present in those lists, there are many other intermediate goals that are thought to help secure that end - learning and applying anger management techniques, setting out and enforcing contracts for reasonable behaviour with teenage children, cleaning up the apartment and keeping the refrigerator stocked, etc. For many families attaining these mediating goals represents enormous achievement and growth; workers and families know this. But evaluations rarely discuss the smaller steps that families take on the road to preserving the family unit, reducing all that work and progress to measuring placement rates. No doubt, this approach loses account of a good deal of forward movement that families make, especially when, in some cases, the child ends up in an out of-home placement for a period of time nonetheless.

It is time to 'unpack' these more modest programme goals for the public to see. This would have a number of benefits. First, it would more accurately enumerate the successes of family preservation: goals such as getting a child to school each day, or establishing and maintaining a drug-free household, have face validity to them; they do not have to be linked to reduced placements for people to appreciate their value. This unpacking would also help the field articulate a more refined theory of the intervention. (We mean here something like, 'when A happens, then it is likely that B will happen, which we expect will yield C'.) This is in keeping with the now popular approach to evaluating community-based initiatives, 'theory-driven evaluation', that Carol Weiss and others are promoting. Finally, in so doing, it would allow for informed discussion about the assumptions that underlie FPS, and whether or how they might be modified to achieve a more effective service.

Implementing family preservation services

To the extent that agencies have adopted the Homebuilders model for their family preservation services, it is important to know the degree to which there is 'treatment integrity' in these programmes. Are the range and types of services available that were originally thought to be necessary to achieve the results? To the extent that they are not, how much and in what ways do these departures appear to affect the power of the programmes to achieve the desired effects?

Understanding the intensity, duration and nature of the family preservation services actually provided also helps develop the intervention theory. By analysing the programme's goals for a particular family, one can understand what intermediate changes are thought to be required in order to achieve a safe home environment. By analysing the *services used*, we can see how providers think those small steps are best taken. Furthermore, describing exactly what the family receives sets up the discussion about continuity of services after FPS ends; again, any reasonable person would appreciate that as intensive services are reduced and then ended, a service gap develops that needs filling. This focuses attention on the community and broader policy context for FPS; there may be a number of reasonable sets of expectations for effects from FPS based on the different characteristics of their community settings.

Modifications to the Homebuilders model

It seems reasonable at this point to explore the ways in which the Homebuilders model has been modified, and the reasons for these modifications. (We are speaking here about thoughtful and conscientious adjustments to the original model, not those made simply to save money.) This is a particularly important line of investigation, given what we have learned over the past decade about the sometimes resource-poor communities into which these programmes have been placed, and the extreme vulnerability of their clientele. If the original model was predicated on a certain mix of services (e.g. after-care family support) being available from CPS or within the community - which it appears to have been - and those services are now not available, then the programme might legitimately and creatively reconfigure itself to fill some of the gaps.

For example, the family preservation programme in Contra Costa County, CA, has developed a service component that allows the families to come back into the programme for brief, intensive interventions, or supportive 'refuelling' for a long while after the original programme period is complete. This modification makes sense if one conceives of family development as cyclical, not linear, with serious challenges for all families, and particularly for those with numerous problems, along the way. If there was a network of family support programmes in existence, perhaps these follow-up opportunities would not be necessary; but in many communities there is no such network.

We also have learned something, largely anecdotally, about the kinds of families for whom the original model makes the most sense, and the kinds for whom perhaps some adjustment is necessary. It is an unpopular notion to programme advocates, but the programme may well have some inherent lack-of-fit with certain kinds of families or problems. This is an issue on which evaluation efforts can, and should, shed some light.

218

Few studies systematically measure the perceived effects of family preservation from the family's perspective, or of families' satisfaction with the programme. This is part of a more generalised problem in child welfare research in the States - the virtual refusal to ask clients, including older children, about their experiences in the system. Here is another opportunity to make a real contribution to improving family preservation.

In essence much of what is discussed above is considered *formative* evaluation activity - investigations that describe the programme and provide feedback for its improvement. Programmes follow developmental trajectories in the same way that individuals do; formative evaluation helps to document and facilitate that growth and is critical to programme longevity and success. Meanwhile, when the public thinks about evaluation, it imagines *summative* evaluation - studies that determine the effectiveness of interventions. To traditionally trained and practised social scientists, the only way to establish these programme effects is with the *sine qua non* of research designs, the experiment.

Now the secret about experimental design is that it does not exactly fit many contemporary social programmes, and it may not fit family preservation well either. That is not to say, necessarily, that it should be abandoned altogether; indeed the movement we have witnessed in family preservation research towards increasing scientific rigour has made important contributions to both the evaluation and programme fields. However, we cannot support an 'all or nothing' approach that views experimental design as the only, or certainly the best at this point. Instead, we propose a genuinely pluralistic approach to evaluation that embraces a range of designs and techniques, thoughtfully and systematically applied, to answer a range of questions. By crediting different ways of learning about programmes we hope to improve family preservation, thereby improving the lives of the families it serves.

Notes

1.Research for this paper was supported, in part, by the Edna McConnell Clark Foundation, New York, NY. The authors alone are responsible for its contents.

References

Bartsch, D., Kawamura, G. and Seeley, K. (1993), *Family preservation services in Colorado*, Denver, CO, Colorado Division of Mental Health and Joint Initiative on Family Preservation.

Bath, H.I. and Haapala, D.A. (1994), "Family preservation services: What does outcome research really tell us?", *Social Service Review*, vol. 68, no. 3, 386.

Bath, H.I. and Haapala, D.A. (1993), "Intensive family preservation services with abused and neglected children: An examination of group differences", *Child Abuse and Neglect*, vol. 17, 213-225.

Bath, H.I., Richey, C.A. and Haapala, D.A. (1992), "Child age and outcome correlates in intensive family preservation services", *Children and Youth Services Review*, vol. 14, 389-406.

Berlin, G. (1992), "Choosing and measuring interventions", *Children and Youth Services Review*, 14, 99-118.

Berry, M. (1993). "The relative effectiveness of family preservation services with neglectful families", in E.S. Morton and R.K. Grigsby (eds), *Advancing family preservation practice* (pp. 70-98), Newbury Park, CA, Sage.

Blythe, B., Salley, M.P. and Jayaratne, S. (1994), "A review of intensive family preservation services research", *Social Work Research*, vol. 18, no. 4, 213-224.

Buchler, B.D. (1993), "Comments on the first outcome measures roundtable", *Protecting Children*, vol. 10, no. 2, 3-4.

Callister, J.P., Mitchell, L. and Tolley, G. (1986), "Profiling family preservation efforts in Utah", *Children Today*, vol. 15, no. 6, 8-11, 23-25.

Collier, W.V. and Hill, R.H. (1993), *Family Ties Intensive Family Preservation Services Program: An evaluation report*, New York, NY, Department of Juvenile Justice.

Cunningham, M.L., Homer, K.S., Bass, A.S. and Brown, M.G. (1993), *Family preservation in Tennessee: The Home Ties Intervention*, Knoxville, TN, University of Tennessee College of Social Work/Office of Research and Public Service.

Family Preservation Evaluation Project (in preparation), *Evaluating Family Preservation Services: A Guide for Administrators*, Medford, MA, Tufts University / New York, Edna McConnell Clark Foundation.

Feldman, L.H. (1991), *Assessing the effectiveness of family preservation services in New Jersey within an ecological context*, New Jersey Division of Youth and Family Services.

Frankel, H. (1988), "Family-centered, home-based services in child protection: A review of the research", *Social Service Review*, March, 137-157.

Fraser, M.W., Pecora, P.J. and Haapala, D.A. (1991), *Families in crisis: The impact of intensive family preservation services*, Hawthorne, NY, Aldine de Gruyter.

Haapala, D.A. and Kinney, J.M. (1988), "Avoiding out-of-home placement of high-risk status offenders through the use of intensive home-based family preservation services", *Criminal Justice and Behavior*, vol. 15, no. 3, 334-348.

Henggeler, S.W., Melton, G.B. and Smith, L.A. (1992), "Family preservation using multisystemic therapy: An effective alternative to incarcerating serious juvenile offenders", *Journal of Consulting and Clinical Psychology*, vol. 60, no. 6, 953-961.

Hornick, J.P., Phillips, D.M. and Kerr, N. (1989), "Gender differences in behavioral problems of foster children: Implications for special foster care", *Community Alternatives*, vol. 1, no. 1, 35-52.

Kaye, E. and Bell, J. (1993a), *Evaluability assessment of family preservation programs: Evaluation design*, Arlington, VA, James Bell Associates.

Kaye, E. and Bell, J. (1993b), *Evaluability assessment of family preservation programs: Final report*, Arlington, VA, James Bell Associates.

Kinney, J., Haapala, D., Booth, C. and Leavitt, S. (1990).' The Homebuilders Model', in J.K. Whittaker, J. Kinney, E.M. Tracy, and C Booth (eds), *Reaching high-risk families: Intensive Family Preservation in human services* (pp. 37-64). New York: Aldine de Gruyter.

Kinney, J.M., Madsen, B., Fleming, T., and Haapala, D.A.(1977). 'Homebuilders: Keeping families together', *Journal of Consulting and Clinical Psychology*, 45(4), 667-673.

Kirk, R.S. (1993), "Methodological issues in measuring outcomes", *Protecting Children*, vol. 10, no. 2, 7-9.

Nelson, D. (1990), "Recognizing and realizing the potential of Family Preservation", in J. Whittaker, J. Kinney, E. Tracy and C. Booth (eds), *Reaching High-Risk Families: Intensive Family Preservation in Human Services* (pp.13-30), Hawthorne, NY, Aldine de Gruyter.

Nelson, K.E. (1991), "Populations and outcomes in five family preservation programs", in K. Wells and D.E. Biegel (eds), *Family preservation services: Research and evaluation* (pp.72 91), Newbury Park, CA, Sage.

New York City Department of Juvenile Justice (1992), *Family Ties: The first eighteen months*, New York, NY, Department of Juvenile Justice.

New York City Department of Juvenile Justice (1993), *Family Ties Intensive Family Preservation Program: A financial analysis*, New York, NY, Department of Juvenile Justice.

Pecora, P.J., Fraser, M.W. and Haapala, D.A. (1992), "Intensive home-based family preservation services: An update from the FIT project", *Child Welfare*, vol 71, no. 2, 177-188.

Pecora, P.J., Fraser, M.W., Nelson, K.E., McCroskey, J. and Meezan, W. (1995), *Evaluating family-based services*, Hawthorne, NY, Aldine de Gruyter.

Posavac, E.J. and Carey, R.G. (1989), *Program evaluation: Methods and case studies*. Third Edition, Englewood Cliffs, NJ, Prentice-Hall.

Rossi, P.H. (1991), *Evaluating family preservation programs: A report to the Edna McConnell Clark Foundation*.

Rossi, P.H. (1992a), "Assessing family preservation programs", *Children and Youth Services Review*, vol. 14, 77-97.

Rossi, P.H. (1992b), "Strategies for evaluation", *Children and Youth Services Review*, vol. 14, 167-191.

Scannapieco, M. (1993), "The importance of family functioning to prevention of placement: A study of family preservation services", *Child and Adolescent Social Work Journal*, vol. 10, no. 6, 509 - 520.

Schuerman, J.R., Rzepnicki, T.L. and Littell, J.H. (1994), *Putting families first: An experiment in family preservation*, Hawthorne, NY, Aldine de Gruyter.

Schuerman, J.R., Rzepnicki, T.L., Littell, J.H. and Chak, A. (1993), *Evaluation of the Illinois Family First Placement Prevention Program: Final report*, Chicago, IL, Chapin Hall Center for Children, University of Chicago.

Schuerman, J.R. and Vogel, L.H. (1986), "Computer support of placement planning: The use of expert systems in child welfare", *Child Welfare*, vol. 65, no. 6, 531-543.

Schwartz, I.M., AuClaire, P. and Harris, L.J. (1991), "Family preservation services as an alternative to out-of-home placement of adolescents: The Hennepin County experience", in K. Wells and D.E. Biegel (eds), *Family preservation services: Research and evaluation* (pp. 33-46), Newbury Park, CA, Sage.

Shaefer, R.D. and Erikson, S.D. (1993), "Evolving family preservation services: The Florida experience", in E.S. Morton and R.K. Grigsby (eds), *Advancing family preservation practice* (pp. 56-69), Newbury Park. CA, Sage.

Spaid, W.M. and Fraser, M. (1991), "The correlates of success/failure in brief and intensive family treatment: Implications for family preservation services", *Children and Youth Services Review*, vol. 13, 77-99.

Staff, I. and Fein, E. (1994), "Inside the black box: An exploration of service delivery in a family reunification program", *Child Welfare*, vol. 73, no. 3, 195-211.

Thieman, A.A. and Dail, P.W. (1992a), "Family preservation services: Problems of measurement and assessment of risk", *Family Relations*, vol. 41, 186-191.

Thieman, A.A. and Dail, P.W. (1992b), *Iowa's Family Preservation Program FY1991 Evaluation*, Ames, IA, Child Welfare Research and Training Project, Iowa State University.

Thieman, A.A. and Dail, P.W. (1993), *Iowa's Family Preservation Program FY1992 Evaluation*, Ames, IA Child Welfare Research and Training Project, Iowa State University.

University Associates (1993), *Evaluation of Michigan's Families First Program: Summary report*, Lansing, MI, Author.

Weiss, C.H. (1995), "Nothing as practical as good theory: Exploring theory-based evaluation for comprehensive community initiatives for children and families", in J.P. Connell, A.C. Kubisch, L.B. Schorr and C.H. Weiss (eds), *New approaches to evaluating community initiatives: Concepts, methods, and contexts*, Washington, D.C., Aspen Institute.

Wells, K. and Biegel, D.E. (eds) (1991), "Introduction and Conclusion", in *Family preservation services: Research and evaluation*, Newbury Park, CA, Sage.

Wells, K. and Whittington, D. (1993), "Child and family functioning after intensive family preservation services", *Social Service Review*, vol. 67, no. 1, 55-83.

Yuan, Y.T., McDonald, W., Wheeler, C., Struckman-Johnson, D. and Rivest, M. (1990), *Evaluation of AB 1562 in-home care demonstration projects, Volume I: Final report* (Contract No. KED6012), Sacramento, CA, Office of Child Abuse Prevention.